What people are saying about

Leonard Sweet

"Leonard Sweet combines theory and practice in life-changing ways. He not only makes me think, he spurs me to live. This book will not only help you cross the finish line strong, it will also help you bring others with you."

—Mark Batterson, lead pastor at Na⁺· urch
and author of '~ ?ay

"In this book, Len Sweet has combined his disᵤ ᵤogizing with really wise, practical insight to concoct a unique ᵤ, ᵤɾ sanctifying relationships. Here is a book that will help us move toward a genuinely biblical form of holiness in a relationally unholy culture. One of a kind!"

—Alan Hirsch, author of *The Forgotten Ways* and
coauthor of *The Shaping of Things to Come*

Praise for *The Gospel According to Starbucks*

"Cultural barista Leonard Sweet serves up a triple venti cup of relevant insights to wake up decaffeinated Christians."

—Ben Young, pastor and author of *Why Mike's Not a Christian*

"Reading this book is a caffeine jolt. Get ready to be accelerated into the future, with Jesus a central part of the experience."

—Dan Kimball, pastor and author of *The Emerging Church*
and *They Like Jesus but Not the Church*

"I have a massive passion for passion. It's my favorite spiritual topic. And I have a nominal coffee obsession, Starbucks being my ritual more often than not. So what a treat to read Leonard Sweet's extra-hot weaving together of the two—all in the hope that each of us will drink in the meaningful and passion-filled life we were designed for."

—Mark Oestreicher, president of Youth Specialties

"Sweet's bottom line? Christianity must move beyond rational, logical apologetics, and instead find ways of showing people that it can offer 'symbols and meaningful engagement.' This whimsical and insightful book offers a fresh approach to a topic of perennial interest."

—*Publishers Weekly*

Praise for *The Three Hardest Words in the World to Get Right*

"Leonard Sweet gets us to examine what it takes to live out love in this world, and he does it beautifully."

—Tony Campolo, coauthor of *Adventures in Missing the Point* and professor of sociology at Eastern University

"Len Sweet has, in his inimitable style, tackled the three easiest-hardest words in the English language, wrestled them to the ground, hugged them, and then let them fly again. His imagination takes us on a journey, his mind is an encyclopedia of wonderful references, and his language is captivating."

—Tony Jones, national coordinator of Emergent-US and author of *The Sacred Way*

"Sweet's work is thought-provoking, insightful, and a must-read for any post-modern thinker."

—Margaret Feinberg, author of *Twentysomething* and
What the Heck Am I Going to Do with My Life?

"Leonard Sweet's book is a tremendous help in guiding us not only to say the words 'I love you' with greater understanding of what they really mean, but also to live them with greater integrity and intention."

—Ruth Haley Barton, cofounder of the Transforming Center
and author of *Sacred Rhythms*

Praise for *SoulTsunami*

"Although Sweet believes that many churches are behind the times, he also notes that the postmodern world offers them new opportunities for mission. In places, these suggestions do little more than urge churches to use the best the culture has to offer.... Sweet goes beyond such commonplaces and also speaks about the spiritual resources that churches possess. Sweet's insistence that postmoderns need to be reminded of the Christian teaching on original sin and human fragility and his sense of the need for spiritual values, such as humility, to counterbalance consumerism are cases in point."

—*Publishers Weekly*

Praise for *SoulSalsa*

"As American culture attempts to find its footing during the transition into post-modernism, Leonard Sweet ... attests that Christians must do the same thing.... By the end of the book, the Christian reader will want to strive to make worship a way of life, the outworking of grace a visible commodity, and his or her allegiance to Christ the revolutionary factor that causes the soul to dance."

—Jill Heatherly for Amazon.com

"This provocative exhortation to a more vibrant Christian life fairly sings with relevance."

—*Publishers Weekly*

11

11

indispensable relationships

you can't be without

Leonard Sweet

transforming lives together

11
Published by David C. Cook
4050 Lee Vance View
Colorado Springs, CO 80918 U.S.A.

David C. Cook Distribution Canada
55 Woodslee Avenue, Paris, Ontario, Canada N3L 3E5

David C. Cook U.K., Kingsway Communications
Eastbourne, East Sussex BN23 6NT, England

The Web site addresses recommended throughout this book are offered as a
resource to you. These Web sites are not intended in any way to be or imply an
endorsement on the part of David C. Cook, nor do we vouch for their content.

Material excerpted from *I Will Not Die an Unlived Life* by Dawna Markova © 2000 with
permission of Conari Press, imprint of Red Wheel/Weiser, Newburyport, MA, and
San Francisco, CA. To order call 1-800-423-7087 or www.redwheelweiser.com.

"Mark Van Doren" by James Worley. Copyright © 1979 by the Christian Century.
Reprinted by permission from the October 17, 1979, issue of the Christian Century.
Subscriptions: $49/yr. from P.O. Box 1941, Marion, OH 43306. (800) 208-4097.

LCCN 2008920365
Hardcover ISBN 978-1-4347-9983-8
International Trade Paperback ISBN 978-1-4347-9981-4

© 2008 Leonard Sweet
Published in association with the literary agency of
Mark Sweeney & Associates, Bonita Springs, Florida 34135

The Team: Don Pape, John Blase, Theresa With, Jack Campbell, and Karen Athen
Cover Design: Christopher Tobias

Printed in the United States of America
First Edition 2008

3 4 5 6 7 8 9 10

112408

To Jules Glanzer
with gratitude for your manifold Withness

Acknowledgments

Two of the most prominent women writers of the nineteenth century, Harriet Beecher Stowe and George Eliot, became friends after Stowe let Eliot know how much she loved *Silas Marner* (1861). In an 1869 letter to George Eliot, Stowe offered this marvelous metaphor for why authors write: "A book is *a hand* stretched forth in the dark passage of life to see if there is another hand to meet it."[1]

As many times have I stretched my hands into the dark, more hands have gone with mine this time than any other. My wife, Elizabeth, most often stretches my palms in directions they don't wish to go, but I've learned to trust her night vision. Other writers have offered "kindred hands" and "kindred minds" by reading the manuscript in its various stages. I especially want to thank Peter Walker (George Fox University) and Michael Oliver (Drew University), two colleagues who kept me from just talking shop and preaching to the converted.

If it had not been for the insistence of Lori Haynes Niles, the editor of the wonderful book *Bold Bible Kids* (Group, 1999), I might not have included a chapter on children. Once I wrote about Rhoda, whom Niles calls "God's Pray-and-Tell Servant," I couldn't imagine ever not considering this Withness. John Blase was assigned the great and grating task of editing this book—in the course of which he must have functioned as each one of my 11 Witnesses at least once. In this very antisocial activity of writing and reading, John has been a social lifeline.

There has been little interest in friendship in the history of Christendom. The move from philia to agape in the Christian tradition was so dramatic that philia was almost left behind. "A book on friendship now means, quite often, a collection of little sayings, attractively illustrated, meant as a gift, and sold in a drugstore" is how Gilbert Meilaender puts it.[2] About the only forms of relationships that have received sustained theological reflection in Christian literature are the two missing from this book: the erotic dimensions of relationships and marriage.

I have two heroes in footnoting: Betty O'Brien, who refuses to let my quotes go to press without signing off with a good-as-gold authentic at the end of each footnote: "(bao)." My second hero in footnoting is John Aubrey, one of the few biographers of the seventeenth century who attended to details in those he was writing about: how they looked, what foods they liked, what personality traits they displayed, etc. Plus he was one of the first to be scrupulous about his sources. He told one anecdote about John Denham mischievously painting out London shop signs and noted: "This I had from R. Escott, esq., that carried the inke-pott."[3] John Aubrey's spirit still lives in Betty O'Brien's "bao" ink-spot.

In a culture where the commodification of relationships is so severe that we have disposable kinfolk, it may come as somewhat of a surprise that "good relationships" are key to a healthy, happy life. This book was written because of the need for more specificity in what kinds of "good relationships" keep us from not needing a therapist. Two colleagues in particular, Carl Savage from Drew and Loren Kerns from GFU, have kept me off couches every week. And Mark Sweeney, the best agent any writer could wish, is the closest thing to a therapist I've ever had.

"My sonnets are not generally finished till I see them again after forgetting them." So wrote Dante Gabriel Rossetti in 1854.[4] The following doctoral students helped me see this manuscript afresh after forgetting it: Sarah Baldwin, Michael Berry, William Alexander (Alex) Bryan, Robert Cannon, James Carlson, James Caruso, Randall Davis, Joel Dietrich, Dan Kimball, John King, Stephen Lewis, Michael Newton, David Phillips, James Regehr, Karen Renner, Stephen Sherwood, Artie Sposaro, Daniel Steigerwald, John Stumbo, Terry Swenson, Jon Talbert. I feel honored to be studying with each and every one of them and wish more criticism came my way with such admirable amenity.

Many other hands have come together and clasped mine in the dark passages of this bookmaking. I am grateful for each and every one, especially one of my 11 Withnesses, Jules Glanzer, the new president of Tabor University, to whom I dedicate this book.

—Leonard Sweet
Thanksgiving Eve, 2007

Contents

Introduction

In the beginning is relation.[1]
—Martin Buber

Rusty: You'd need at least a dozen guys doing a combination of cons.
Danny: Like what, do you think?
Rusty: Off the top of my head, I'd say you're looking at a Boesky, a Jim Brown, a Miss Daisy, two Jethros, and a Leon Spinks, not to mention the biggest Ella Fitzgerald ever!
—*Ocean's Eleven*

Ocean's ???

As good-looking and savvy as George Clooney is, one of his recent movie offerings emphasized his need for help. In 2001, director Steven Soderbergh's *Ocean's Eleven* gave us a visual reminder that if it's going to get done, it's going to take more than just one. Clooney (the idea man) needed Brad Pitt (the pro), Matt Damon (the rookie), Andy Garcia (the target), and even Julia Roberts (the wild card). Reunions in 2004 and 2007 with *Ocean's Twelve* and *Ocean's Thirteen* brought the gang back together, with a couple of new faces, to drive the message home once more: You need others to get the job done. And it's also a lot more fun that way. That's what this book is about—you need others to get where you're going. And they make the ride a lot more fun as well.

Journey or Destination?

Life is a journey of journeys. Each one of us is on multiple journeys at the same time, some short, some long (some have dubbed marriage "the longest journey"),[2] with some being closer to ports of arrival than others. To be on the right path, we might take journeys to places we would rather not go.[3] Other times, to get where we are called to go, we follow detours we would rather not take. Sometimes, as Homer, Augustine, Dante, and Freud all realized, we get lost in order to find ourselves. And other times, we go on pilgrimages to lose our way.

"It's not about the destination; it's about the journey," preaches the UltraMarathon Cycling Association to its members.

"Life is a journey. Enjoy the ride," counsels Nissan in one of its advertising slogans (advertisements … proverbs of our day).

"It is good to have an end to journey toward; but it is the journey that matters, in the end" is the poetic formulation of one of my favorite writers, Ursula K. Le Guin (1929–), as she reflects on the fact that the race of life does not always go to the swift.[4]

<blockquote>

11

To *journey without being changed* is to be a nomad.

To change *without* journeying is to be a chameleon.

To *journey* and be transformed by the *journey* is to be a pilgrim.[5]

—Mark Nepo, *The Exquisite Risk*

11

</blockquote>

Then there is the opposite perspective. It doesn't occur often, since the idea of journey is a founding myth of Western culture (*The Epic of Gilgamesh*, Dante, etc.). If it does, the destination doesn't win out over the journey for long. American Airlines once had as its slogan "We understand, it's not about the journey; it's about the destination."

But not for long. It was quickly changed to a more "American" rendition: "After all, life is a journey."

In fact, it's easier to find voices mediating the journey and destination than the naming of life's meaning as destination: "It's not about the journey or the destination; it's about what you do once you get there."

And my personal favorite: "Life is not about journeys or destinations; it's about how you look while you're traveling!"[6]

The Only Way to Travel

> The church is a community of people
> on a journey to God.[7]
> —psychologist Larry Crabb

Journey or arrival? Result or process? Either-or? Both-and?

Take a poll of our goal-oriented society, and I suspect a surprising result: The journey-over-destination people would win hands down even while their hands and feet are busy living the "are we there yet" lifestyle.

I suspect this because I am a prime participant in this kind of hypocrisy. I profess one thing and I live another. While saying that the journey is more important than the destination, I still haul my carry-on luggage into the express lane and flash my e-ticket at the flight attendant. It seems that I'm always in a mad dash to some finish line or deadline.

We know the journey has value, we know the roses need our attention along the path, but instead of making time we keep kidding ourselves, faking polls, and pretending to live something increasingly foreign to us.

11

> I'm not a liar ... I am gifted in fiction.
> —David Mamet's film *State and Main* (2000)

11

Maybe one reason I am not more repentant for my hypocrisy is that I come by my "are we there yet" drive genetically. The founder of my tribe, John Wesley, logged thousands of miles on horseback, causing one biographer to call him "the Lord's Horseman." Wesley used to annoy the great Dr. Johnson because he couldn't seem to simply relax and enjoy the moment. "John Wesley's conversation is good, but he is never at leisure," Samuel Johnson complained. "He is always obliged to go at a certain hour. This is very disagreeable to a man who loves to fold his legs and have out his talk, as I do."[8] For Dr. Johnson, Wesley lacked the joy of journeying that comes with spending time together, sometimes in speech, but sometimes even more deeply in silence.

The deeper I go into my spiritual life, and the more years I use up, the more important "finishing" and "finishing well" become. Disciples of Jesus are "finishers," sprinters who finish races, who "press toward the mark," toward "what lies ahead" and end up at the places to which they are summoned.[9] If there's no end to pursue, why undergo the journey in the first place? A journey without a destination is a vagrancy, not a voyage. And Jesus himself said, "He who stands firm to the end will be saved."[10]

11

> I have finished the race, I have kept the faith.[11]
> —apostle Paul

11

But at the same time, the Bible clearly makes the journey important. In fact, you might call the gospel a theology of journey. To keep our "eyes on the prize" doesn't keep our hands from racquets, or our mouths from Godiva chocolates, or our noses from lily of the valley flowers, or our feet from dancing. If you don't meet God along the way, you'll never meet God at the destination. That's the dynamic tension.

The Relationship Question

[Jesus] appointed twelve—
designating them apostles—
that they might be *with him*.[12]
—Mark 3:14

The real meaning of life is not a journey question or an arrival question. It's a relationship question. Your journey *and* your destination are both important, but neither is possible without an answer to this prior question: *Who do you have with you?*

Life is a handicap event. We can't get to our destination without the help of others. Who are you taking with you on the journey toward your destination? Or as my friend/Episcopal rector Michael Blewett puts it, "The joy is not in the journey; it's in the relationships. The joy isn't found where the rubber meets the road, but where I meet you, in Christ. It's not about 'me becoming we'; it's about us becoming him."[13]

This resolution of the journey-arrival debate shouldn't surprise those of you who have read some of my previous books. The divine revelation is not a story about divine being, but about divine love and God's desire for relationship with us. Jesus came to reveal a God of love who will love you to the end.[14] In fact, what is the ultimate purpose of the Creator for you? God wants you with him. For eternity: "that where I am, there you may be also."[15]

God wants to spend eternity with you and me.

There is no one formula or secret method that can bring you home. More than seven principles of this or five practices of that, we need relationships, guides, and guards who can help us on our journeys and be with us when we reach our destinations. We also need the dynamic power that is released by these relationships, a power that draws us beyond ourselves to the Beyond itself.

So here's another phrasing of the real question: Will you be holding hands when you cross the finish line?[16] Or did you try to go it alone? Without these 11 indispensable relationships this side of heaven, life can get hard—hard enough to make a boxer throw in the towel, a conductor throw in the baton, a gardener throw in the trowel, a runner throw in the shoes, a theologian throw in the library card. Hard indeed.

11

> Anyone who doesn't need company is either
> greater than a man, and is a God,
> or lesser than a man, and is a beast.[17]
> —Aristotle, as quoted by Saint Thomas Aquinas

11

My favorite Robert Fulghum Kindergarten Rule is the one that said, When you go out into the world, watch out, hold hands, and stick together.

This book is an exploration of the 11 Withnesses every person needs on life's journey. *Withnesses* is my shorthand for "indispensable relationships." I could have shortened "indispensable relationships" to IR, but when I did, it kept coming out ER. Besides, I like the word *Withness* better as an abbreviation for "indispensable relationships" for a couple of reasons.

No doubt you are more familiar with the word *witness* than *Withness*, but if *witness* means anything, it is only because there was or is a *Withness*. The Greek word *marturos* means "witness," from which we get our word *martyr*. Martyrs were people who "witnessed," who put their lives where their lips were.[18] Witnesses like the eleven apostles who put their lives on the line. Their actions spoke louder than their words. Witnesses are people who are willing to be martyrs, to "witness unto death."[19] But before the apostles could be "witnesses to him,"[20] they first had simply to "be with him,"[21] to be "Withnesses."

11

> Therefore, since we are surrounded by such a great cloud of witnesses,
> let us throw off everything that hinders ...
> —Hebrews 12:1

11

Yes, sometimes we are surrounded by a great cloud of witnesses.[22] Other times we're surrounded by a great cloud of witlesses. But most of all we need to be surrounded by a great cloud of Witnesses. "The LORD God said, 'It is not good for the man to be alone.'"[23]

Your Triple Fs (FFF): Faithful Friends Forever

Each of the 11 Witnesses presented in this book is a biblical character made into a metaphor that constitutes God's Indispensable Dream Team for you. Your success or failure in life is shaped to a significant degree by the success or failure of these 11. Who you surround yourself with, how you interact with this network of relationships, the range of your relationship repertoires or "friendship repertoires"[24] is crucial to your future—whether you spend your life happy or miserable, well or sick, well-to-do or make-do, it's all about your entourage.

In each of our lives there are landmark moments, swing moments when our whole history hinges, turning one way or another. At the heart of these "landmark" moments are usually landmark people. Witnesses.

Your fate is not the result of your faith alone, for no one stands alone. Relationships don't stand alone either. All notions of self-sufficiency need abandoning. Without the involvement of others in your future, you have no future.[25] Outside of relationships, there is no "you" or "I." In fact, it is not "I think, therefore I am" (ala Descartes). It is "I'm with, therefore I am." Or more precisely, "We are, therefore I am."

11

> Faithful friends are life-saving medicine.
> —Sirach (Ecclesiasticus) 6:16 NRSV

11

For Vincent van Gogh, there was only one pathway out of the hell that besieged him and the nightmare that ultimately cost him his ear and then his life. When Vincent stumbled onto that magic path, he shared his excitement with his brother Theo:

> Do you know what frees one from this captivity? It is every deep, serious affection. Being friends, being brothers, love, that is what opens the prison by some supreme power, by some magic force.[26]

There are spaces between each of us. Each of us fills in those spaces with something, someone, and those filled-in spaces determine our destiny. I'm suggesting that we need to fill in those spaces with 11 relationships.

Here are two of the biggest hoaxes of all time:

First hoax: "I am a rock, I am an island." Every hoax is a profound half-truth. What makes it a hoax is that it trumpets only the wrong half. In a sense, we are all islands. The universe is composed of "island universes," and planet Earth is composed of island individuals.

But ask anyone who lives on an island (e.g., the island dwellers of ABC's *Lost*), and they will tell you that they learn the "no man is an island" dance with each new season. Whether your island is a prison or a crossroad, a place of repellent insularity or entrepôts of cultural and communal exchange, depends on the nature of the relationships you form with other islanders and with mainlanders. Island living requires "no one is an island" relationships if you are to survive. Islanders learn to depend on each other and to live with and even love people they can't stand. You can't carry a grudge with the septic man when your toilets back up at 2:00 a.m.

> **11**
>
> If you have not first of all lived rightly with men,
>
> you will not be able to live rightly in solitude.
>
> —maxim found in the *Apothegmata*, a collection of desert fathers' sayings
>
> **11**

Second hoax: the romantic notion that one person can meet all the needs of another person. Each one of us lives on many levels, and we need multileveled relationships with many different kinds of people to be healthy and whole. With the decline of extended families in Western cultures, this becomes all the more pressing. The closest thing to this book is a two-sentence insight from the Regius Professor of Divinity at Oxford University, Marilyn McCord Adams:

> It is a lie that any one person can be everything to another. Even in the blessed Trinity, the Father needs both Son and Holy Spirit, the Holy Spirit both Son and Father, the Son both Father and Holy Spirit—even each Divine person needs at least two others to be fully itself![27]

Mind *My* Business

This book argues that every person needs at least 11 others to be fully himself or herself. You need people who will not just mind their own business, but mind each other's business, and especially mind *your* business. That's called "intimacy."

In a hyperactive, hyperspeed, hypertext society, intimate relationships are not only uncommon, they're impractical. Depth takes time, and time is a commodity few of us are prepared to sacrifice. Withnesses walk alongside us and require time to fully develop. Are you prepared for the cost of Christ's discipleship?

Life is about the huddling together of verbs and prepositions. While faith resides in the verbs (not nouns), religion resides in the prepositions (not adverbs). *With* is the word of relationships. Just as the physical universe at bottom is a web of relationships, and it is these relationships that hold the universe—and you and me—together, so our life is a web of relationships or Withnesses. In the fight between "for" and "with," the armies of "for" are winning over the forces of "with."

There is an old African American spiritual about Jesus and Death Valley. Jesus "walked this lonesome valley, / He had to walk it by himself. / Nobody else could walk it for him, / He had to walk it by himself." No one could walk it "for him," but there were those who walked it "with him." *For* is the word of colonialism. It's also the word of laziness. After all, it is easier to do things *for* people than *with* them. When we do things *for* someone, we automatically position ourselves (purposefully *or* inadvertently) as the "givers"—which immediately implies that we have attained a certain level of wherewithal or some modicum of success. It allows us the indulgence of being identified with a benevolent "upper echelon." Simultaneously, it classifies recipients of our giving as "receivers" or, more disparagingly, "takers." We unavoidably demean Christ's "least of these" when we refuse to roll up our sleeves and walk with them. The incarnation is just that.

It used to be that the need for these 11 Withnesses was addressed in a complex kinship network along with an elaborate system of guardian angels and saints. In medieval times such a portrayal of life's 11 would probably have been classified as angelology: Here is the cast of angels God has promised to walk alongside you and camp on your shoulders. We were made to consort with angels,[28] most of whom need no wings to accomplish their ministering work of ramping up of life's resources. In these more therapeutic times, life's 11 might be seen as the outside story of insiders, our inner circle.

The angel of the LORD encamps around those
who fear him, and he delivers them.
—Psalm 34:7

In other words, these 11 are your insiders, but "insiders" who need to include "outsiders." The worst thing you can do is to create a matched community, an inner circle of people who see life exactly as you do. Life is becoming more complex, not less, which necessitates an ever-greater diversity of counsel. These 11 will most likely have little in common with one another and, if you got them all together in one place, may not like one another that much either.

That's why, in a world beset by chance and change, your 11 need to be as diverse as you can make and take them, with varied experiences, attitudes, politics, even theologies. Your 11 are people to help you be creative, not merely to help you implement your creativity. Each has her own culture, his own climate patterns and range of social weather.

The whole will add up to no more than the sum of its parts only so long as the parts themselves are isolated from knowledge of one another or of how they interact. Your soul has the power to weave a tight braid. The strands are all connected. Extricate one strand and there is no telling what happens … without the 12th Withness.

God's "Pocket Handkerchiefs"

You aren't in the recruiting business. There is no need for spiritual cajolery and cunning. No need for conjuring (although maybe some coaxing at times). There is no need for amulets engraved with the names of your 11 by which you could abduct their powers and annex their participation in your life. One of the worst things I could have done would be to make this into a how-to book of "Finding and Keeping Your Perfect 11." With each Withness, the fit is never perfect.

You don't need to hunt down and trap each one of these Withnesses. Most often the 11, like all good things in life, don't come from the directions you expect them to. The magnificent 11 will find their way to you … if only you are in the prayerful modes of attention and reception, willing to stop, stoop, and pick up one of these "handkerchiefs" that fall to earth from God's pockets.

> In his holy flirtation with the world, God occasionally drops a pocket handkerchief. These handkerchiefs are called saints.[29]
>
> —Frederick Buechner

One more thing: This book is not just about *your* 11 Withnesses. You need to serve in Withness roles for others too. Life is not lived solely for our own benefit. To whom are you a Barnabas? To whom are you a Nathan? Etc. Life goes both ways.... Are you there for people in the tough times as well as the good times? It is your high and holy calling. To paraphrase Ralph Waldo Emerson ("The only way to have a friend is to be one"), the only way to have a Withness is to be one. In fact, our first and best goal might be to become some of these Withnesses to others.

Just as in knowing others we come to know ourselves, it is only by being a Withness for others that you can have a Withness yourself. When we engage in authentic, vital relationships, we participate in something that is far greater than our own ability to affect another person; we're participating in the fabric that unites us as God's creation. In other words, our investment in another's life is always an eternal investment and proceeds according to an eternal wavelength.

Who's on Your Shoulder?

We live in a digital iPhone world where you're never alone, but you'll always be lonely without the 11. Every person needs 11 companions on life's journey. Each Withness is what the ancients called a *donum dei*, a gift of God: a Jethro, a Jonathan, a Nathan, a Barnabas, a Peter/Paul, a Timothy, a Deborah, a Zacchaeus, a Lydia/Lazarus, a Rhoda, and a Jerusalem. Here is life's best buddy system:

WHO'S YOUR NATHAN:	You Need an Editor
WHO'S YOUR JONATHAN:	You Need a True Friend

WHO'S YOUR JETHRO:	You Need a Butt-Kicker
WHO'S YOUR TIMOTHY:	You Need an Heir
WHO'S YOUR BARNABAS:	You Need an Encourager
WHO'S YOUR PETER/PAUL:	You Need a Yoda
WHO'S YOUR DEBORAH:	You Need a Back-Coverer
WHO'S YOUR ZACCHAEUS:	You Need a Reject
WHO'S YOUR RHODA:	You Need a "Little One"
WHO ARE YOUR VIPs:	You Need a Lydia and Lazarus, Rich and Poor
WHERE'S YOUR JERUSALEM:	You Need a Place
THE INVISIBLE 12TH:	You Need the Paraclete

You aren't strongest when alone; you're strongest when together. In fact, in a very real sense, your 11, like your spouse, are not outside of you but part of you. The most important thing is not to try to go it alone.

> Let us swing wide all the doors and windows
>   of our hearts on their rusty hinges
>   so we may learn how to open in love.
>
> Let us see the light in the other and honor it
>   so we may lift one another on our shoulders
>   and carry each other along.
>
> Let holiness move in us
>   so we may pay attention to its small voice
>   and give ourselves fully with both hands.[30]
>
> —Dawna Markova

Introductory Interactives

1. Author Michael Bywater says, "We place too many eggs in the basket of our relationships, regarding our spouses or partners in the way an infant regards its mother: as a cornucopia, guardian, protector, and fount of all gratification."[31]

   What do you think? Is he right?

2. To what extent do you think that the current rage for "coaching" is an expression of this hidden hunger for Withnesses?

3. What if we were to replace all job descriptions with "people descriptions" or "spirit descriptions"? Draw up what one such "spirit description" might look like.

4. If we started with the best people, would we come up with the best ideas and best outcomes? Why or why not?

5. When the book was first an idea in the mind, I drew up a list of possible candidates for Withnesses and each one's defining attribute. Here are some that didn't make the cut or whose attribute was integrated into one of the 11.

   You need a Sarah: a funny bone (sense of humor)
   You need a Mary Magdalene: stubborn faithfulness
   You need an Abram: a sense of adventure
   You need an Issachar: a sign-reader
   You need a Jacob: art of improvisation (clever adaptability)
   You need a Joseph: mature wisdom
   You need an Eli: listener
   You need an Epaphras: a prayer warrior

You need an Esther: who helps you say no and yes

Can you think of other attributes that go with biblical characters? Would you have chosen differently?

6. When you're in trouble, Martin Luther used to say, "Remember your baptism." What do you think he meant by that? What would it mean for you to "remember your baptism" in your life today?

7. My friend and colleague John Ed Mathison calls his change team the "Joel Committee." In his book *Tried and True* (1992), Mathison talks about how the Hebrew prophet encouraged the old to dream dreams and the young to see visions (Joel 2:28). His "Joel Committee" is a handpicked group on which he, the senior pastor, serves as well as influences both older and younger leaders.[32]

What might a "Joel Committee" look like in your life? Or do you already have one by another name?

8. Leadership guru Tracy Goss, in *The Last Word on Power*, suggests accepting this "gift":

1) Life does not turn out the way it "should."
2) Life does not turn out the way it "shouldn't."
3) Life turns out the way it "does."[33]

Is this a profound or silly statement? Might it be a profound half-truth? If so, what's the other half?

9. Here's a fun pop quiz (fun because there are no right or wrong answers) I sometimes give my students. I ask them to take out a sheet of paper and map

the genealogy of relatives whom they have met in person since the previous Christmas. It's always amazing how many have not run across a close relative, much less a brother or sister, in months.

Try it as a group. Is there a decline of active kinship ties in your life? If so, what are the implications for the need for relational networks?

10. "Having been warned in a dream not to go back to Herod, they returned to their country by another route" (Matt. 2:1–12).

How have you turned and gone a different way this past year? Or are you only turning and going in directions you want to go?

11. I have an angel story: I could never prove to you that it was an angel, but you could never convince me that it wasn't. Do you have one of these angel stories as well?

12. Check out the HBO show *Entourage*. Does the program encourage the kind of entourage spirit being outlined in this chapter?

Withness 1: Who's Your Nathan? You Need an Editor

Truth comes as conqueror only to those who have
lost the art of receiving it as friend.[1]
—Rabindranath Tagore

Someone to Give You the Finger

There is a moment in *The SpongeBob SquarePants Movie* when Plankton roars, "I'm going to rule the world!"

Towering over him, SpongeBob says, "Good luck with that."

In that moment SpongeBob SquarePants was Plankton's "Nathan."

The name *Nathan* means "gift."[2] Nathan the prophet was a "gift" to King David, a man we would describe today as being of Renaissance interests and Rabelaisian urges. During David's reign, Nathan provided him with expert counsel on a vast range of issues from architecture[3] to music[4] to dynastic succession.[5]

But Nathan went beyond just advice for the throne; he spoke directly to the heart of the king. Nathan confronted David about his sexual relationship with "that woman" Bathsheba and had the courage to stick his bony finger in David's face and say, "You are the man!"[6] Without Nathan, David would have continued his adulterous, murderous, lecherous behavior and corrupted the Davidic line.

You need a Nathan. When you are living in grand squalor, you need someone to point his or her bony finger in your face and say the words with double meaning: "You The Man." Yes, "You THE MAN" God wants to use. But also, "You THE MAN/WOMAN" who has stumbled or slumbered into immorality.

If you think you can't fall into sexual sin, then you're godlier than David, stronger than Samson, and wiser than Solomon.[7]

—Bill Perkins

Who is not afraid to haul you before the tribunals of truth?

Who is that person who can tell you that if you routinely run into more than three jerks a day, it's probably YOU. YOU Da Jerk! In life, you find fewer scoundrels than jerks, and you're the biggest one of them all.

Who can tell you you're not speaking with a Jesus voice?

Who can tell you when to turn the cheek less and the hands and feet more?

It's easy to gloss over this little moment in David's life: "Then David the king went in and sat before the LORD."[8] Did you hear it? "Then David the king went in and sat before the LORD." Then Leonard, the writer … then Randy, the dentist … then Samantha, the physician … "went in and sat before the LORD." *Someone* got David's attention and convinced him to sit down.

Love's essence, like a poem's, shall spring
From the not saying everything.[9]

—Cecil Day-Lewis

Who is that person who can get you to come in and "sit before the LORD"?

That's your Nathan. And your Nathan is more than a wagging finger. Or as Eudora Welty might put it, a Nathan is less about pointing a finger than parting a curtain.[10]

Your Nathan is your editor, someone who lifts the veil of your own voice.

From Accountability to Editability

I borrow that metaphor of "editor" from one of my favorite authors, Joe Myers. In his book *Organic Community*, Joe argues for the concept of "edit-ability" rather than "accountability." I have never liked the whole "accountability" theme for a couple of reasons, so I am jumping all over Joe's idea.[11]

First, the world of "accounting" is a foreign territory for someone who never did like math and never could balance a checkbook. Besides, "accounting" concerns focus on the world of numbers and finance, not relationships. My proof-text verse is Paul's misgivings about the accounting world of chart making and record keeping when he warns that love "keeps no record of wrongs."[12]

Second, the person who is the first to volunteer to be my "accountability partner" or who promises, "I'll help keep you accountable," is the very person I most want to flee from. These "volunteers" seem to hate not only the sin, but also the sinner (and secretly hate themselves as well, I suspect).

The accountability mentality has given us umbrageous politics in the church, which is constantly on the lookout for offenses: monitoring others for sins and trespasses. On the liberal side, it's sins of racism, sexism, ageism, homophobism, etc. On the conservative side, it's opposing stem-cell research, picketing the war in Iraq, and anything having anything to do with condom use.

Third, the "accountability team" has not worked well in the past. It has not kept religious leaders from every kind of moral failure, as the spectacular case of Ted Haggard demonstrates. No one had better accountability structures and procedures in place than Haggard. But the problem with "accountability" is that it is too easy to keep double books: one book for your accountability team, and another secret book for yourself.

An Editor's Heart

Joe Myers illustrates the editability theme with the story of his wife, Sara, handing him back an essay she had edited for him, and all he could see was red. Every page was dripping in blood. As he tried to find one pure white page, she said these words: "Joe, this is fantastic! This is one of the best things I have ever read! This is going to change people's lives."

"You're kidding. You hate it …"

"No, I love it."

"But look at all the red. You hate it."

"Joe, I love it. I just want you to get your ideas out as powerfully as you can. Every time you see red on the page, you should hear me saying to you, "Joe, I love this, I love you, and I want the whole world to read this book."

When Joe told that story at a mountain advance in Canaan Valley, West Virginia, it made me understand why I had just dedicated an entire book to my editor Ron Lee. Here was someone in my life whose greatest ambition was to help me be the best writer I could be. He labored for hours over my stumblings and mumblings, making sentences less convoluted but without destroying my voice in the process. Whenever we talked on the phone, or met in person, his entire dedication was toward making my voice stronger and helping me speak out of my voice. He often told me what to think about, but never what to think.

Belly Voice versus Heart Voice

Isaiah raged against what he called the "belly-speakers."[13] These were the mediums and spiritists of his day—what we might call ventriloquists. When you're speaking out of someone else's voice, you're speaking from the belly, not the heart. An editor helps you to speak from your own voice, and when you lose your voice, an editor helps you hear it again. When the well starts to run dry, an editor rushes to prime it with fresh water: Wells that go dry quickly become hellholes.

Accountability is designed to prevent you from doing bad. Editability is designed to help you do good. The real question is not "Are you accountable?" but rather "Are you editable?" Do you mind your manuscripts being overhauled by other thumbs? What if the script being "edited" is your life? What if the subject being sculpted is your soul?

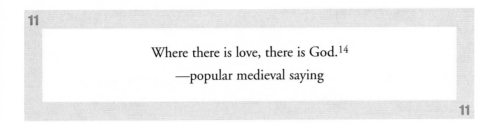

11

> Where there is love, there is God.[14]
> —popular medieval saying

11

Even the best writers in the world need editors. In fact, the more something glitters, the more it is in need of spit and polish. Don't believe me? Here is someone you might know through his writing. Some have called him one of the greatest writers of this or any time.[15] His name is Henry James, and here is what he wrote, unedited, in the *Times Literary Supplement* on April 2, 1914:

> Mrs. Wharton not only owes to her cultivated art of putting it the distinction enjoyed when some ideal of expression has the whole of the case, the case once made its concern, in charge, but might further act for us, were we to follow up her exhibition, as lighting not a little that question of tone, the author's own intrinsic, as to which we have just seen Mr. Conrad's late production rather tend to darken counsel.[16]

If you can make heads or tails of this, you're a better reader than I am. Or you're psychic.

What makes the Nathans unique in your life is that they are fundamentally best understood as welcome intruders. They tend to pop in unannounced to take the moral temperature of a particular moment, especially at the most inconvenient and disturbing times. But because you are already in a relationship with them, and authenticity is your brand, their temperature taking is always welcome. In a culture of increasing transparency, thanks to the Internet and ubiquitous surveillance (the average Londoner is captured on camera over three hundred times a day), you refuse them entrance at your peril.

A Welcome Intrusion

Nathan had already given David good advice on a variety of subjects when he dropped in at court that fateful day. In other words, as a trusted adviser, Nathan wasn't a general nuisance to David. He had access to the king because he was already in a valued relationship with David, one that had contributed significantly to the success of David's kingship. And even though David didn't invite Nathan to edit this part of his life, Nathan had a standing invitation to drop by and carpe momentum when the script desperately needed a rewrite.

Sometimes God specializes in the bony finger in the face, and sometimes God specializes in the still small voice from behind. But before either the finger or the whisper, there's always the story. Everyone welcomes a story. Nathan didn't come to David and say, "Bro, you done wrong." He came to David and told a story, a story that appeared totally unrelated to the situation and that drew David into the trap.

Every Nathan has a modicum of Machiavelli. Editors know how to spring traps with stories. Nathans don't tell stories to play games or beat around the bush. They tell stories because story and image are the most infectious transmitters of truth. Nathan's narrative sounded deep within David long before he felt the sting in its tail.

The gospel story always has a sting in its tail: the sting of truth or, more accurately, the double sting of truth and consequences.

Nathans care as much as you do about finding the right word or putting the right foot in the right place. A Nathan is welcome because this is not an editorial critic with icicles in his or her heart. This is a person who believes in you and wants the best for you, even when he or she shows up at the door with a sword. Who in your life is able to wield what William Blake speaks of as "the spiritual sword that lays open the hidden heart"?[17] A Nathan is not a hooded, anonymous executioner who wields a sword, but a trusted surgeon who heals the heart with a scalpel. Even though the knife is sharp and painful and cuts you deeply, red-drenched is the color of healing and wholeness.

In biblical language, Nathans "speak the truth in love."[18] Or as Paul put it, if someone is "detected in a transgression, you who have received the Spirit should restore such a one in a spirit of gentleness." Did you catch that? "Gentleness." Besides, "take care that you yourselves are not tempted."[19] Some people want to catch you in your sin. Nathan wanted David to catch himself in his sin. A Nathan is not someone who rushes to "tell you the truth" but someone who helps you to "do the truth."

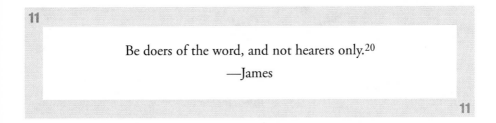

11

Be doers of the word, and not hearers only.[20]

—James

11

Do It!

This world has a lot of high-octane but low-grade leaders who need special editing. But whatever your octane or grade, we all need a Nathan. No one has ever been closer to God than Moses. But even the divine face didn't cause the greatest of all prophets to take off his shoes. He had to be told what to do: "Remove the sandals from your feet, for the place on which you are standing is holy ground."[21]

Without a Nathan to give what is often very simple advice, "Do the Word!" we remain oblivious to the obvious. Sometimes God is saying to you, "Do this!" and you need help hearing it. The last words the mother of Jesus speaks in the Gospels are these: "Do whatever he tells you."[22]

Especially when the word is to go to places of power. Some Nathans speak the truth and "Do the Word!" to political power: for example, Dietrich Bonhoeffer, Martin Luther King Jr., and Bishop Oscar Romero. And some Nathans speak the truth and "Do the Word!" to economic power: for example, Gandhi.

Both are often also known as "martyrs."

> We make out of the quarrel with others, rhetoric, but of the quarrel with
> ourselves, poetry [or if we have a moral sense, sanctity].[23]
> —William Butler Yeats

Just So You Know

It's not fun being edited. It's not always fun having a Nathan around. But it's necessary. What follows is a list of "just so you know" character traits of the editor you need. Knowing them doesn't always make the process easier; in fact, it may make it more difficult. But most things worth something are difficult. The only similarity between the words *edit* and *easy* is that they both start with the letter *e*.

A Nathan Will ...

1. Get Under Your Skin

A Nathan helps you get under your skin—ideally without getting under your skin, but often the irritation comes with the intrusion. You see, the problem is never out there; the problem is always in here. Without a Nathan, you might spend your twilight years wondering what you might have become if you hadn't gotten in the way.

The same thing that stirs our basest motives also inspires our noblest acts. Good and evil cohabit in each one of us in ways we don't want to admit. That's why the more you allow God to use you, the more you need a Nathan.

This is exactly what happened in Jesus' life; not that he had evil in his heart, but that his "Your will be done" stance was a green light for Satan to full-steam-ahead. Right after his highest moment, where he is riding the crest of the wave—his baptism where he accepts his sonship of the Father—Satan immediately enters the scene to tempt him into a traditional ministry of messiahship.[24] The deepest steps on the downward path are when you reach the summits of success.

The word *Satan* means "accuser" in Hebrew. Part of our "accusing" is to have four horsemen sent our way to knock us off our feet: fear, despair, rage, and guilt.

For some people, the Devil has only one subject of conversation: sex. Of course, the Devil would love for us to think that sex is the only thing evil is all about. The only thing the Devil likes better than this is to be portrayed as an "imp"—a small, trivial being that is more of a joke than a scourge.

11

> The more I'm around people, the more I love my dog.
> —T-shirt/bumper sticker

11

When Paul talks about the "works of the flesh" (*sarx*), he talks about hostility, jealousy, anger, envy, and competitiveness.[25] The "desires" of the flesh are not bad—it's when our ego wants those desires for selfish purposes that they become "works of the flesh." We mishandle our souls, and we can do it in a blink of an eye.

2. Ask Questions

Relationships need questions, and questions by definition are intrusive. Questions can comfort ("Is there anything too hard for God?"), questions can challenge ("Adam, where are you?"), and questions can convict ("Peter, do you love me?").

It is quite possible to accomplish much but never amount to much. When it comes to goodness, we confuse "good" with "good at." It's an editor's job to get you to ask the question: Is God's name glorified or smeared in my life? We easily bind the spirit of Christ in the fetters of our imagination, our religion, and our systems. An editor helps to let the spirit of Christ break free from our mind-forged manacles.

In a world full of people who never even look you in the eye, a Nathan looks straight through you … and asks questions like "Sweet, do you think God's going to ask you one day, 'How many books did you write?'"

It's not usually a Nathan's job to help you find a way out of your problem, or midwife your midlife crisis. I had a friend who, when he turned fifty, came to his wife and said, "Dear, it's your choice. A Mazda Miata or a mistress." But a Nathan asks intrusive questions about those ill-fitting parts of our personalities and problems that need fixing. A Nathan also inspires in you the virtue of resilience—the ability to bounce back from adversity.

> To fall is human. To get up again is divine.
> —T-shirt

3. Tell the Truth

A Nathan helps us see the truth about ourselves. And maybe even speak it. And the truth is, you aren't as good as you imagine you are; however, you aren't as bad as you fear you are. You're probably worse, but that's another book.

The line in us separating humbug from hero gets thinner and thinner the wiser we get.

It is hard for us to have a correct valuation of our own strengths and best assets. Linus Pauling won the Nobel Prize for chemistry in 1954. He won the Nobel Peace Prize in 1962. But he was totally wrong about what he deemed his greatest discovery and contribution: the cancer-fighting value of vitamin C.

We always know less than we think and, in some sense, speak more falsehood than truth if approximate truth is less a species of truth than a species of falsehood. We all can only come close to "the whole truth" at best. I take perhaps too much pleasure in knowing that Augustine changed his mind over time and came to different answers to the same questions. At nearly sixty, Augustine wrote to a friend: Cicero, greatest author of the Roman language, says of someone that "he never uttered a word which he would wish to take back." High praise indeed—but more applicable to a complete moron than to a genuinely wise man.[26]

Truth telling is a major role of an editor. Not "truth-dumping," which psychiatrist Willard Gaylin warns, "can be every bit as cruel as habitual lying."[27] A Nathan finds ways to come and get us and make us—proud, rebellious, impatient, and all—own up to the truth, even when we're in hiding. It's not that Nathan's editorial self haunts you, casting a critical eye over everything you do. Rather, Nathan's editorial eye helps you see the very things you are running from.

The difficult truth can concern little things. Our sins make us look ridiculous more than anything. Who tells you how ridiculous you look walking around with dandruff on your shoulder or a booger in your beard? Christianity quickly becomes Niceianity, and a Nathan doesn't live on Planet Nice, at least when we're around. You know you've been pricked and prodded by a Nathan when you leave an encounter smarting, but thinking, *There are kinder words that could have been said to me, but there aren't truer ones.* Nathans practice radical honesty even about the little things.

Or the truth can be about big things. Some of the most frightening words of Scripture occur in one sentence: "But he did not know that the LORD had left him."[28]

Or sometimes the little things are the big things, like a Nathan telling you which hat to wear. Savonarola, preaching against the excessive pomp and circumstance of worldly popes in the 1400s, was offered a cardinal's hat, which certain Nathans close to him warned was the institution's attempt to silence him. From the pulpit, Savonarola announced his decision: He sought a red hat, he admitted, but one red with a martyr's blood, if need be, not the red hat of papal, worldly glory.

We are tempted to think of a Nathan as the kind of person who likes short skirts on women, but only because it saves on material. But Nathans come in many shapes and sizes, and your spouse often makes your best Nathan. Who else can tell you what sucks, what struck out, what stuck out? Who else can see faster when you have crossed the line from beguiling to bewildering, when your strangeness becomes estrangement? Who will tell you that "it" is annoyingly cloying, or that "it" appears a trifle cozy, or that "it," despite your enthusiasm, is no great shakes? Who else will tell you that you've just crossed that moving line of "one thought too many"[29] or "one oddness too many," as my wife puts it; that your overexcited executions added an extra layer of icing on an already rich and well-decorated cake; that you've gone "too far" and violated that unspoken pact with the general audience (which, I have just been told, I've just done with this paragraph)?

Tie a Gift to the Saddle

Everybody needs a Nathan. Even Nathan needs a Nathan.[30]

Your Nathan may sometimes be a donkey that refuses to move or a whale that rescrambles your relationships, restructures your realities, and regurgitates a purged you up on the shore.

But whatever or whomever your Nathan, tie a gift to the saddle.

The seventeenth-century haiku master Bashō was walking around the island of Japan in 1689 and got lost. He asked a farmer for directions, but the farmer said, "It's easier if you just take my horse. He knows the way. When you get to the next town, just let him go and he'll come home."

So Bashō let the farmer's horse lead him. Once they arrived safely at the next town, he sent the horse home. But not before tying a gift to the empty saddle.[31]

I love that image of the riderless horse with a gift tied to its empty saddle.

It's incredibly important to tie a gift to the saddle for all your Withnesses. Relationships dissolve and decay. They are broken off, connections are severed, distances become too great (sometimes physical and other times emotional). We change, and with it our interests and circumstances, our enjoyments and our education are altered. So, too, are there changes in the relationships built on the old interests and circumstances. This is not a matter of our need to "totally reconfigure our network" periodically (to use the language of business). But it is a reflection of our constant reconfiguration and of the impact of that change on our relationships.

No matter how walk-on a role they played, former Witnesses should have a hallowed place in our lives. As much as we would like Cicero to be right—that the end of a relationship should be more like one having been "burned out rather than to have been stamped out"[32]—many of the 11 relationships will be broken by deceit and betrayal. Even so, we must honor our past and tie a gift to the saddle. We must speak well of every bridge that carries us across.

The Obligation of Oblation

You will get lost.... Let me repeat: You will get lost.

We all lose our way. Everyone gets lost for a while.... Anyone reading this not take some charming byways of irrelevance and some dangerous back alleys of irreverence? When I was a teenager, I didn't sow wild oats. I planted a prairie.

Can you imagine former president Bill Clinton naming one of his children "Kenneth Starr Clinton"?

Do you recall what David named his son? That's right: Nathan.

And that's the line through which Jesus came (through Mary's side).

Naming his son Nathan was David's way of tying a gift to the saddle, fulfilling the obligation of oblation. When a rewrite happens, and you've had a Nathan, tie a gift to the saddle.

Nathan Interactives

1. Discuss this quote from Marilyn McCord Adams: "The deep truth about us is that we are all morally flimsy, covertly willing to sell out at some terrible price. Does this mean we flunk the course without the possibility of a rewrite? ... God our Creator is our Re-Creator, healing, repairing, confronting, consoling, forgiving, sending us out with the power to strengthen one another, right now, immediately."[33]

2. Read Mark 1:32: "That evening after sunset the people brought to Jesus all the sick and demon-possessed."

   Now pause and reflect in silence on what you've just read. Now read verse 33: "The whole town gathered at the door."

   Who showed up needing healing from Jesus? Everyone.[34]

   How do you convince someone that he or she needs to show up?

3. Do you think there are times when a Nathan needs to "knock you out" just like an anesthesiologist? A surgeon can't save your life unless he first "knocks you out."

   What are ways a Nathan can deliver that knockout punch?

   If you don't think a Nathan should ever knock you out, what prevents you from messing with the healing if you weren't knocked out?

   In Europe, when you ask someone to "knock me up in the morning," it means to wake you up, to function as your alarm clock. Is this a better metaphor of "knocking" for a Nathan Withness—someone who awakens you to your life coordinates and trajectory? Why or why not?

4. With all that goes on in life, and especially those who are straight-to-the-edge thinkers and on-the-edge leaders, you can very quickly find yourself landed in what writer Robert Anton Wilson calls "Chapel Perilous, that vortex where cosmological speculations, coincidences, and paranoia seem to multiply and then collapse, compelling belief or lunacy, wisdom or agnosticism."[35]

What is he getting at? Do you agree with him? Why or why not?

5. We are not bulletproof. But should we wear some bulletproof vests, knowing that they are still penetrable? What might those bulletproof vests be?

Or do you think that we should be more like Jesus: vulnerable to attacks, without the added protection of bulletproof vests?

6. Martin Luther said that ridicule is one of our most effective weapons against the Devil. What do you think? Is ridicule becoming Christian? Is there a difference between ridicule and humor or satire? If so, what? Does it matter what we ridicule? Are there certain things that should never be ridiculed? If so, why?

7. The bigger our God, the safer it is to take risks, because the less life's contradictions seem dangerous or threatening.

Would you agree? Why or why not? Do small gods lead to small people?

Do you feel more alive when God becomes a bigger part of your life? Why or why not?

8. We all turn to dust, some before the same fate overtakes others. But we all turn to dust. In the nineteenth century, the "office" or "study" would most likely have a skull to remind all who enter of their impending death. What reminds you of your mortality? Do you have artifacts around your home or office that remind you of "ashes to ashes, dust to dust"?

9. My definition of the "four horsemen of the apocalypse" is rather different from most: fear, despair, rage, and guilt. Do you think the more traditional riders of the apocalypse are more compelling? Why or why not? Or are these states of soul more the causes of the four traditional riders?

10. There are no limits in life, but there are limitations. Everything that lives has limitations. And each one of us has different limitations: drinking, gambling, shopping, eating, and other attempts to negate life.

    What is your personal kryptonite?

    Do we prosper by those very limitations under which we live? Why or why not?

11. Ten percent of the Christmas trees the Boy Scout troop on Orcas Island sold last year were stolen. Of 190 trees, about 18 were stolen, including the demo tree in the stand. What does this say? Do you think this says something about the little island where we live? Would the statistics be any better (or worse) in your area?

When I registered my horror at the theft, Scout Master Steve Guilford responded, "Hey, I'm just glad we sold the 90 percent."

How would you have responded?

12. Do you think a Nathan can take social form with the function of finger wagging? What "Nathan" organizations can you think of? Do all Nathans need to not just point out what is wrong with the world, but provide answers? Or is finger wagging significant in and of itself? Support your response.

Withness 2: Who's Your Jonathan? You Need a True Friend

There are only two people who can tell you the truth about yourself—an enemy who has lost his temper and a friend who loves you dearly.
—philosopher Antisthenes the Cynic

Joseph Heller is famous for his cult-status novel *Catch 22* (1961), often cited as one of the greatest literary works of the twentieth century. But Heller wrote another novel that is equally as provocative and mockingly humorous, yet unknown.

God Knows is a novel about David, a figure who has captured the imagination of many people both within and without the Christian tradition. U2 singer Bono, the new Mother Teresa, has dubbed David the "Elvis of the Bible" and celebrated this "King's" songwriting ability as a formative influence on his own life as a musician and as a follower of Jesus.[1]

In Heller's novel, David says, "I don't like to boast … but I honestly think I have the best story in the Bible.… Old Sarah's fun.… Abraham, of course, is ever up to the mark.… Joseph is pretty lively as the pampered, late-born, bratty favorite of his doting father.… Moses isn't bad, I have to admit, but he's very, very long.… Moses has the Ten Commandments, it's true, but I have better lines. I've got the poetry and the passion, savage violence and the plain raw civilizing grief of human heartbreak."[2]

What both Heller and Bono fail to mention is that David has one more thing, the best thing anybody can have: a Jonathan.[3] Jonathan, the son of King Saul, loved David "as himself."[4]

A Jonathan is a true friend. There is a biblical text that lists increasing degrees of relational intimacy and intensity: "your very own brother, or your son or daughter, or the wife you love, or your closest friend" (Deut. 13:6). Your friend who loves you "as himself [or herself]" is the biblical definition of a true friend, a Jonathan.

> The true friend is, so to speak,
>
> a second self.[5]
>
> —Cicero

Your Second Self

A Jonathan believes in you when no one else does.

A Jonathan is loyal even when you make it hard to be loyal.

A Jonathan is the first to call in good times or in bad.

A Jonathan gives and gives and wants no payment.

A Jonathan walks with you in all seasons, like the winter of your discontent, when a miasma of gloom settles like a fog around your soul and nothing can be done until it lifts.

A Jonathan stanches the internal bleeding from your blanched body when depression (which shows up frequently in David's psalms) drains the life from your soul. If "melancholy prepares the devil's bath," as Martin Luther liked to put it from personal experience, a Jonathan fights to turn off the faucets.[6] A Jonathan won't let you surrender to your dark side. A Jonathan holds on to you for dear life when you're about to fall into that grave of a black bottomless pit, where death hides.

> Why is it that all men who have become outstanding in philosophy, statesmanship, poetry or the arts are melancholic, and some to such an extent that they are infected by the diseases arising from black bile.[7]
>
> —Aristotle (fourth century BC) in history's first-known reference to the "melancholy" of creative people

A Jonathan has seen you naked, in all your treachery and lechery, at your most heinous and most luminous, and loves you anyway.

A Jonathan keeps you in check when you want what you can't have.

A Jonathan grants you grace when you take him or her for granted.

A Jonathan defends [your] life's meaning, when [your] life has no meaning.

But most of all, a Jonathan sacrifices himself for you, even knowing, as the original Jonathan knew, that the more your song rises, the more his or her own song fades into the background.[8] A Jonathan is willing to lead a life of decreasing significance, or as John the Baptist put it so eloquently about his younger cousin Jesus, "He must become greater; I must become less."[9] The greatest act of true friendship in history? Jesus' death: "Greater love has no one than this, that he lay down his life for his friends. You are my friends."[10]

Harry Potter had Ron, his Jonathan, who, in a dramatic, life-size game of chess, was willing to take a sword that his friend might move on to the next level. Do you have a Jonathan who is willing to take a bullet for you, who is willing to say, "The finest thing I could ever do in my life would be to lay down my life for you"?[11]

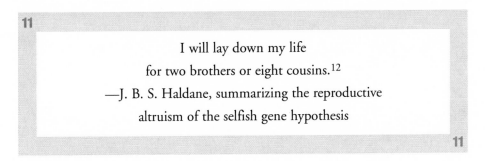

11

I will lay down my life
for two brothers or eight cousins.[12]
—J. B. S. Haldane, summarizing the reproductive
altruism of the selfish gene hypothesis

11

Not "Best," but "True"

A Jonathan is more than an acquaintance or a companion. The writer of Proverbs warned about confusing the two: "One who has unreliable friends soon comes to ruin, but there is a friend who sticks closer than a brother." Or in my favorite translation of this verse: "Some friends play at friendship but a true friend sticks closer than one's nearest kin."[13]

Who is "closer to you than a brother or sister"? Who is that "second self" who stands firm in your life? Who stands by you in good times and bad? Susan Sontag said we all carry two passports: one for the land of the well, one for the land of the ill. Any minute, the passport of the land of the well can be revoked, and you're in another land entirely. Who's still with you then?

Notice I didn't say "best" friend, but "true" friend. Each one of these 11 is your "best" friend. It all depends on where you are in life which best is "best." The worst thing you can do is to play favorites with your Withnesses. God doesn't play favorites with us—we mustn't fall into the trap of relational hierarchy. Sooner or later, that game forces us to pit friend against friend—whether directly or indirectly. The Irish defined "Jonathan" as the *anam cara*: the soul friend. The true friend.

11

Faithful friends are a sturdy shelter:
whoever finds one has found a treasure....
Faithful friends are life-saving medicine.
—Sirach (Ecclesiasticus) 6:14, 16 NRSV

11

Endangered Species

In 1961, near the end of his life, baseball legend Ty Cobb confessed, "If I had the chance to live my life over, I'd do things a little different.... I'd have more friends."[14] He had plenty of "acquaintances," "hangers-on," and "Washington friends" (defined as someone who stabs you in the front). But Ty Cobb died without a Jonathan.

A Jonathan may be the scarcest species on planet Earth (especially to a Saul). At least the Roman philosopher and politician Cicero (106–43 BC) thought so.

My high school required one foreign language course, so I took Latin. I didn't *want* to take Latin. Most of my buddies sat in the front row of French or Spanish class— and bowed adoringly (at times, bow-wowed!) at the "hottest" teacher in school. But my parents, insisting that those I called "friends" didn't know nearly as much as I thought they did and weren't nearly the friends I thought they were, made me take Latin. It would help me understand English better, they said. So I slouched in the back row and listened to Mr. Garno, a short, balding, serious, uptight, white-shirted instructor, hoping he wouldn't call my name to come up front and read out loud a poem or conjugate a sentence or explain how the English word *satire* came from the Latin *satura*, which means "a mixed dish filled with various kinds of fruit."

In my third or fourth year of struggling to bring this dead language to life, Mr. Garno assigned me the task of translating from scratch Cicero's essay "On True Friendship." My closest seatmate got what I thought was an infinitely more interesting assignment: She translated Cicero's detailed description of how to hold the index finger or the middle finger when gesticulating in oratory.

Life has a few landmark moments. This was one, translating what I now believe is the greatest essay on friendship ever written. Its landmark moment status came about because my translation took place while I was suffering from the crushing betrayal of a so-called friend. This personal Judas told my *don't-tell-anyone-but-I-have-a-crush-on-Linda-Armstrong confidence* to that same Linda Armstrong! I avoided Linda after she knew my dark secret, and never really talked to her again in high school (we spoke often, but I never made eye contact). At our fifteen-year high school reunion, Linda came up to me, we looked each other in the eye, and she said, "How come you never liked me?"

"Liked you?" I exclaimed. "You don't remember? My first serious college essay was 'God, Death, and Linda Armstrong.'"

Cicero's essay challenged me to take out my one hand and count my fingers. If when I die I can count "on the fingers of one hand" the number of true friends I have, Cicero said, I would be the wealthiest person on the planet.

Cicero awakened me to the reality and the rarity of a Jonathan. And as I learned later, Cicero was deemed an optimist by Montaigne, who thought that the bonds of true friendship ("one soul in bodies twain") could only be shared by one.

What makes having a Jonathan so rare, and what makes it so hard for you to be a Jonathan to others? Why is it so hard to maintain a friendship as an adult?

Three things. Three syndromes. We might even call them sin-dromes.

11

Nothing among human things has such power to keep our gaze fixed ever more intensely upon God, than friendship for the friends of God.[15]
—Simone Weil

11

1. "What's in It for Me?" Egosystem Syndrome

First and foremost, egoland. No, it's not a theme park; it's our homeland, our ecosystem, or what I call the egosystem. We're highly adapted organisms thriving in the egosystem habitat, where the law of the jungle is "what's in it for me?"

For example, today's "friends" are all about "networking," and if "friends" can't advance our career and connect us to sources of power and prestige—if "friends" can't make the net "work"—it's time for a new set of friends who can "work" to your advantage.

Sound familiar? Or in denial? As a society, we're forgetting the purpose—the art—of friendship at an alarming rate. Rather than the "what's in it for me?" syndrome, the Jonathan genome asks, "what's in it for *you?*" Only when the energies and motives of the ego are blocked, only when the ego is banished from the front to the back of the line, only when love does not seek its own, can the higher Jonathan consciousness step up. Weighed down by self-absorption, pride, and ambition, with undisciplined selfish impulses, most people don't wear themselves lightly enough to be a Jonathan.

Jealousy, rivalry, greed, distances, indifference, indebtedness … poisons all.

And all kill our Jonathans. Yet all are the most prominent features of the egoland landscape. Every time he painted a portrait, John Singer Sargent said he lost a friend.[16] "Every time a friend succeeds," Gore Vidal has famously admitted, "I die a little."[17] A millennium earlier, Anselm felt so severely the pain of success-severed relationships that he cried out, "Do not love me less because God does his will in me."[18]

11

> It is easier to forgive an enemy than it is to forgive a friend.[19]
> —William Blake

11

2. "No Down Elevator" Syndrome

Second, some of us are better at friendship than others. Males are notoriously culturally disadvantaged in the "friends" department. Newspaper columnist Laura Marcus claimed that the typical male idea of a best friend is "someone they haven't seen for ten years."[20] Men are surprisingly gifted at taking elevators up but suffer immensely when taking elevators down.

Clinical psychologist Dan Montgomery uses the image of "taking the elevator down" to explore what it means to reach deeper levels of truth and trust in a relationship.[21]

> The intimacy elevator starts with the *facade level*, or level of public appearances. Here, people relate through social custom. Conversations are filled with small talk about the weather, sports, earthquakes, families, and the state of the world. This is a valuable and necessary stage for getting acquainted and for doing business with people we don't know well.

The next floor down is the *acquaintance level*. We reveal some of our private sentiments and opinions. At this level, we present more of our views on politics, religions, sex, and marriage. There is some risk that people will take offense. However, most people know how to participate in these exchanges without taking it personally.

To reach the third floor down, the *friendship level,* we must willingly experience emotional vulnerability. At this level, we share all sorts of feelings, yet hold back on the deeper ones. We look for compatibility, empathy, and mutual trust. If all goes well, and the other person responds at this same level, we may choose to take the elevator down another floor.

The fourth floor down is the *intimacy level*. We come clean with the dark side—the memories, wounds, and reflections that make us who we are, but that can feel shameful to disclose. We also share the heart's desires. People who cannot reach this level in friendships or marriage may need a pastoral counselor or therapist to help them.[22]

> 11
>
> If we stick together we can see it through,
> 'Cause you got a friend in me.
> —Randy Newman, *Toy Story*
>
> 11

According to psychologists, whether you can completely trust at least one person is the test of whether or not you are a psychologically healthy human being.[23] For most of us, this is more difficult than we care to admit. Should we be surprised at the level of our dis-ease?

3. "What, Me Sacrifice?" Syndrome

Third and finally, Jonathans are so rare to find and be because a Jonathan is willing to pay the price of being a friend. Perhaps the highest cost of true friendship is our most precious commodity: time. An ancient Greek proverb (referenced by Aristotle and others) submitted that friends must have eaten the required pinch of salt together—which is a fancy way of saying that true friends invest hefty amounts of time in each other's company. In a culture where money is time and time money, the "cost" of friendship requires great sacrifice.

A God who expects sacrifice, or a relationship that requires sacrifice, is not a sensibility well suited to the twenty-first century. But sacrifice is the embodiment of a Jonathan relationship, where love has two components, both of which are unfashionable: duty and sacrifice. "What, me sacrifice?" is the signature phrase of a "Yes, me worry" twenty-first century that refuses to sacrifice to rid itself of those worries it knows it must face.

> 11
>
> "What does a woman want?" Freud famously asked.
> "Simple. She wants a partner who cares what she wants,"
> Daniel Goleman famously answered.
>
> 11

But ...

If you find that Jonathan, that true friend, that *anam cara*, that sticks closer-than-a-brother, that what's-in-it-for-you-elevator-down-lay-down-their-life-for-you person, then you'll have something that feels warm, like a familiar song:

Carole King wrote these lyrics, but James Taylor sang them best: "All you have to do is call, and I'll be there. You've got a friend."[24]

Everybody needs a Jonathan. Everybody.

Jonathan Interactives

1. Discuss my understanding of a Jonathan as someone with whom you can strip your soul, and when the skeleton of the soul is stripped bare, your Jonathan will not laugh or gasp at how ugly you are. What is the strength of this definition? Its weakness?

2. What do you think Teresa of Avila meant when she said, "Take God very seriously, but don't take yourself seriously at all"?

   Do you think you take yourself too seriously? Do you think you take God seriously enough? Why or why not?

3. Some recent research suggests that women will sacrifice achievement for the sake of a relationship, but men will more likely sacrifice a relationship for the sake of an achievement.

   Does this ring true with your own experience? Do you agree with those who argue for gender differences in terms of relational skills? If true, what are its implications if strong relationships hold both families and societies together?

4. Do all friendships have sexual dimensions (but only one friendship leads to sexual intercourse)? Support your answer.

5. In some cultures, one's spouse is most often one's Jonathan. In other cultures, one's spouse is most often not one's Jonathan (e.g., "An ideal husband is one who is always well and never home," according to an old Japanese

proverb). What are the advantages of having a spouse as one's Jonathan? The disadvantages?

6. What is the difference between giving yourself to God and giving yourself to another person?

7. Listen to yourself talk sometime. How ego-centered is your conversation?

8. Is this a good rule of thumb? Never assume that other people are interested in your problems.

    Is that what makes a Jonathan so special and rare—a person who genuinely cares about your problems? Which of the 11 will be most there for you during sickness and disability? Which of the 11 do you want with you when the two worlds kiss, as the ancient rabbis referred to the last hours of your life?

9. Do you think God's presence can be found and felt as much in the valleys as in the mountains, or is this just pious pablum? Do you have stories to back up whichever way you argue?

10. If someone were to ask you, "What is the greatest honor you can pay to someone?" what would the candidates be? What would be the greatest honor someone could pay to you?

    How about these words: "I trust you"? Or would "I love you" be a higher honor?

11. How do you respond to Irish playwright George Bernard Shaw's (1856–1950) dictum that "the quantity of love that an ordinary person can stand without serious damage is about ten minutes in 50 years"?[25] Do you find this philosophy reflected anywhere in his play *Pygmalion* (*My Fair Lady*)?

12. Do you think the whitewashed tomb syndrome is especially true among pastors? Are we (or too many of us) lone rangers to the core, the treasurers of relational poverty?

Withness 3: Who's Your Jethro? You Need a Butt-Kicker

In the first place you can't see anything from a car;

you've got to get out of the ... contraption

and walk, better yet crawl, on hands and knees, over the sandstone and

through the cactus. When traces of blood begin to mark your

trail you'll see something, maybe.[1]

—Edward Abbey

My father seldom woke up my brothers and me in the morning, but when he did, these were his alarm-clock lines: "Leonard, get up, dress, up, show up." For my father's generation, that shorthand formula equaled "success" in life.

You grow up and don't have parents to kick you out of bed. But you still need someone to kick you around when you're intellectually/morally/spiritually lazy, dumb, and fat: "Leonard, get up, cowboy up, or for God's sake at least look up." Basically, you need a butt-kicker. You need a Jethro.

Go *to* Peace versus Go *in* Peace

An ancient Japanese proverb says you should never rely on the glory of the morning, nor the smiles of your mother-in-law.

If you live in the Seattle area, you know how fickle that morning glory can be.

If you are married, you know how much you look forward to the smiles of that mother-in-law.

But to count on those smiles? To build on those smiles? To rely on those smiles?

Moses did. He built on the smiles of his father-in-law and the glory of the morning.

Moses' father-in-law was a Midianite high priest named Jethro. He was part of a camel-riding desert tribe that we would today call Bedouins. Without any sons, Jethro offered Moses one of his seven daughters, Zipporah ("bird"), and Moses happily spent years looking after the flocks of his father-in-law.[2]

But one morning, Moses woke up and the glory was gone and his father-in-law was grinning, not smiling. Jethro kicked Moses' butt out the tent and into the mission God had given him.

When Jethro said farewell to Moses, he used the Hebrew phrase *lech l'shalom,* which means, literally, "Go to peace."[3]

Little Things Mean a Lot

When David said good-bye to Absalom, he used another more familiar Hebrew phrase, *lech b'shalom,* which means, literally, "Go in peace."

Did your nose twitch suspiciously? Sometimes the smallest of grammatical changes can make the biggest differences: like the world of difference between "to" and "in."

What followed Jethro's blessing of "go *to* peace"? Moses returned to Egypt and liberated his people.

What about David's blessing of "go *in* peace"? Absalom died,[4] and David's heartache cried out these words: "O my son Absalom! My son, my son Absalom! If only I had died instead of you—O Absalom, my son, my son!"[5]

We often bless one another with the good-bye dismissal of "go in peace." Be careful of this "blessing": The "go in peace" blessing is the blessing of death. Going "in peace" is a resting in wholeness or perfection, possible only in the RIP (Rest in Peace) posture of the grave.[6] Going "to peace" is a wresting of beauty, truth, and goodness out of the jaws of death, and is a push to make the best use of whatever life remains.

Quite different blessings: "Go *to* peace" versus "Go *in* peace."

Be careful whom you wish *lech l'shalom* ("Go *to* peace"). But be even more careful whom you wish *lech b'shalom* ("Go *in* peace").

"Peace" is not the "peace and quiet" kind of peace. If you want a life of peace and quiet, then don't follow Jesus. Jesus was crucified in the name of peace and quiet. Jesus didn't die on some soft mattress. Jesus died nailed to some hard wood.

"Go *to* peace" has the peacemaking sense of *shalom*, the channeling of energies that brings wholeness and wellness to the world.

It's one of the most powerful acts you can do to another human being: Bless them forward. When you're spiritually neutered, or when you've become complacent and complaisant, when you begin to shrink from your mission, you need a Jethro to keep you loyal to your dreams. You need a Jethro to wake you up from your lazy laxities with these spiritual laxatives: Go to peace or go to pieces …

You can't be *at* peace until you *go to peace* so that one day you can go *in* peace and rest in peace.[7] For as Dante puts it, "In His will is our peace."[8]

Get Your Kicks from Jethro

You need a Jethro: someone who kicks you in your posterior and gets you off the seat of your pants and into the future. Or, to put it more civilly, a Jethro is someone who asks you, "What's your favorite future?" and who blesses you forward.

You need a Jethro: someone who boots you awake so you *look at* rather than *look away,* and blesses you forward with, "Go in vigor and strength in what you are going to do."

You need a Jethro: a conductor who punts you off the gravy train so you can climb aboard the gospel train where you hear the challenge, "How can you 'hold your piece' when others are without peace?"

You need a Jethro: a conscientious kick-in-the-pants objector who confronts your tut-tutting and hew-hawing, who unglues you from the boob tube or YouTube, and makes you face up to your capacity to wallow in mud baths of your own making. Because of Jethros, genes don't have to be a life sentence.

11

Who squanders talent praises death.[9]

—a character in Cynthia Ozick's first novel

11

You need a Jethro: a nagger who kicks open the doors and windows of your house, makes you rise to the midnight hour, and spotlights your hidden resources. A locked house quickly becomes filled with stale, toxic air.

You need a Jethro: a squeaky wheel that kicks you attentive and keeps you moving. If you're on a mission, you must keep moving.

You need a Jethro: a laxative that pushes you out the door and ends the "after you, Claude" syndrome—where you say, "I'll only do it if you do it," and the other says, "We'll only do it if you do it," and meanwhile nobody goes anywhere, everyone just sits around, and nothing gets done.

You need a Jethro: someone who puts the boot to the backside and tells you to live life, not just with your brain but with your backbone … and that "telltale tingle down the spine" that confirms you are living the truth.[10] Who makes sure you do nothing by halves?

You need a Jethro: a commanding voice that kicks it up a notch and asks, "How are you?" to which your soul responds by asking itself, "How should I be?"

Who is your Jethro? And who are you Jethroing?

Jethros bless you to go to what God is calling you to do so that you can receive peace in your life. Everyone needs someone (often older) who is wild and crazy about them, who believes in them, and cares enough about them to wake and shake them up to dream big and live large. The older you get (and the transition from "young turk" to "old geezer" is alarmingly fast), the more you need a Jethro to help you make the transition from blazing comet to fixed star, rather than shooting star.

A Jethro is a blesser, not a flatterer. There is a vast difference between blessing and brownnosing, between consecrating and ingratiating.[11]

Note that Jethro was *not* a part of the Hebrew community. You need people in your life who are not part of the community of faith, people who are more "doers" than "believers." Your Withness may be from another religious tradition or from no faith at all. In fact, Jewish households needed their "shot of Goy" for strict Sabbath observance. The term, a Gentile corruption of the Yiddish term *Shabbes Goy*, refers to Gentiles hired to do work on the Sabbath forbidden to a Jew (e.g., extinguish lighted candles, make fires in the oven, put out the candles in the synagogue after the Sabbath-eve prayer). In fact, some Gentiles made a good living being a "shot of Goy" for Jews (both Elvis Presley and Colin Powell worked as *Shabbes Goy* in their youth). We need people of other cultures and faiths in our lives, not just to "witness" to them but also to keep us honest and faithful in our own rituals and beliefs and to purify our own understanding of the faith.[12]

11

> We are not called to be microcosms of the gospel
> but members of the body.
> —Canadian theologian John Stackhouse

11

"You're History, Sweet!"

A Cheyenne Indian song says, "Only the stones stay on earth forever."[13] When you look at the Rolling Stones, it seems like that. But even the Rolling Stones will roll to a stop one day, for all the reasons that stop the rest of us from rolling along forever. Even the Rolling Stones can't stay on earth forever.

We all end up in the same box. We all become a box lunch for worms. We only have a short time to fulfill our mission. That's why we need some Jethros to hear the two "shaloms" every day, for one without the other is a profound half-truth.

Lech l'shalom: Live each day as if it were your first.

Lech b'shalom: Live each day as if it were your last.

The Jethro blessing is the blessing of "you're history!" with the double meaning of "you're history."

The first meaning is this: With everything you do, every action you take, you're making history. "You're history, Sweet."

The second meaning is this: Every day could be my last, and at any moment, it could be over, finished, the end. "You're history, Sweet."

Your butt-kicking-"you're-history!" Jethro pushes you out the door with these questions haunting your every step: Will you look back on your life and see a succession of sorrows, missteps, missed moments? Or will you look back on your life with a sense of satisfaction and joy? If life matters, you have to give your life to mattering. Will your life matter? Or will you live one of those Paris Hilton lives that have nothing to say?

11

> The clouds you so much dread
> Are big with mercy, and shall break
> In blessings on your head.[14]
> —depressed poet William Cowper

11

Butt-Kicking Blessings

We have ample people in our lives who curse us and what we are doing. Some curses are innocent, merely mischievous. Yankees coach Casey Stengel used to cross his fingers and point to the opposing teams: He used to "pox" them with the early-church sign of the cross, and smile as he "cursed" his competition. My all-time favorite "mischievous" curse, though, is this one by Robert Desnos titled "Dove in the Arch":

> Cursed!
> be the father of the bride
> of the blacksmith who forged the iron for the axe
> with which the woodsman hacked down the oak
> from which the bed was carved
> in which was conceived the great-grandfather
> of the man who was driving the carriage
> in which your mother met your father.[15]

And then there are some curses that are not mischievous and light-years from innocent. Did you know that there are entire Web sites expressly devoted to cursing me? I still smart from one denomination's banning of my book *Out of the Question, Into the Mystery* (2004). How could they order my book purged from the shelves in all their stores? I had written about something I thought I had learned from them. Sometimes our cursers are as close to us as a brother or a sister, but the fact that we were hit by friendly fire doesn't make a punch in the mouth any less painful.

Sticks and stones can break your bones, and friendly fire can knock the spirit out of you.

Unless a Jethro reverses the curses.

The Breath of Life

In both the First Creation passages of Genesis, and the New Creation passages of the Gospels, the Spirit of God "breathes" new life into the world. In John 20:19–22 (NRSV), Jesus "breathed" on his disciples while saying, "Peace be with you. As the Father has sent me, so I send you"—and the Spirit is released, the same Spirit who incubated the deep "In the beginning" and who breathed soul into the first Adam "in the garden."

With this "Second Breath," however, two things are different. First, with this second breath the curse of the garden is reversed, and our connection with the earth is reinstated.[16] Second, when Jesus breathes the breath of life into the "new Adam," the church is conceived and sent out into the world "in peace," not to rest but to charge and champion God's healing work in the world.

If the joy of the Lord is our strength, the jeers of the crowd are our weakness. At a moment in my ministry when I began to lose my charge, withering in self-pity for having my DMin demeaned by a friend who pooh-poohed behind my back anything other than a PhD degree, a Jethro by the name of Jim Carlson kicked my butt, reversed the curse, and breathed new life into my ministry. Before I could even start enjoying the fantasy of repairing to my lair, replacing speech with

silence, and looking backward for my thrills, he sent me this e-mail as I was sched-
uled to begin mentoring a new doctoral cohort:

> Len: It's 2:26 a.m. PST on Friday and I am up: thinking
> and praying and listening to your latest podcast (the Napkin
> Scribbles on "mercy"). You mentioned that you were in
> Portland with new DMin students and I thought back to
> my beginning as a member of your cohort. What strong
> and rich glue was formed those first few days together with
> you and with our colleagues. So my prayer is this:
>
> I pray that this new cohort will find the same and give
> themselves fully to their learning for much has changed
> this past year. I pray for the opening of hearts and minds.
>
> I pray that each one will find that place among the whole
> … that place that feeds them all.
>
> I pray for Loren Kerns that he will be embraced and that
> they see what a blessing and friend he will become.
>
> I pray for Len Sweet as you open and lead and stretch
> and sacrifice for this new and precious method of touch-
> ing and teaching our restless hearts.
>
> I pray for Len Sweet again, for wisdom, for stamina, for
> the very words of God.
>
> I pray that the mechanism of the mystery, the incarnate
> paradox, that precious name … Jesus … may bless you
> all as you begin the ride together!

Without this one e-mail, I might have sold my soul for a bowl of stew. A Jethro is one of God's angels sent to help us handle the "dark night" of the soul and the "dry well"[17] of the spirit.

In their butt-kicking blessing, Jethros give us a "mind to work."[18] In other words, there is something of a Nehemiah in every Jethro. You remember Nehemiah. The year was 445 BC, the year Nehemiah held high office at the court of the Persian king, the year he heard of the desolation of Jerusalem, the city of his fathers, and heard the call of *lech l'shalom* to help rebuild the city.

Nehemiah mobilized people not only from Jerusalem, but also from the neighboring communities of Jericho, Thekra, Mizpah, and other surrounding towns. Nehemiah didn't recruit or conscript anyone: The old and the young, the rich and the poor, the priests and the laity—everybody with a "mind to work" came freely to rebuild the city. A Jethro blesses you with a "mind to mission" and reminds you that there is something of a Nehemiah in you. One of the greatest tragedies of our world today is this: people with a "mind to mission" but no mission to mind.

11

> For the past eighty years I have started each day in the same
> manner.... I go to the piano, and I play two preludes and fugues of
> Bach.... It is a sort of benediction on the house. But that is not its
> only meaning.... It is a rediscovery of the world in which I have the
> joy of being a part. It fills me with awareness of the wonder of life,
> with a feeling of the incredible marvel of being a human being.[19]
> —Pablo Casals

11

"The Way Will Open"

As you recall, your Jethro blesses you forward ... *forward*, not backward. And that forward may be right into someone else's life, someone else who needs a Jethro to bless him or her. That's the ongoing challenge of the Withnesses: seeing them around you *and* being them to others around you.

Who in your life right now needs a good butt-kicking? Remember, this is not flattery, but blessing. And it's not whopping on somebody either. The butt-kick startles into attention; it doesn't bruise the reed. Above all, do no harm. Being a Jethro to others is opening a way.

> The Quakers have a saying: "The way will open."

Jethros push us out the door while telling us, "Trust God. The way will open." Who keeps your feet to the fire, your hands to the plow, both in your blessedness and your brokenness? Just as bruised apples make the best pies, bruised and broken people make the best blessers and blessings. And whose feet need to have the temperature raised on them a little? Their hands reacquainted with the grip on the plow? Their curse reversed and their spirits lifted up? Ah yes, the joys of a boot to the caboose.

Jethro Interactives

1. Canadian theologian John Stackhouse notes that Billy Graham experienced at least three, possibly four, major spiritual turning points in his life. Has this been your experience as well? What were your spiritual turning points?[20]

2. African American Franciscan Sister Thea Bowman offered this prayer when she learned she had cancer: "Lord, let me live until I die."[21] The price of life is death. It's your Jethros who enable you to die, not just full of years, but to die full of life. Tell some Jethro stories from your own experience.

3. What spiritual practices and disciplines help you maintain a harmonious life of saving and savoring the world?

4. Bishop John Sperry, the retired Anglican bishop of the Arctic, had been a missionary bishop in the vast Yukon Territory, where there was no Inuit (Eskimo) translation of the Bible. So, he set about producing one, but fairly quickly came to a sudden halt. In the Inuit language there is no word for joy, just images and metaphors. When the translators came to the resurrection story (John 20:20; Luke 24:41; Matt. 28:8), they had to find a word to express joy, and the closest metaphor to what joy meant in Inuit culture was "wagging the tail." That explains why in Inuit, John 20:20 became, "When the disciples saw the Lord, they wagged their tails."[22]

    What tales get your tail wagging?

5. Name one "shot of Goy" that keeps your faith honest and alive. Could read-ing a book by an atheist (e.g., Sam Harris's *The End of Faith*) be considered a "shot of Goy"?

6. Look at Exodus 18, where Jethro comes again to Moses incognito and blesses him in a different butt-kicking way. Moses is neglecting his family. He is tak-ing too much on himself and needs to learn to delegate. Moses was so busy blessing others that he forgot to bless his own family.

    When is the last time a Jethro got through to you that you needed to bless your own family?

7. Paul commented about one group of people: "For this reason God gave them up" (Rom. 1:26 ESV). God didn't hurl thunderbolts at them or strike them down. God merely left them to their own devices.

    What do you think is the greater danger: that God will punish us and be angry with us for our failings and rejections, or that God may leave us alone with our choices, and just let things take their course? Why?

    When God does nothing … is that the time to be afraid? Why or why not?

8. Name some people who are good blessers. Who are some people who help you bless others?

9. What would it mean to really "bless the food"? Not in some rote fashion, but with full attention? The next time you "bless the food," trying blessing

it at full attention: "Here is shrimp cocktail in front of me. Someone caught these shrimp for me. Someone carted it to land for me. Someone refrigerated this shrimp, then skinned it. Someone placed it in this beautiful container.... And we must not forget the cocktail sauce.... Thank God for sauces of all kinds, but especially cocktail sauce rich with horseradish."

Withness 4: Who's Your Timothy? You Need a Protégé

We are all treading in someone else's footsteps.

An old African proverb tells about a band of elephants happily traversing the terrain when they suddenly came upon a raging river. The big elephants did not have a problem stepping into the rough, dangerous waters. However, the small young elephants in the group were afraid to take that first step.

Elephants are known for never forgetting. As the big elephants were "crossing over," one of the elephants in the middle of the river shouted to the front of the line, to those who had already crossed over, and said, "Brother leader, we have some folks still standing on the banks of the river who haven't made it into the water."

"Brother leader" didn't call a town meeting, or write a government grant, or seek any congressional legislation. These lead elephants turned around, got back into the water, and stood shoulder to shoulder, allowing their bodies to create a dam that parted the waters to allow those little elephants (and the more fearful adult elephants) to cross over on dry ground.

How many people who make it in life, who get to the other side, forget to remember? Or they refuse to take the time to turn around, get back into the water, and help Timothys cross over on to dry ground?

> You, however, know all about my teaching, my way of life, my purpose, faith, patience, love, endurance, persecutions, sufferings.[1]
> —Paul's charge to Timothy

A "Timothy" is a protégé, an heir, an apprentice, a younger (usually), less mature version of yourself. A "Timothy" is someone who knows your mind better than anyone almost ought to be allowed to know someone else's mind. The historical Timothy was a single-parent son, probably sixteen when he was first called by Paul "my son," the same term of endearment Peter calls his protégé John Mark.[2]

Not every pupil inherits the mantle of his master: Sometimes the cream of Peter and Paul turns out skimmed milk. But of whom can you say "my son" or "my daughter"? Will you have any heirs? Who will inherit your work? Who will continue your legacy? Will you even have an heir, not of your possessions, but of your life and soul? Have you ever considered that your Sistine Chapel might not be a place or a project but a person?

My New Zealand friend Alan Jamieson puts it like this in his book that comes as close to a theology of journey as anything yet written: "Like Abram, the question that we, too, must consider is whether we will have descendants: not children in our own line but descendants in faith and life. Will we love and care for others in such a way that they become descendants? People to whom and through whom the lessons of faith we have learned are passed on and the richness of our experience of God's presence and God's absence is carried?"[3]

Before Paul had a Timothy, he first had to *be* a Timothy. Paul was a protégé of Gamaliel, the most important rabbi in Jerusalem during the time of Jesus. Gamaliel was the grandson of Hillel, one of the greatest interpreters of the Torah in Jewish history, as evidenced by the title bestowed on him of Rabboni ("our teacher") rather than Rabbi ("my teacher"). Even though Gamaliel recommended patience with those who claimed that Jesus was the Messiah,[4] his star pupil Saul didn't agree with him and set upon and stoned "blasphemers." Before becoming an evangelizing Paul, Gamaliel's star pupil was a persecuting Saul.

Have you ever noticed how Paul, whenever he begins a letter to a church, pushes Timothy to the front and brings greeting from both of them? Consider the following examples.

1. 2 Corinthians 1:1—"*Paul*, an apostle of Christ Jesus by the will of God,

and *Timothy* our brother, To the church of God in Corinth, together
with all the saints throughout Achaia."

2. Philippians 1:1—"*Paul* and *Timothy*, servants of Christ Jesus, To all
   the saints in Christ Jesus at Philippi, together with the overseers and
   deacons."

3. Colossians 1:1—"*Paul*, an apostle of Christ Jesus by the will of God, and
   Timothy our brother."

4. 1 Thessalonians 1:1—"*Paul*, Silas and *Timothy*, To the church of the
   Thessalonians in God the Father and the Lord Jesus Christ: Grace and
   peace to you."

5. 2 Thessalonians 1:1—"*Paul*, Silas and *Timothy*, To the church of the
   Thessalonians in God our Father and the Lord Jesus Christ."

In the words of Reggie McNeal, "Paul knew that ministry reproduction would
be necessary for the movement to survive."[5]

Shunammitism versus Sharonism

Shunammitism

The Bible references two Shunammite women, both unnamed. One provided
hospitality for prophets and preachers, hence the tradition of "Shunammite households"—homes with sleeping quarters for preachers also known as "prophets'
chambers."

The other provided warmth and stimulation for an ailing king. This became
known as Shunammitism, the notion that old men are rejuvenated by being with
young women, with the emphasis on closeness, not commerce. The name comes
from the young girl Abishag of Shunem who was brought to lie with the seventy-
year-old king David (1090–1015 BC) in a nonsexual embrace[6] because it was
believed that the breath and moisture of someone younger is "warmer" and hence
therapeutic than the "colder" breath of older people.[7]

I combine these two Shunammite traditions into one and call it Shunammitism: the cultivation of leadership by the old in the young through the hospitality of teaching, mentoring, and deploying. Shunammitism keeps the old young and gives age and wisdom to youth.

> In the final analysis,
> knowledge is but the luminous radiance of love.[8]
> —Karl Rahner

In my own life I tend to shut down, circle the wagons around what and whom I know, and befriend the familiar. Fortunately, for eleven years[9] I was a Timothy to a Shunammite woman who was still making new friends and investing time, energy, and resources in new projects when she became a centenarian. Marie Aull was a gardener/philanthropist/environmentalist who created in Dayton, Ohio, the largest learning center of the National Audubon Society.[10] Well into her eighties when I first met her, Marie was still open to new ideas, new perspectives, and May-December friends, and she became such a Yoda to me that I paid tribute to her influence on my life by dedicating a book to her.[11]

Marie Aull "took me on," as she put it, because "you are so into books and your own creativity, Leonard, you need to be introduced to God's creativity." In her upstairs loft, which served as an orchid greenhouse, she offered me a protected space for writing and reading when the phones in the president's office would not stop ringing. When the words did not want to stop flowing, she would send up meals to me. But Marie always insisted I take time out for an early-morning or late-afternoon walk in the garden.

That's when she painstakingly and peripatetically introduced me to the out-of-doors, the world of night, the ways of a sycamore tree, the red-cedar reclamation, and the "Sunset Effect." And she taught me to always look for the

Timothys. A healthy tree is not a single tree, no matter how beautiful it may look. A healthy sycamore tree is a tree with heirs ... a sycamore community with trees in various stages of growth and development. Not only did you never plant one tree (always odd numbers: 3, 5, 7, etc.), but you fostered sycamores in various ages and stages. "Always look for a tree's successors," she would say over and over again, "before you judge its health and vitality."

Not until she died did it hit me that our friendship had been a brilliant reflection of that Shunammite "look for the heirs" philosophy of life.

Sharonism

Every great leader and teacher has been a Timothy: Jesus apprenticed to John the Baptist; Paul of Tarsus, about five years younger than Jesus of Nazareth, apprenticed with Gamaliel; Elisha apprenticed to Elijah; Joshua apprenticed to Moses.

But Joshua did not pass on his baton. Joshua had no heirs ... and then came the judges, spawning the most horrible times recorded in the Hebrew Bible for Israel. Or in the Bible's scalding words, the judges came because the baton-less generation "did not know the LORD or the work that he had done for Israel."[12]

Not to have a Joshua or a Timothy (or a John Mark, who was Peter's protégé) is what I call "Sharonism." Ariel Sharon (b. 1928) had no Joshua when a massive stroke ended his political career in 2006. As defense minister and minister of agriculture, Ariel Sharon was a hard-line settlement builder and Arab fighter. For his military exploits, he was seen as a war hero by some and a war criminal by others.

When Sharon became prime minister, he did an abrupt turnaround and, to the surprise of both his friends and his foes, turned into his country's greatest peacemaker and settlement demolisher. In words that should be entered in every book of quotations, he confessed, "You see things from here that you don't see from there."[13] With the courage to admit he was wrong, Sharon began cleaning up his mess, even to the point of leaving the Likkud party, which he crafted to build a raft of defiant Jewish settlements in the West Bank and Gaza.

Just when it looked like he would use his considerable weight to muscle into being an Arab-Israel resolution, a massive stroke brought everything he had worked for to a halt. Without a Joshua to wear his mantle, Sharon's power was a spent force, and the Middle East was thrown into even more ghoulish grips.

It is not just that you can get a lot more done if you have heirs, but that sometimes you can't even do what God is calling you to do without heirs. One of the worst things you can say about a musician or a scholar or any artist is this: "He left no progeny." It ought to be one of the worst things anyone could say in your obituary. One of the highest honors a musician or a scholar or an artist can receive is a Festschrift: a book of essays about their life and work created by their Timothys. A Festschrift of one's own works and words would not just be given short shrift; it would be laughed off the shelves.

11

> When nature removes a great man, we explore the horizons for a successor. But none comes and none will, for his class is extinguished with him.[14]
> —Finnish runner Paavo Nurmi

11

Where Have All the Timothys Gone?

If you're going to have a Timothy in your life or be a Timothy in someone else's life, you're going to have to learn the ways of holy dissonance. These are daring, mold-breaking, life-giving ways, but don't expect them to make "sense" or be able to put them into a spreadsheet.

Ministry by Osmosis

A lot of life is sheer osmosis, and we don't have the patience of presence to allow the slow labor of apostolic exposure and experience to take place. Osmosis was how protégés like Timothy, Titus, Epaphroditus, Erastus, Epaphras, Silas, Luke, John Mark, and others learned from Paul. They traveled with him, watched what he did, and then were given "tests" or assignments to complete to see how well they were developing their potential. Wherever they went, however, they carried the aura of Paul's authority and name with them. But the Timothy relationship cannot develop without the patience of presence.

For at least ten years now, I have been arguing against the desk dominion of the "Pastor's Office" in favor of the apprentice environment of the "studio" model.[15] Instead of private, personal "office" space, what if we reconfigured our space to allow for open areas with large tables and other architectural elements that could encourage collaboration, discourage possessiveness, and allow for osmosis to take place. The number of pastors who have taken me up on this "don't do desk" refrain is virtually zero. Have we lost the team eldership and relational models of the biblical story for solo leadership patterns and principles?

A final neglected part of ministry formation by osmosis is shared silence. Ours is a culture that has little use for sanctums of silence. A Timothy is someone with whom you can share vast amounts of silence. You don't have to say a word, or call every other day, to let him know you still care.

11

> There should be in the soul halls of space, avenues of leisure and high porticos of silence, where God waits.[16]
> —Jeremy Taylor

11

Evolution in the Church

If church members have a responsibility to replicate themselves in the form of new converts, how much more should church leaders replicate themselves in the form of new ministerial candidates?

When the baton is passed, however, we tend to grab the wrong end of the stick. That's the end our mentor was holding, not our own end. In other words, most Timothys want to be clones, not heirs.

It is natural to want to reproduce in ourselves others' experience of God. But even nature (the true "natural") doesn't copy itself. Reproduction is a process of inaccurate, flawed self-copying, which is the key insight of Charles Darwin: Authentic "nature" is not cloning but evolving.

Cloning isn't present in the Bible either. Joshua is not a Moses clone. Timothy was not a Paul clone. What you find in the Scriptures is what today we would call a "mash-up"—the putting together of material in fresh ways. Mash-ups remix the same song with a different beat, sometimes in a different key. Almost all creativity is some form of mash-up, whether it's Starbucks' mash-up of third place with Internet access, or the "1984" anti-Hillary ad in 2007 that mashed up George Orwell and George Lucas. For mash-ups to take place, what Timothys need most is "sounding boards."

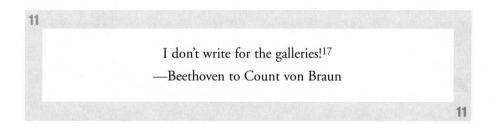

I don't write for the galleries![17]
—Beethoven to Count von Braun

Superstring physics defines matter very simply: You and I are "vibrating strings of energy." We are string instruments … sounding boards by nature. Life plays those strings, and the notes of life are your thoughts and emotions. That's the danger of holding things in and keeping the notes to yourself. Those notes have to

witness 4: who's your timothy?   83

burst forth in song, and if they don't burst forth in song, they burst forth and explode in destructive ways.

Neglected strings break when finally played. Some people never get the opportunity to play their song ... so we medicate our numbness rather than play the song we've been given. The process of being a Timothy is a gradual revelation of the song your life is composing ... that one-of-a-kind, unrepeatable, irreplaceable song that only you can sing. But Timothys need sounding boards to find their songs.

Remember the Winnie the Pooh story about losing his song? He gets his friends to go on the hunt for his song and then he finds that his song is within him. Too many Timothys are being told to "play the part" of corporate Christendom: Sing all six verses from the hymnal.

Instead, the song of the gospel is a ballad of daring, mold-breaking, lie-rejecting, life-giving dissonance. Holy dissonance.

> **11**
>
> A friend is someone who, when you forget your
> song, comes and sings it for you.[18]
>
> **11**

The Ears Have It

Leadership is more of a sound check than a vision test, and the primary Timothy organs are the ears. When Power (Pilate) confronted Truth (Jesus), Jesus said, "Everyone who belongs to the Truth hears my voice." He did not say, "Everyone who belongs to the Truth sees my vision."

Jesuit professor Walter Ong has written an important book about the war between the eye and the ear in Christian history. The Protestant Reformation was a triumph of the eye, with the printed text winning out over spoken word.[19]

Ong argues that the ear engages with voice, with call, with revelation. Go into a room, and you are anonymous until you speak. It is your voice that activates a relationship.[20]

The challenge for a Timothy is to learn how to hear. If there were one word that indicates the success or failure of being a Timothy, it would be this one: *listening*. Some things can only be heard by those with ears to hear. The more our layers of interference—iPods, cell phones, BlackBerries—the more our inner voice is blocked and the more help we need to hear. Timothys learn how to hear themselves think and to eavesdrop on eternity with newly attuned ears. Most important, Timothys learn to recognize Jesus as God's middle C, God's tuning fork to the eternal, God's perfect pitch.[21]

It is not an accident that music is the language of the emerging culture. And not just in the West. The greatest communal event in Cairo's recent history was the four-million-strong procession that escorted the singer Umm Kulthum to her grave.[22] Music helps to grow the biggest grapes[23] and to grow the best disciples of Jesus.

The Church Has Only Half a Brain ... and It's the Wrong Half

Wanted: Right-Brained Timothys

In the twentieth century, a Timothy's key assets were a right arm and a left brain. The future belongs to the right brained and the left armed. The era of left-brain dominance is over. In fact, most left-brained items—rational, logical, linear functions—will be outsourced to computers.

A right-brain world is aborning, a world where inventiveness, empathy, and meaning predominate and where the forces of creativity and imagination will be the most important resources for every Timothy.

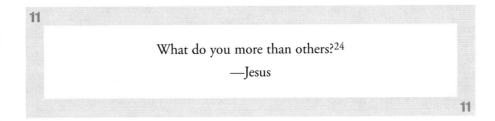

> What do you more than others?[24]
> —Jesus

The Meaning of More

Faith is the art of imagining. When God said, "Let there be light," God was saying, "Let there be inquiry and imagination." Humans are less "made in God's image" than "made in God's imagination" and invited to *participate* in the divine imagination. Imagination is participation in the divine nature.

The power behind the creation of the universe is the power behind all inquiring and imagining. The Christian life is creative and imaginative. The Russian Orthodox writer Nicholas Berdyaev has argued that the revelation of God to man must be complemented by a *revelation of man to God*, meaning our creative response to life that serves as a gift of gratitude to God.

That means that the greatest crisis in the world today is not political or economic or religious. The greatest crisis in the world today is a crisis of the imagination. Trace every crisis back to its roots, and you will find the same thing: a failure of the imagination.

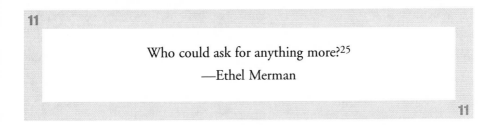

> Who could ask for anything more?[25]
> —Ethel Merman

Imagination splits into two kinds; both are differing interpretations of Jesus' question to his disciples: "What do you more than others?"

What did Jesus mean by "more"? The meaning of more is a matter of utmost urgency since postmodern culture is on a search for "something more," and that "something more" is the subject of many books and articles. In fact, sociologists in Holland have begun calling this "something more" cultural phenomenon "something-ism," a phrase that will no doubt catch on. But the problem with "something-ism" is that its meaning depends on that four-letter word—*more*.

11

Somewhere, something incredible is waiting to be known.[26]
—astronomer/atheist Carl Sagan

11

More as "Better"

Two primary candidates arise when determining the meaning of *more*: better and different. There is the imagination of "better," and the imagination of "different." In the past, Timothys were trained in the imagination of more as "better."[27] In the future, Timothys will need to be trained in the imagination of *more* as "different."

More as "better" means doing what you're already doing, except doing it bigger, faster, with added value, reinforced reliability, improved scalability, and ever-more-narrow-casted nichecraft. The winner of the 2005 Berry-AMA Book Prize was *Simply Better*, a defense of low-risk, high-return "inside the box" thinking that imitates and elevates what is already being done.[28] For the imagination of *more* as "better," excellence is working harder at delivery of the basics. There is a lot of money to be made in the imagination of better. Inside-the-box packing of wooden furniture has generated more wealth for its owner than Microsoft Man's innovations in software.[29]

More as "Different"?

More as "different" means doing something unique and "outside the box." Rather than doing the same thing better, break the mold, embrace change, and try something new. For the imagination of difference, doing the same thing "better" is called a rut. Or in the words of architect Robert Venturi, "more is a bore."[30] In fact, there is strong textual support for the "different" understanding of *more*. Where the King James and Revised Standard and NIV translate the Greek as *more*, other translations offer these alternatives: "out of the ordinary or extraordinary (Good News Translation/New English Bible), "remarkable" (Goodspeed), "exceptional" (Phillips/Jerusalem Bible), "unusual" (New American Bible).[31]

The imagination of "better" has given us Hummer-houses, megachurches, supersonic jets, IKEA, Microsoft, and spiritual-gifts inventories.

The imagination of "different" has given us cohousing, noncongregational churches, "mash-ups," Segways, Linux, Google, Apple, and spiritual-weakness inventories.

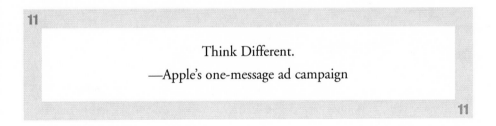

11

Think Different.
—Apple's one-message ad campaign

11

Sounds Like "We"

Rather than abandon the category "more" completely, I would argue that the kind of imagination the world needs today is one that understands *more* less as "better" and more as "different." "Get different" is now a more required imagination than "Get better." Our current times require the imagination of conception more than improvement.

The imagination of "better" is what characterizes Sony's PlayStation 3 (PS3) and Microsoft's Xbox 360. Tokyo-based Sony and Seattle-based Microsoft produce video-game experiences that are "better" than anything that has come before: They are faster (the PS3 has a cell processor that is forty times faster than the chip used in the PS2), more powerful, with unsurpassed graphics, extensive online services, the most lifelike characters ever seen on a screen, and a host of other "extras."

The imagination of "different" is what characterizes Nintendo's Wii (sounds like "we"). With a console only one-tenth as powerful as Sony's and Microsoft's new offerings, Kyoto-based Nintendo produced a menu of video-game experiences that were all about interaction, participation, "we."

Go into any video-game store, and you stumble over tall stacks of PlayStation 3s and Xbox 360s, seeking buyers and sucking wind. Meanwhile, Nintendo Wiis are nowhere to be found—so hot you have to be in the store at the right time to get one. Nobody in Nintendo anticipated the demand. Within a year after the console was introduced (November 2006), Nintendo sold four million Wii players in the United States alone, and the stepping up of Wii production at Chinese factories[32] and the fast-tracking of new games still can't keep up with the demand.

Altered States and Timothys

The desire to imagine a better world has been the root of much idiocy and crime as well as beauty, truth, and goodness. If "imagination" is not to feed our "need" to buy more stuff, get bigger and better body parts, and medicalize our passion, perhaps it's time that Christians ought to use our imagination less to "better ourselves" than to "difference ourselves." If truth be told, Christians don't so much live "better" than others. We live "different." The Greek word we translate as "repentance" is *metanoia,* which literally means "change your mind." I translate it as "altered imagination." The gospel is more than mind altering. It alters our imaginations as well.

Of course, the imaginations of "better" and "difference" are both needed. Christians need to both better ourselves and difference ourselves. But at this time in history, our mission is not so much to create a "better world" as it is a "different world." In a world that prides itself in its love of force, difference yourself: Be known for imagining the force of love.

The meaning of *more* as "better" feeds into the image of a "ladder of success." All we need to do to achieve success is to keep climbing rungs, each one predictable, each one higher, each one building on what went before it, each one safe.

Different isn't safe. Timothys have to take some leaps into the unknown when they go the "different" route. But I ask you: When you come to the top of the ladder, when you come to the top step in that ladder of "better," what's the next one?

A leap into the unknown. Even the ladder makes us step out in faith. Why not leapfrog the ladder and go right to the leaping? The future is wide open to those who do.

In August 1953, a truck driver arrived at a Memphis studio and announced he wanted to start a singing career. "What do you sound like?" asked the secretary.

"I don't sound like nobody," answered Elvis Presley.[33]

Timothy Interactives

1. Saint Benedict, in his Rules, says a couple of times that "the young should respect their elders, and the elders should love their juniors."[34]

    Which group do you think has the harder task?

2. My Rule #1 for reading the Bible is this: "Every story about Jesus is about me." Do you agree with me? Why or why not?

3. Lord Alfred Douglas belongs to an elite club: individuals (Mark Twain was another) who have had the shock of reading their own obituary. On the afternoon of February 4, 1921, he bought a copy of the *Evening News* and was halted by the headline: SUDDEN DEATH OF LORD ALFRED DOUGLAS—FOUND DEAD IN BED BY MAID. What followed was worse:

    > A brilliant and most unhappy career is ended.... The charity which is fitting at all times, but most fitting when we are speaking of the newly-dead, urges that much should be forgiven to this poor, bewildered man, who, with all his gifts, will perhaps only be remembered by the scandals and the quarrels in which he involved himself.

    He was fifty-one when he read this. He sued the paper for defamation: His obituary omitted what he deemed significant about his life. What about his poetry, his horsemanship, his fame? Douglas actually won the suit, but history has agreed with his first obituary.[35]

Who is helping you to write your obituary, and what will it feature? What do you hope it will feature?

4. "Left-brain dominance" is shorthand for how the left hemisphere is sequential, textual, and analytical, while the right hemisphere is simultaneous, contextual, and synthetic.

    When someone says, "You sure do think different," do you take it as a compliment? Why or why not? Is it meant (sometimes) as a compliment, or is it almost always negative in its implications? What about when you say it of others?

5. Do you agree with me that the gospel is less about "better" than "different," that disciples of Jesus are not just called to be "better" but to be "different"?

    What do you think of my motto of discipleship: "I beg to differ"?

6. Eli failed twice as a father before he "parented" Samuel. How difficult do you think it was for Hannah to trust Eli with Samuel? Did it make a difference that Hannah was known to be a pray-er? Why or why not?

7. Seeing aids are now high fashion: What about walking aids or hearing aids?

    Go around the room and explore the different kinds of eyewear. Compare the style of seeing aids with walking aids … one-color, elderly gray canes, wheelchairs, or crutches. Why not have Harley wheelchairs or Donna Karan walkers or iPod hearing aids? Come up with your own ideas and combinations that reflect more as "different" rather than "better."

Check out the Web site for Rollator, which is trying to bring design to walkers. The "Walking Assistant" (invented by Andres Berl) puts a grabber as well as a magnet on the bottom of the cane and a flashlight in the handle.

What other ideas can you think of?

8. Do you have any stories of people in your life who have enjoyed patronizing young preachers, trying to build cubs into lions? Any Shunammite households you know of or been privileged to be a part of?

9. Research the tradition of the "Parson's cupboard" in nineteenth-century homes. Interview some of the older members of your community who might know of homes where this was still a feature in the fireplace. Was this a somewhat abbreviated version of "prophets' chambers"?

10. Invite some of the youth of your church to give a demonstration of the different video-games systems.

11. Do you think Timothys need rites of initiation? Can you think of any other culture in history that has been without initiation rituals that have helped young people find their places in larger communities? How much of youth's experimentation with high-risk behaviors is an attempt at self-initiation? What are some of those high-risk behaviors?

12. If you don't have a father, how do you know how to be a father?[36] Many today have never had a Peter/Paul, so they don't know how to be a Yoda to others or

they don't know how to entrust their kids to mentors. What do you think of the thesis that mentors of the future may need to go after their Timothys, not wait for Timothys to choose them?

Is to be a Timothy more a bequeathing or more an inheriting?

13. Studies of tortured prisoners have revealed that one of the best ways to survive torture is to sing. When James Mawdsley was imprisoned in Burma, he sang to give himself courage:

> After [the prison guard] left, still unable to sleep, I began singing "How Great Thou Art." My voice got louder and louder until I was belting it out. I could feel strength coming back to me; I was not going to bow yet. A gaggle of guards came running and told me to be quiet. They were excited and afraid. I sang to the end of the song, congratulating myself on my defiance, then crumpled back into bleakness.[37]

We should have known this simply by understanding the power of slave spirituals. When you go back to your cell, sing. Better yet, sing in your cells with other prisoners, as Chilean political prisoner Luis Muñoz did. Become a choir. Give voice your pain and anguish.[38] Sing what you cannot say.

A choir director once said, "When you're nervous, just sing for Jesus." But there's even something more liberating than singing for Jesus: Let Jesus sing through you. It's the difference between "singing for God" and "letting God sing in and through you." When God sings in and through us, liberation happens.

The vibrations of Paul and Silas, singing in that miserable jail in the Macedonian city of Philippi, brought the prison building down.

It's story time: What prison bars have come crashing down when you have let Jesus sing in you?

14. By the time you read this book, you will know whether my prediction is right: I predict that more Wiis will be sold in 2007 than PS3 and Xbox 360 consoles combined in spite of slashed prices by both Sony and Microsoft.[39] I also wonder whether remotes in the future might be called "Wii-motes."

Withness 5: Who's Your Barnabas? You Need an Encourager

"Where shall I find courage?" Frodo asked.
"For that is what I chiefly need."[1]

A Barnabas is an "encourager," someone in your life who is constantly saying, "Atta boy!" or, "Atta girl!" When you have had more than your fair share of jabs to the ribs and stabs in the back, who puts his or her arms on your shoulders and whispers, "Don't let them get to you. I believe in you"?

That's your Barnabas.

You need affirmation, attention, and encouragement as much as you need food, shelter, and rest. You need what church culture calls an "acolyte"—someone to light your candle, to keep it lit, and to encourage you when it does get dark.

Every word of praise you receive is a star in the night sky.

In fact, the physical benefits of encouragement are demonstrated by that elite club of actors who get to take home an Oscar, what I prefer to call the "Oscar Barnabas" of the movie industry. Demographic studies of Oscar winners reveal recipients have abnormally long life spans compared with those who are passed over or are in the general population. An Oscar is the statistical equivalent of a complete abolition of coronary heart disease for the person receiving it. Why is an Oscar that good for your health? Because it symbolizes the constant encouragement of your peers.[2]

Barnabas was called a "son of a prophet," not because he was abrasive, but because he was positive. Barnabas was originally known as Joseph, a respected leader of the church. He was a Levite by birth, a member of the Jewish tribe that functioned as scholars and teachers when they weren't conducting temple duties. Because Joseph's family had moved to Cyprus, he didn't serve in the temple.

Joseph sold a field he owned and gave the proceeds to the apostles.[3] The disciples were grateful and gave Joseph a new name of endearment: "Barnabas," which means "Encourager."

Multi-Sight Ministry

Barnabas's ministry of encouragement was multidimensional:

- ✓ When the apostles were frightened of Saul, Barnabas vouched for his good character[4] and sought him out to encourage him in his missionary journeys.
- ✓ The church in Jerusalem sent Barnabas to check out the situation in Antioch, and he welcomed the new converts with joy[5] and encouraged other struggling churches.
- ✓ Barnabas sought out Paul to minister with him in Antioch, where believers were first called "Christians."[6]
- ✓ Even when he and Paul disagreed, Barnabas went on to mentor another young Christian and continue the work of the Lord.
- ✓ Barnabas sided with Peter in the battle with Paul at Antioch. Surprising? Inconsistent?

A Barnabas is an encourager, not an embalmer. Some people will embalm you in flattery. That's not a Barnabas, that's a sycophant.

Do you have a Barnabas, a peer-encourager who is

someone to hold up those tired and weary arms;

someone to add a hand when you rarely or barely hear the sound of one hand clapping;

someone who gives you permission to fail, permission to write a bad first draft;

someone who can remind you that God gives us a portion adequate for us to make it through the day;

someone who can dare you to remember that the God who called you to life is that same God who called you to ministry;

someone to remind you that you have the privilege of loving for a living;

someone who, when life takes your breath away and you hold it in, will slap your back and "inspire" you with the enlivening Spirit who makes you want to breathe again;

someone who will lift you up when you're road-whipped, world-weary, bone-tired, blood-thin, when you feel buttonholed and browbeaten;

someone who will encourage you when you're tempted to think that the only difference between yogurt and the church you're a part of is that yogurt has active, living culture?

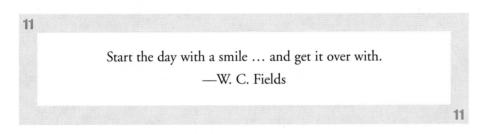

Start the day with a smile ... and get it over with.
—W. C. Fields

A Barnabas leaves a porch light on, not the 100-watt spotlight so as to ferret out where you've been, but more like the 10- or 15-watt soft white energy-efficient compact fluorescent bulb—something warm to welcome you home and let you know you were missed.

Who works like steroids to your spirit? Who sets you free for mission and ministry?

But don't forget the vice versa. To whom are *you* a Barnabas? Do you "encourage one another"?[7] To whom do you regularly speak words that put wind into their sails?

Worry makes a heart heavy,
a kindly word makes it glad.
—Proverbs 12:25 NJB

Two Kinds of Handlers

Human beings need two kinds of "handlers," two kinds of "hands-on" Withnesses. Just like there are two sides of the brain, there are two types of "hands." One kind of hand makes a fist. The other kind of hand makes a palm.

Nathan? That's the fist. But Barnabas? That's the palm: They give strokes, they pat on the back, keep in touch, and "feel" your pain (the word *feel* derives from roots meaning "palm of the hand"). A "fist-handler" is your Nathan. A "palm-handler" is your Barnabas.

Do you have two-handed Withnesses?

Who's your Barnabas? Who have you nicknamed with a term of endearment as you call him or her into a mission that can save the world?

Up until Acts 13:7, Paul is Barnabas's assistant. Barnabas is Paul's senior and sponsor, hence the order of "Barnabas and Paul." From the moment they parted company, it becomes "Paul and Barnabas." In fact, Saul becomes Paul when Paul and Barnabas have a falling out to the point where Paul pulls Barnabas, and Paul becomes the lead member.[8] Later Paul has another quarrel with Peter and Barnabas in Antioch, which pulls him further away from Barnabas.[9]

What was the nature of their first falling out?

Paul lost faith in John Mark. But Barnabas didn't.

We have no idea why John Mark lost his fire. Clearly Paul didn't "buy" the reasons he heard for John Mark's return to Jerusalem.

Why do we forsake the mission? What makes us want to run and hide? What tempts us to leave the path, to shrug off our charge? What prompts us to release our hand from the plow?

We will always have moments of weakness—of compromised resolve. When John Mark (author of Mark) ran back home to his mother, his cousin Barnabas went after him, bucked him up, and brought him back. Barnabas then insisted that the disciples give John Mark another chance. Paul, not always the best team player, refused to take him back.[10]

Mark's mother was one of the first supporters in Jerusalem. Peter and other disciples enjoyed her hospitality. John Mark grew up listening to the stories of these apostles. His boyish ears picked up the stories of those who lived and talked with Jesus. One can only imagine what John Mark's mother thought of her son's return; she was not looking forward to this homecoming.

But Barnabas so believed in his first-cousin John Mark that he took him and went in one direction (Cyprus), while Paul took Silas and went in another. Only later in life, after John Mark became a confidant of Peter and proved himself fit in the field, did Paul seek his companionship. Indeed, Paul asked for John Mark's presence as he was facing certain death.

We all feel like giving up, and sometimes we will give up. You may cast away. Others may cast you off. But God never casts us aside. You may not keep up. And others may not see you as a "keeper." But because God is your keeper, God will keep vigil over you with a host of encouragers.

The House of Barnabas

The house of Barnabas has many mansions and many outhouses.

Or as Dante would put it, a Barnabas is "polysemous."

In a famous letter to his Veronan benefactor, Can Grande della Scala, Dante set forth his purpose behind writing *The Divine Comedy*, a masterpiece now recognized as one of the greatest writings in the history of Western literature. Dante described what he had written as "polysemous." It is a matter of some debate what Dante meant by this, but mystery novelist and Anglo-Catholic Dorothy L. Sayers (who valued her own translation of *The Divine Comedy* as her greatest achievement) argues that it refers to the many layers of meaning that mark the uniqueness of sacred and secular scriptures.[11]

"Polysemous" is another way of saying that something is so profound, so split-at-the-root it can only be understood in terms of its multiple levels and outcroppings. Here is a polysemous understanding of the various Barnabas Witnesses that you may need at any one time or another. And that you may be. The five energy fields of a Barnabas encourager may be symbolized as follows:

1. The Good Samaritan Barnabas

The Good Samaritan Barnabas makes support a sport.

Often anonymous, this spontaneous Barnabas speaks that perfectly timed "word fitly spoken," which Proverbs compares to golden apples in silver settings.[12] You could be pulling out your credit card at a checkout counter, or apologizing for a misdialed phone number, or asking for directions at a gas station, or sitting at the front of the bus next to the shuttle driver when the spontaneous Barnabas says something to lift your chin up, to buck you up and cheer you up, to help you regain your sea legs.

I ran a marathon … once. I half-jokingly call marathons the "ultimate postmodern sport" because you don't enter to win, but to finish. No one asks, "Did you win the Boston Marathon?" but, "Did you finish?"

The marathon was held in Dayton, Ohio, and all of us who were running had our names emblazoned on the backs of our T-shirts. I'll never forget the experience of having those along the route encouraging me as I panted through my paces and staggered toward the finish line. Onlookers did more than stand there and gawk. The sidelines became part of the marathon's mainlines by the constant yelling from mile one of "Go, Len! Go, Len!" or, closer to the end of the race, "Don't give up, Len. Don't give up." These people didn't know me from a number on a license plate. But these anonymous, spontaneous Barnabas Withnesses helped me finish that race in a near-record (for near last-place) time.

Sometimes we are called to encourage people we don't know. But we're all in the same race.

Some people have entertained angels
without knowing it.
—Hebrews 13:2

In fact, one of my most favorite spiritual practices is to dedicate at least one day a week to being a spontaneous Barnabas to every person I meet that day. At one point in my life I resolved to do this every day of my life,[13] but for someone with a hermit's heart who reads and converses with the dead while he walks, the expenditure of gregarious energy is simply too great. However, something as simple as recognizing a piece of jewelry someone picked out to wear that day ("Love that pin") or preceding a "Thanks!" with "You're fantastic! Thank you!" can be as life giving to the giver as it is to the receiver.

This kind of Barnabas is admittedly more style than substance, more good manners than good works. But in our pursuit of a "deeper" spiritual life and depth of relationships, we should not forget the importance of the shallow— the smile, the wink, the hand squeeze, the slap on the back, the kiss on the cheek. The shallow is a beginning for us all, dipping our toes at the shallow end of the pool, preparing for deeper waters. There are moments when Muzak is fine, and there are moments when only Mozart will do. Sometimes to plumb the depths of a problem a submarine is required; sometimes a dipstick will do.

I'm a big defender of shallow friends. We need people in our lives who do shallow well. Not every conversation needs to end in confidences. Not every moment or interchange must "suck the marrow." The worst company in the world is that person who can't chat or engage in small talk.

11

Deep calls to deep in the roar of your waterfalls;
all your waves and breakers have swept over me.
—Psalm 42:7

11

Every depth has a surface, and when you live deeply, you still need surface people in your life. Barnabas types can be surface people. You don't need a "heavy, deep, and real" relationship with every person you meet. In fact, you don't need to be "heavy, deep, and real" at all times yourself. I love to imagine Jesus being shallow with a great sense of fun: joking with his disciples, laughing at a burp, telling Peter that the one who smelt it dealt it.

Your Barnabas is often found in the shallows, but a spontaneous Barnabas helps you to see life's inexhaustible epiphanies even from the shallow end of the pond. Sometimes you're a "diver in." Other times you're a "dipper in." But remember that the mundane is never inane. Your Barnabas helps you see how the holy haunts the everyday, and to see those holy haunts in all their splendor and significance. Everyday and eternal matters are always mixed.

When you find out who you really are—a child of God—each person you meet and every place you visit becomes an epiphany. Or in the words of Hopkins' famous sonnet ("As Kingfishers Catch Fire"), every human being

> acts in God's eyes what in God's eyes he is—
> Christ—for Christ plays in ten thousand places,
> Lovely in limbs, and lovely in eyes not his
> To the Father through the features of men's face.[14]

2. The Onesimus/Big Brother Barnabas

The Onesimus Barnabas encourages us by name, not by number.

Poet Philip Larkin once said of jazz clarinetist Sidney Bechet: "On me your voice falls as they say love should, / Like an enormous yes."[15] Whose voice falls on your ears "like an enormous yes"? Who knows your name well enough to understand the hesitancies of your heart, and yet helps you know every hesitant moment that you are loved, and out of that love you are an instrument of God's love? Paul was fixated on John Mark's defects; Barnabas was fixated on his promise. Who is reminding you that God's nature and name is Love, especially when you think it is Judgment and Fear? Who is close enough to you to challenge you not to compromise your promise?

That person is your Onesimus Barnabas, the person who is helping you to learn to … simply be.

Sometimes you grasp life with both hands. Other times life grabs you, by the throat, in a headlock, trips you up, and takes you down. Crumpled up and keeled over, you can lose confidence in your abilities and lose sight of your responsibilities.

What curls you up in the fetal position? Death of a loved one? Depression? Fear of the unknown? Collapse of a relationship? Dreaded diagnosis? Sickness?

When I'm sick, here's my routine: go home, shut the door, close the blinds, and crawl in bed. And go into the fetal position. I unconsciously want to re-create the conditions of the womb: darkness (hence close the curtains or blinds), warmth (hence hot water bottles and warm blankets), quiet (turn off loud noises—only simple, soothing rhythms), cramped quarters (tuck in bedsheets, comforter). I want to re-create that time in my life when I felt most secure and taken care of … the womb.

No one can keep you from going into that fetal position, but they can encourage you to uncurl. No one can keep your soul from breaking, but they can lift you up when your soul is broken. This Barnabas is the person who is close enough to awaken the best in you when you start sleepwalking through life in some dreamy detachment. Your Barnabas can also put you to bed when you enter a dreamless absence from your existence. Like sweet rockets at the end of May, we lie down and play dead when the nights are cold but perk up and become pretty when kissed by the morning sunshine. Whose kiss, whose fingers wipe away the tears from your eyes so that you can see the beauty, truth, and goodness through the marring maze of ugliness, evil, and injustice? That's your Big Sister Barnabas.

This is the person or presence who climbs into the foxhole with you. There are no Peters or Pauls in foxholes. They're focused on their own battlefronts. But for Batman there was Robin, for Pancho there was Lefty, for the Lone Ranger there was Tonto, for Don Quixote there was Sancho Panza, for Robin Hood there was Little John, for Frodo there was Samwise, and for Arthur there was (for a time) Lancelot.

> But in the mud and scum of things
> There always, always something sings.[16]
> —Ralph Waldo Emerson

"Close enough" doesn't mean that you've necessarily met this person. I took time out from writing these words to thank an Onesimus Barnabas in my life. His name is Ken Brown; he's a historian, author, and antique bookseller from Pennsylvania. I have never met Ken even though we have exchanged hundreds of e-mails and I have purchased dozens of books from him privately and on eBay. No one knows more about the tradition from which I hail (the holiness movement) than Ken, and no one is a better guide to the primary resources my library requires than Ken.

In negotiating the purchase of a Phoebe Palmer book I needed for a research project, I mentioned to Ken that I had just visited the Amazon sales figures for a couple of my books and logged off a craven creature suffering from the Amazon Blues. Immediately he fired back this response:

> Len: I sure do understand those feelings, my dear friend!!
> Been there, and it can be as nasty as, as, —as much as it
> is a blessing! Do this: Take long walks, bounce rocks off
> the water, watch the birds, fish or hunt (even if it's just
> with an old BB gun!), read Psalm 23, and go antiquing
> with your wife—a lot!
>
> THEN—write like mad! Ken

So here I am once again writing like mad. I didn't do exactly what my Onesimus Barnabas told me to do. But I did take a walk, throw rocks into the waters of Puget Sound, watch the birds at the bird feeder outside my study, and listen to two of my most reliable Barnabas Withnesses: John Coltrane and Søren Hyldgaard. I dare you to spend fourteen minutes with jazz genius John Coltrane's "Out of This World" and not be taken, well, "out of this world." And nothing can lift me out of the blues, whether caused by Amazon or the Zeitgeist, like the trombone solo and wind music in Danish composer Søren Hyldgaard's Nordic "Rapsodia Borealis."

It is only when, as the psalmist put it, our "cup runneth over" that we can be triumphantly creative and bless others. When our cup is depleted or dry, we have barely enough to survive, and everything we slosh stays inside. But try to carry a full cup. What's inside will inevitably "run over" and jostle out. Your Onesimus Barnabas keeps your cup full of love, hope, and faith (and a little bit jazzy) so that what's inside can spill out and splash others in the face.

3. The Epaphras-Prayer Barnabas

Epaphras Barnabas, your most Dangerous Barnabas.

Prayer is the most powerful force in the universe. So your Epaphras Barnabas, who keeps the prayer wheel turning your direction, is one of the most powerful people in your relationship repertoire. This Barnabas is not the one who says, "I'll pray for you," a dismissal with the same meaning as "Don't call me, I'll call you." This Barnabas has entered into a covenant of prayer for you, often ritualized with a prayer ceremony.

Pray-er, beware: Before you unleash the power of an Epaphras Barnabas, make sure you're ready to give up who you are for who you might become. Make sure you're ready to move mountains, slay dragons, and leap into the abyss.

Epaphras was part of the Colossian community who was "always wrestling in prayer for you," as Paul put it, even when the conditions (i.e., prison) weren't the best for praying for others besides yourself.[17] Who is praying for you? Who is bathing you in prayer energies as you read this? Right now, at this very moment? Do you have a Dangerous Barnabas like Epaphras who is "unceasing in prayer" and keeps the energy field of prayer hot and healing? If Jesus' specially chosen disciples could sleep through their prayer life, how much easier it is for us to live prayerless lives? And if we "have not" because we "ask not,"[18] then we need people to ask for us when we are sleeping.

An Epaphras Barnabas does wonders for your ears.

First, your ears are imperative to your sense of hearing. Prayer is another way of talking about listening. Prayer opens up our ears to hear what God is saying and to find our "voice." I almost lost my mind once because I couldn't find my voice. Without an Epaphras Barnabas who covenanted to pray for me every day, I'm not sure I would ever have heard God's voice or rediscovered my own.

A Barnabas helps us to hear God's "no" as well as God's "yes," to recognize the true sound of our own voice, and to listen thoroughly (which is the literal meaning of obedience).[19]

Second, your ears have *everything* to do with your sense of balance. Without prayer, our equilibrium is off and we lean in Devil-on-stilts directions. It is almost as if planet Earth were tilted on a negative axis, making it easier to be bad than good. Life is a slippery slope, and humans slide into savagery quickly. Or to use a metaphor quite popular in the early church: One thing is certain about a boat—it will always and everywhere drift off course. Your prayer partner helps you stay on course and not "drift away."[20]

Do you have an Epaphras Barnabas whose prayers keep you from slip-sliding away?

Third, your ears pick up the vibrations of life's ticking time bombs before your vision brings these dangers into focus. Prayers help you to prepare for the sudden faults and seismic shifts that crack open on your path and threaten to swallow you up. Certain things in life, in the words of poet A. S. Byatt, who lost her son in a cycling accident, "can scythe through the fabric of dailiness, and change things forever."[21] Life moves in a blink from birth to death, from blessing to curse, from good to bad, from health to sickness. Prayer can turn death, curse, bad, and sickness inside out—back to life, blessing, good, and health.

I love the famous story of Saint Francis and the giant wolf of Gubbio. While the townspeople trembled, Francis called the wolf to come forward. When the wolf appeared, Francis gave it a stern sermon about its bad behavior in scaring the town and prayed for the wolf to change. The wolf was so moved by Saint Francis's sermon and prayer that it became an honorary town guardian instead.

Your Epaphras-prayer Barnabas is your secret weapon in fighting the dangers of living in a world of big, bad wolves.

4. The Sarah-Humor Barnabas

What happens when you go into a spiritual slouch? We all do from time to time, and most often it is brought about by a skulking, skunking attitude. In Alcoholics Anonymous this is called "stinkin' thinkin'." When you feel like a sparkling stream, you stand up straight. When other times you feel like a polluted river, you start to bend over and walk wounded.

When we slouch over, we need someone with Sarah-Humor to correct our spiritual posture.

This type of Barnabas is someone who supports you, not always by agreeing with you, but by propping you up or poking fun at you. When we smell bad from our "stinkin' thinkin'," our Sarah-Humor Barnabas sprays us with some "good news" cologne.

Although the Genesis story has both Abraham and Sarah laughing hysterically upon hearing that they would have a child in their dribbling, doddering, Depends-wearing dotage, only Sarah is remembered for her sense of humor. Actually, Sarah laughed at God's sense of humor. Her laughter was not of disbelief ("Mission Impossible, God"), or sarcasm ("Sure, right! Pregnant at ninety–*hello*?!"). Her comic ear picked up the utter humor of it all. While you're frantically ironing out the wrinkles from your face and life, God ironizes your life with more twists and turns, more folds and creases than you ever thought possible. And so far from fearing a punitive God for her laughter, Sarah continued her humor in a pun. This child of laughter was named Isaac, which means, "he laughs." Sarah's child was the gift of laughter.

Faith and humor are tightly allied. In fact, Dante's *Divine Comedy* presupposes a Divine Comedian who came down and comes back to surprise us with the pleasures of being human. Sarah-Humor Barnabas laughs in the midst of life's jokes and twists, and makes fun of the cussed ironies of existence.

> Be joyful
> even though you have considered all the facts.[22]
> —Wendell Berry

A Sarah Barnabas's gift of humor is as important to your well-being as his or her gift of tears.[23] By keeping you laughing at a Jokester, Trickster God, a Sarah Barnabas bolsters your immune system. Some studies seem to suggest that people who use humor as a coping mechanism are more resistant to infections than those who don't. Sarah-Humor limits negativity and brings joy so that the stops-out organ swell of good news can fill every grim place.

We forget that the gospel is "good news." Christianity has become too much of a "bad news" religion. What does it mean to give people "good news"? It means news that encourages them whether we agree with them or not. Why aren't we encouraging one another more? In a society of face-lifts and facials, it is hard to look beyond face values to the inner beauty, the deeper meaning, your hidden giftedness and native greatness. But the incubation of the integral is the essence of what it means to be an encourager.

When was the last time you found someone slouched over and encouraged him or her with, "Weeping may endure for a night, but joy is coming in the morning" (Ps. 30:5)?

When will be the first time you say to someone with bad spiritual posture, "Here is your mantra. Say it over and over again until you straighten up: When you're down to nothing, God is up to something"?

When you encourage someone, you stiffen his or her spine.

When you encourage your spouse, the reception is rewarding.

When you encourage your children, they blossom and bloom.

When you encourage your antagonist, you aim not to deliver arguments that compel assent so much as arguments that further discussion, dialogue, and relationship.

My physics professor at the University of Richmond once encouraged me not to drop his class. When I protested that quantum mechanics was beyond my intellectual abilities and the only thing I understood about Einstein was his refusal to wear socks, he said, "Leonard, just think about this: At one point Einstein was the only person on the entire planet who fully understood the theory of relativity." I stayed with it and twenty years later wrote a book titled *Quantum Spirituality*. Encouragement is fertilizer, delivering nutrients we need to grow for the long haul.

5. The Ruth-Endurance Barnabas

Life is full of moments, some magical, some malignant. I have an old brass spittoon in my study because sometimes I feel so low I know how that big golden spittoon in the brothel felt. Who stays with you when you feel like a room with all the gloom left in? Who are the people in your life who will "lamentate" when you "tribulate," as my preacher mom liked to put it? Who will share your lamentations when your tribulations leave you weak and abandoned. Who will gift you with their patience?

Who will pledge to you, like Ruth did to Naomi (her mother-in-law, no less): "Whither thou goest, I will go."[24]

The Greek word for *patience* is most properly translated as "a conquering endurance."[25] Who conquers your depression with their sheer endurance? Who endures with you in times of crisis or failed relationships, when those contrarian naysayers are getting their kicks out of kicking you in the rear? Who stays with you and accompanies you while you journey through that foreign country called "Pain"—a landscape with its own language, culture, rituals, and climate? Who is your Ruth-Endurance Barnabas?

Jesus asked three of his disciples to stay near him while he cried and prayed. We all need companions in our suffering, which is the deepest meaning of "bear one another's burdens." Not who carries your burdens for you, but who bears with you, stays with you, and endures with you, while you are carrying those burdens. Who bears you up when you get beat up? You need a Ruth Barnabas.

Kurt Vonnegut thought that AA might turn out to be America's most important contribution to Western civilization because it gave us two gifts. First, it pioneered mechanisms to combat alcoholism and other addictions. Second, and more important, it provided a networked family of encouragers around the world.[26]

If the Christian church had been more encouraging than judging, it could have been that global family of encouragers. In the Byzantine Divine Liturgy, the passing of the peace is introduced this way: "Let us love one another." The world has its four-letter word, and we have ours: *L-O-V-E*. A Ruth Barnabas uses it and says it as often as the world does its four-letter word. Hopefully, more often.

11

> God descends through mercy as far as
> the human intellect ascends through love.
> —Maximus the Confessor

11

Conclusion

> Long life,
> honey in the heart,
> no evil,
> and 13 thank yous.
> —a parting blessing of the Tzutujil Indians of Guatemala

I have met more ministers than I care to count who, after thirty years of ministry, are so beaten and discouraged that I call them "Tin Men," after the Tin Man from *The Wizard of Oz*: if only he had a heart. The truth is he once did: a heart with a calling, a heart with a passion. But without a Barnabas, those ministers succumbed to the bloodsucking despair that can leech into the heart itself. At the end of that brick road, only a lie hides behind the wizard's curtain. The lie goes like this: "You can go it alone."

> 11
>
> I'd be tender—I'd be gentle. And awful sentimental
>
> . . . .
>
> If I only had a heart.
> —*The Wizard of Oz*
>
> 11

The word *encouragement* is from the French *coeur:* It means to put "heart" into someone.

Your Barnabas is a heartening presence and power in your life. Your Barnabas helps you live, not by rote or by rules, but by heart.

Barnabas Interactives

1. Do you have memories of times when you "lost your first love," when Jesus was more in the grave than out of it? Is there anyone who comes to mind who helped move you from a full tomb to an empty one? How did that person encourage you?

2. Name names. Name the Barnabas Withnesses who are helping you move from self-consciousness and self-centeredness to self-surrender and other-centricity. Who boosts your morale? When are you most in a Barnabas mode? Least?

3. Augustine said it will take a lifetime for your heart to be stretched wide enough to contain the beauty and blessings of God. The heart is hollow. You decide what to fill it with. What can we fill our hearts with that will allow them to stretch toward God's beauty and blessings? To what extent are we "full of ourselves" and not God?

4. The ancients believed that the self emerged from the activities of the heart. We know now that the primary organ is the brain, but the brain isn't nearly as useful a metaphor as the heart. There are 592 references to the heart in 550 verses of the Christian Bible. Study a couple of these references. Here are a couple to get you going:

    a) "I will remove from you your heart of stone and give you a heart of flesh" (Ezek. 36:26).

Are you open to a change of heart? What opens our hearts to change? Do our hearts often need to be cracked open? Cracked open by brokenness? Cracked open by what else?

b) "God has poured out his love into our hearts" (Rom. 5:5).

What things are you allowing to be "poured" into your heart?

5. An open heart will yield new beginnings and surprises. What new beginnings and surprises do you sense God preparing you for right now?

6. What do you think Saint Gregory of Sinai meant when he said, "Only by participating in the truth can you share in the meaning of the truth"?[27]

7. Have you ever noticed that people with a good sense of humor are sick less than those who don't have a good sense of humor?

8. Do you believe with me that faith and humor are tightly allied? What is one of the running jokes of your life? If you have a spouse, does your relationship have any running jokes? Are you brave enough to bare one of them? Are you brave enough to laugh with God?

9. Andrew Carnegie once observed firsthand that "millionaires who laugh are rare."[28] Does this coincide with your experience of the wealthy? Or does the lack of a sense of humor have more to do with being possessed by possessions and less to do with wealth itself? Explain.

10. "Fathers and teachers, I ask myself, 'What is hell?' And I answer thus: The suffering of being no longer able to love." Discuss this quote from Dostoevsky.[29]

11. The best of saints make the worst of company.… Only joking … Or is it true? How crucial is joy? Might the lack of joy be what keeps the best of churches from doing the best of things in the worst of times?

12. Is it always the foods of our childhood that become our "comfort" foods? Do you have "comfort foods" that aren't associated with your childhood?

Why can't there be such a thing as "comfort books"? What would some of your favorites be? Here are a couple of mine:

For dealing with all sorts of loss, see Rabbi Alan Abraham Kay's *A Jewish Book of Comfort* (Jason Aronson, 1993).

For the role of the healing and transforming power of love and compassion in the medical world, see Erie Chapman's outline of his approach to hospital health care in *Radical Loving Care* (Baptist Healing Trust, 2003). Have someone do research on the Institute for Research on Unlimited Love founded in 2001 by Stephen Post, professor of bioethics at Case Western Reserve University, and report back to the group. Read "Why Good Things Happen to Good People" for some of the results of the IRUL's ongoing research.

13. Are Big Brothers/Sisters ideal Barnabases? Take Miriam as a case study. All her life Miriam was a big sister to Moses, beginning when she tracked her baby brother as he floated down the Nile in his waterproof papyrus basket and planted the idea for Pharaoh's daughter to take Moses as her own child and hire Moses' real mother to nurse her brother until weaning.[30]

Withness 6:
Who's Your Peter/Paul?
You Need a Yoda

Always two there are, no more, no less:
a master and an apprentice.
—Yoda

Who's Your Yoda?

Yoda, of course, is the Jedi master and instructor of Obi-Wan Kenobi and Luke Skywalker in the epic myth known as Star Wars. And whether your last name is Skywalker or Sweet, each one of us needs a Yoda—a mentor, a guru, a coach, a spiritual teacher/director—if we are to complete successfully the missions to which God is summoning us. As life's catalog of choices expands, trustworthy mentors become ever more necessary.

In *Good Will Hunting*, Ben Affleck was a Peter to Matt Damon.

In *Spy Game*, Robert Redford was a Paul to Brad Pitt.

In *The Matrix*, Morpheus was a Peter to Neo.

In *Spider-Man*, Aunt May and Uncle Ben were Pauls to Peter Parker/Spider-Man.

Each one of us needs someone to look up to, a wiser, (usually) older, God-energized guide who can help us find our way through this new and unfamiliar landscape that is not for faint hearts or weak stomachs. Who can help us navigate those rivers of life that seem or we deem uncrossable? Who can help us move to new levels of perception and experience?

As much as I like William Wordsworth as a poet, his lines inspired by the statue of Sir Isaac Newton in the Antechapel of Trinity College, Cambridge—"… a mind forever / Voyaging through strange seas of thought, / alone"[1]—fail to adequately appreciate that even the greatest geniuses who ever lived didn't voyage alone. Newton prophetically rebuked what Wordsworth would later say about him in these words for which he is most famous: "If I have seen further, it is by standing on the shoulders of giants."[2]

Whose shoulders are you standing on?

Who do you look up to? Who do you see and say, "I want to be like them someday"? Who sets standards to which you aspire? Who is turning your tinkling tin can of insight into the sounding gong of wisdom? Who helps make you, a homo sapien, sapient? What person are you seeking out to help you find your voice and be true to your own voice? From whom are you learning when to suppress and when to express yourself?

Whose blessing do you seek?

The Abbas and the Ammas

The ancient rabbis said that even one who has memorized the whole Bible, and the Mishnah too, is still only an ignoramus, heretic, or even worse, unless he has also "served the Sages," that is, has carried out a proper apprenticeship with a master.[3] In the desert tradition, these venerable masters and mouthpieces were known as abbas (some of whom were holy hermits) and their female counterparts, ammas. Who will your sages be, your abbas and your ammas? And to whom will you be an abba or an amma sage?

> He will be our guide even unto death.
> —Psalm 48:14 KJV

There is always someone wiser than you with whom you need to apprentice. In earlier times, your Yoda was often a favorite uncle or a godfather/godmother.

Today you need to find people to attach yourself to who is further down the road than you; not too far ahead, but just a little. They may be well educated, they may be uneducated. They may not even dwell or do well in the academic derby or religious circuit. The issue is not education, but instruction by the Spirit in life and in what the Scriptures mean and what they mean for your duty and destiny.

Being a disciple of Jesus has not come easy to me. I was born without a prodigious religious temperament. Without my share of Yodas, old hands who helped this Timothy discern new ways, I never would have learned to walk by faith and not by sight.

There is even a chance your Yoda may be younger than you. Father Baltazar Alvarez became Saint Teresa of Avila's spiritual director in 1559. She was forty-five and he was twenty. Her other spiritual director was Saint John of the Cross. He was twenty-seven years her junior. My kids are techno-Yodas for me. I sit at the feet of my children about some things. Who do you take with you to buy an iPod? Who tells you what kind of computer to buy? Sometimes Peter and Paul need to sit at the feet of Timothy.

It's not as if we don't have sufficient models from which to learn. Jesus himself apprenticed to his cousin John the Baptist. The greatest example of mentor-student relationships in history is the Jesus school—"They were amazed at the disciples' knowledge for they had been *with* Christ"[4]—even eclipsing the most celebrated master-pupil relationship: Socrates and Plato.[5] But don't forget John and Polycarp or, more recently, Reinhold Niebuhr and Dietrich Bonhoeffer. One of the most moving letters ever written is the one Bonhoeffer wrote to his Yoda in June 1939, explaining why he had to leave the shelter of Niebuhr's cozy nest in New York City and go back to Germany and into harm's way, a decision that cost him his life.[6]

Who's your sage? Are you serving him or her well by complying with his or her mentorship[7] and sharing "all good things" with those with whom you apprentice?[8] Who is your spiritual and theological colossus? Who is ramrodding your spinal cord for life's spine-chilling challenges?

As a pump-priming trick to debut his first collection of poems called *The*

North Ship (1945), poet Philip Larkin used to limber up every night after supper. His exercise of choice? Turning the pages of Yeats's *Collected Poems*.9 Whose pages are you turning? Who is teaching you how to form simple sentences in the language of life? Who is helping you weave them into something more complex?

Your Yoda or Your University?

Question—which is more important: your Yoda or your university? Up until now, we would've answered, "The university," but in the future, who you studied with will be more important than where you studied. In fact, people are already filling their résumés with the names of people with whom they studied, alongside the schools where they attended.

Our institutions of higher learning and their accrediting bodies are slow to acknowledge this shift. For example, according to ATS (Association of Theological Schools), the North American accrediting body for seminaries, Billy Graham, Bill Hybels, Jim Cymbala, Brian McLaren, etc., are not qualified to teach in a seminary even though they are some of the most successful practitioners of that for which seminaries profess to educate. Brian McLaren didn't go to seminary; neither did Bill Hybels. Jim Cymbala? Nope. Surely Billy Graham went to seminary. Sorry, he didn't either. Then again, John Calvin didn't go to seminary (law school doesn't count). But let's not forget that Jesus never studied in any rabbinical school.

Learning the Finer Things

A great spirituality is like great art. For there to be truly original art, there must be submission to discipline, a mastery of the basics, close brushwork accomplishments, a tutoring in the traditions and texts of the faith—all so that we can author our own fifth gospel and become a Third Testament. The adventure continues in us …

We have to learn apprenticeship before we can offer mentorship. We have to serve sages if we are ever to grow to become a sage.

The "finer" things of the spiritual are like the "finer" things of life: a matter of "fine" and subtle distinctions. The failure to appreciate art is this failure to make "fine" distinctions. These distinctions—e.g., between the "good" and the "excellent," between artiness and art—can't be picked up on your own. They are acquired tastes, and you acquire them from sitting at the feet of a Yoda who trains your tastes to be "discriminating" (a good word, by the way).

The ability to discriminate is what makes a vast difference between amateurs and connoisseurs of the Spirit. The key to discrimination is recognizing what makes for "differences," and what makes for "distinctions." The failure to distinguish between the two leads to indiscriminate sex, indiscriminate talk, and indiscriminate lifestyles. But you'll never even be aware of the need without a Yoda.

Some distinctions are easy and blunt: like the distinction between being a plow horse and a show horse, or a Madonna and a madrona. These distinctions you can learn on your own.

But some distinctions are delicate and nuanced: like the distinction between a Cabernet Franc and a Cabernet Sauvignon, a smile and a smirk, a stretch and a strain, a one of a kind and a weird. These distinctions require a Yoda.

If I had come from a Czech culture, I would not need a Yoda to appreciate the differences and the distinctions in beer. Czechs drink more beer per capita than anyone else in the world. Their consumption of beer is about one bottle per day for every man/woman/child in the country. There are about 100 Czech breweries making 450 different Czech beers. To be Czech means to "know your beer."

I came from a holiness Wesleyan culture where you not only didn't have beer in your house, you weren't even allowed to watch beer commercials. For me to appreciate the beauty and benefits of beer, I would need a Yoda, someone who could teach me in the ways of evaluating and appreciating beer and the variety of foams that go with it. Without that Yoda, I am stone-blind, tone-deaf, and taste-dead to suds. And because I am clueless to the differences in beer, I am indifferent to beer, rarely drink one, and can't understand why other people do. Indifference stems from an immunity to difference.

11

> Those who can, do.
>
> Those who believe others can also, teach.[10]
>
> —lawyer/aphorist John E. King

11

Peter/Paul Withnesses

There are two different kinds of Yodas: a Peter and a Paul.[11] Peter is not a Paul, Paul is not a Peter, and neither of them is Jesus. Some people need a more hands-on master-novice Withness, others a more hands-off relationship. So, are you more of a Peter person? Or a Paul person?

The answer to that question depends on who and what feed you emotionally and spiritually on a regular basis, and where you are in your life and vocation. Depending on the seasons of the soul, you may need more of one than the other, or even both. But we all need *either* a Peter or a Paul Withness.

What is the difference? An old joke says that the difference between anthropology and sociology is that the former is about them and the latter is about us. If you're more of an anthropologist, you want to study with a Paul. If you're more of a sociologist, you want to study with a Peter. Peter was intellectually and culturally slow but interpersonally quick and rich. Paul was intellectually and culturally quick but interpersonally slow. One example: It took awhile for Peter to understand that the gospel was addressed for all humanity; Paul got it immediately. Paul had polemical verve; Peter had relational nerve.[12]

All of the Above

In a lifetime of Peter/Paul Withnesses, you might think there would be one single experience. However, this is one of those where "all of the above" is the correct response.

a) You will study with several Peter/Paul Withnesses during your lifetime, and will form a different relationship with each. This means each Peter/Paul will play a different role in your life.

b) Not every Peter/Paul Withness is equally accomplished.

c) The appropriate relationship between you and your mentor depends upon the spiritual level of each of you.

d) Your relationship with your Peter/Paul Withness will deepen and change as you proceed along the spiritual path.[13]

e) You will never cease apprentice work.

Neither Peter nor Paul was afraid of a fight. But a mentor can tell you which battles are worth fighting and which ones aren't—a lesson that both Peter and Paul learned the hard way. Here is an example of a fight not worth having: The Church of the Holy Sepulchre is locked every night by a Muslim brother, because the Christians couldn't agree on who should get to lock it. The various Christian factions fought with one another over who should have the honor. The only resolution they could arrive on? Give the honor to the Muslim. Who gets the keys is *not* a fight worth having.

If you're going to fight, let's fight about this: A fight broke out in Jerusalem on Good Friday. As the procession began to make its way on the Via Dolorosa, ending at Calvary, two Christian leaders of different denominations began fighting over which of them got to carry the cross.

If only more fights were conducted over "Must Jesus bear the cross alone?"

11

> Much of the history we teach
> was made by people we taught.[14]
> —West Point recruitment poster

11

How to Choose a Yoda

Choose your Yodas carefully. There must, as Anna Karenina said of "kinds of love," be as many kinds of Yodas as there are heads, minds, and hearts.[15] Don't hitch your wagon to any single star or listen to any voice that seems to attract a following. It is said that the mere presence of Napoleon on the battlefield was worth forty thousand additional soldiers. The Allies soon learned to "avoid battle when Napoleon was commanding" and to "seek it when he was away."[16] Napoleon was one of history's greatest military commanders but one of the worst mentors you could imagine. Just because someone is at the top of the best-seller lists, or at the top of his or her profession, is not sufficient authentication for being your Withness. If anything, top-dog, prima-donna status should invite as much skepticism as would any venture on a volcano. Beware of the name-dropping, head-lopping, chest-thumping, knock-and-mock mentor.

My all-time favorite Charles Swindoll analogy is one that I personally experienced with my kids at Kruger National Park in South Africa. Swindoll says that if you're going to stalk wild game in Africa, you need a tracking guide. But the guide is not the one who takes the pictures or fires the rifle. The guide is there to guide you. And when you come back home, you don't have five hundred pictures of your guide, and you don't take your guide to the taxidermist and have him stuffed.

That's why we don't lift up the preacher or the teacher or the Yoda. Their function is to guide and guard us into a living, dynamic relationship with God, to help us grow in grace and in the knowledge of our Lord Jesus Christ, and to help us live in a daily relationship with the divine.

Three Wise Points

If you could base your choice of a mentor on only three things, then choose these: Watch how they treat their spouses. Are the walls of their study permeable to their kids? And do they spend time reading and reviewing, blurbing and blogging other people's books and manuscripts, or do they consider themselves too famous for that? And don't forget that when others are looking for a Yoda, they'll ask the same questions about *you*.

11

> Any writer who is polite, who acknowledges a letter or the receipt
> of a book, does not believe himself to be famous.
> —attributed to Jules Renard

11

But if you've got time for more than three, here are some additional tips on what to look for in a mentor.

1. Humility ...

> I am just a simple monk.
> —often the first words out of the mouth of the Dalai Lama
> (his title means "Ocean of Wisdom") before he speaks

A pivot verse of Scripture comes when Jesus is mentoring his disciples and Peter objects to this reverse mentoring of Jesus—humbling himself to wash their feet. Jesus challenges Peter: "You do not realize now what I am doing, but later you will understand."[17]

The whole story of the spiritual life (and of Christianity, for that matter) is encapsulated in that one sentence: "You do not realize now what I am doing, but later you will understand." Wisdom comes over time, and we must learn to trust the Spirit even if it doesn't make sense to us at the time. A Yoda worth learning from accepts fallibility and makes it into a driving force of his or her life.

Unfortunately, the disciples were most often the "duh!-ciples" because they just didn't "get it," even while they were mainlining his teachings. In fact, the very last words of these "duh!-ciples" before Jesus ascended were these: "Lord, will you now restore the kingdom to Israel?" Talk about "Duh!" After three years of teaching, three days of waiting, and forty days of postresurrection appearances (christophanies), they still didn't "get it." But Jesus didn't give up on them. He revealed all things, in time.

> **11**
>
> Adults are always asking kids what they want to be when
> they grow up 'cause they're trying to get ideas.[18]
> —Paula Poundstone
>
> **11**

An ideal Yoda is a One-who-knows ... but a One-who-knows who knows he or she doesn't know it all. True Yodas see themselves as always a student and will not allow the student to withhold wisdom from the teacher.[19] True Yodas want to study *with* you, not demand you to study under them.

My undergraduate Yoda was W. Harrison Daniel, a Baptist historian (and baseball fanatic) at the University of Richmond. I found the way he organized the story of religion in America so fascinating I took dictation and transcribed to holy notebooks his interpretation of American religious history.

The fact that he had a student who was interested in what he had to say humbled him, and though he never invited me into the archives to be part of any of his research, he mentored me in the art of how to work with primary documents.

When it came time to pick a graduate school, Professor Daniel encouraged me to visit a distinguished historian teaching at Richmond's own Union Theological Seminary. Maybe this scholar would like to take me on, and I could go to seminary and graduate school right there in Richmond. I made my appointment, and to this day I remember the excitement of sitting outside his seminary office and smelling the musty, stale scent of centuries-old books and documents emanating from his office. It was like a narcotic to my nose and made me want more than ever to study with him.

The interview lasted ten minutes. Not only was he disinterested in me person-ally, but he rang the death knell of the profession. The discipline of church history was moving toward religious studies. And besides, there were already too many church historians around. The best advice he could give me was to consider some other career. There are Yodas and then there are Vaders.

When I returned to report on my interview, I shall never forget Dr. Daniel's words: "Mr. Sweet [he was very formal with his students], you got just one man's opinion. I recommend you go to graduate school, but I would encourage you not to pick a graduate program but to pick a mentor."

"I'm not sure I understand," I interrupted. "You're telling me not to choose a school or a seminary for graduate work, but pick the faculty?"

"No, I'm saying pick a mentor you want to study and write your dissertation under. And you just discovered the reason why."

"Do you have anyone in mind, Professor Daniel?"

"I know Baptist circles the best, and the best historian I know of there is the author of the primary text I assign for all my introductory courses in American religion: Winthrop Still Hudson. In fact, some call him 'the dean of American reli-gious historians.'"

Unlike my earlier interview, Professor Hudson got up from his seat to greet me. When I first heard Winthrop Still Hudson speak my name, my spine trem-bled. And it's been that way ever since. He gave me and all his students the illusion of equal standing as part of our standard training. He and his wife, Lois, invited all his students with spouses to his home for dinner once a year. He never bragged about his latest book, article, or award but focused on what we were working on. He instilled in us the sense that the truth about God was more than what he (or we) happened to be thinking about God at that moment. And his generosity of spirit, giving full credit to others and to us even when we didn't deserve it, left an indelible imprint to this day. That's why all my books have hun-dreds of footnote citations, so that I can acknowledge my debts, give credit to others who have influenced me, and make it easy for people to follow my tracks and even argue with me.

> The one who knows much says little;
> an understanding person remains calm.
> —Proverbs 17:27 MSG

Winthrop Hudson went from being my mentor to being my father … the father I wished I had. Even when I left "pure scholarship" for academic administration, he continued to mentor me in what it means to be a man and what it means to be a scholar. To my everlasting shame, he never knew how much I loved him until I tried to tell him when he was at the Mayo Clinic.[20] By then it may have been too late.

The greatest symbol of his humble spirit, however, was the fact that when he submitted an article for publication, he enclosed a self-addressed stamped envelope. Even when he was invited to write the article, he still did it and taught us to do it. Later I learned that while John Masefield was Poet Laureate, Masefield (one of Win's favorite poets) submitted with a self-addressed stamped envelope every poem he wrote for the *Times* to mark significant events "so that they could be returned if not acceptable."[21]

The gold standard for Yodas is not educational status, but spiritual status. It is not who has the most right answers, but who has the best right spirit. It is not who has it all worked out, but who has an awareness that he or she doesn't have it all worked out, and needs Jesus and others and you to help him or her work it out.

When Jesus asks Peter, "Do you truly love me," Peter gives a strange answer. Before the crucifixion and his betrayal of Jesus three times, Peter would have had the confidence and know-it-all-ness to say, "I truly love you." But Peter has a much more subtle answer now. He knows that his love will fail, and that he will more than once break Jesus' heart. So it is his humility that makes him say "Lord, you know that I love you."

2. Honesty ...

Only the initiated are parlay to the greatest secrets. The best Yodas will be honest enough to share their secrets with you.

But they will be honest enough to tell you the truth, even to rebuke you, especially when you settle for easy answers.

When a student sent a manuscript to Russian playwright and physician Anton Chekhov, he read it and told the truth: "What you have here is not a short story or a novel, not a piece of artistry, but a long row of heavy, dismal barracks."[22]

Have you ever had a teacher willing to be that spare and unsparing with you? Have you ever had the theological stuffing knocked out of you? How about crucified out of you?

You are going to get crucified on some cross. A Yoda helps you make sure that your cross is heavy enough (but not *too* heavy), and that you're carrying your own cross, not someone else's.

Part of a Yoda's value is in honestly identifying of masterpieces without bias, a loving explaining of their significance and place in the ongoing tradition, and a nut-and-bolts dismantling of how and why they work so powerfully. Here is poet Worley honoring the teacher he remembered most—Mark Van Doren:

> It must unfold as grace, inevitably, necessarily,
> > as tomcats stretch: in such a way he lolled upon
> > his desk
> and fell in love again before our very eyes
> > again, again—how many times again!—
> > with Dante, Chaucer, Shakespeare, Milton's
> > Satan,
> as if his shameless, glad, compelling love
> > were all he really wanted us to learn ...[23]

However, a Yoda goes beyond conveying knowledge yoked to love. A Yoda reveals secrets and awakens your own revelations. In fact, the mentor-student relationship is more an exercise in subtraction than addition: less adding new knowledge to our database than disabusing us of false notions, misleading navigations, and trapped assumptions that become theological pitfalls and pratfalls.

But rest assured, Yodas don't tell all their secrets. The Persian poet Sa'di tells the story of the master wrestler who taught his favorite pupil all his tricks except one. The inevitable happened: The pupil challenged the master, who only won the bout when he employed that one trick he held back from his best student.[24]

3. Honor ...

Honor is important because in honoring (like praising), you become what you honor.

A Yoda is someone who has won his or her honors fair and square. That means he or she will want people to mentor who will honor him or her by demonstrating both a love of originality and a love of conformity.

One of the worst things you can say about a person is that greatness passed by and he or she did not recognize it.[25] We all need the experience of feeling like dwarf gnomes who hew wood among the giants. To be blessed by and to bless a mentor are two of life's richest blessings.

There is a rabbinic saying that a person has a greater obligation to honor his teacher than to honor his father since his father brought him into this world, while the teacher who taught him the Torah brings him into the world to come.[26] But how is a Yoda best honored?

> If you meet the Buddha on the road, kill him.
> —traditional Zen koan

Paul believed that a Yoda was worthy of what he called a "double honor": meaning an extra measure of financial support and an extra measure of protection against false charges.[27]

Nietzsche claimed that the best way to express gratitude to one's mentors is to be a thorn in their flesh. In other words, you must go beyond the illumination of the ancestors, even those who passed on to you the vials of ancestral light. For example, Margaret McMillan (1860–1931) is known as the "Albert Schweitzer of the Bradford slums" because she did for England what Maria Montessori did for Rome: opened a slum school based on the theories of the French psychologist Edouard Seguin. But she took his teaching one step further, and insisted on school baths for her children. Up until then teachers stitched sulfur inside the hems of their own skirts to keep out the vermin.

But there are thorns in the flesh that honor Yodas, and thorns in the flesh that drain the life right out of them and thereby dishonor them.

Relationships are about questions: Who gets you to ask the questions? In fact, relationships need questions like fire needs air. Two Withnesses get you to ask the right questions: your Editor (Nathan) and your Yoda (Peter/Paul).

Yodas love questions. They love to ask them, they love to listen to them, and they love to turn them into more and better questions. Every good Yoda trains a student to ask questions like lawyers are trained: to "think otherwise" and to find their own way to think and do things. Indeed, you honor your mentors when you take them seriously enough to ask hard questions, argue with them, and disagree with them. The founder of my tribe, John Wesley, had no problem with his itinerants or anyone else disagreeing with him. But there are ways to argue and disagree without dishonoring the person. Or in Wesley's own words, "I have no more right to object to a man for holding a different opinion from mine than I have to differ with a man because he wears a wig and I wear my own hair." But then Wesley kept the metaphor going: "But if he takes his wig off and shakes the powder in my face, I shall consider it my duty to get quit of him as soon as possible."[28]

You can honor difference without dishonoring your Yoda or the integrity of your own commitments. But you always speak well of the bridge that carried you across.

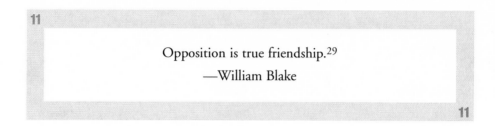

11

> Opposition is true friendship.[29]
> —William Blake

11

Part of the need of some to belittle or behead their mentors is a reflection of the lack of "otherwise" thinking encouraged by the mentor. There is a fine line sometimes between being tutored and being tortured. When Yodas are "unready to believe that there is any work of God but among themselves,"[30] as Wesley put it, the students then feel that the only way to gain unique identities and voices is to slay the ancestors.

But there is another "thorn in the flesh" that dishonors Yodas. Perhaps a smattering of stories will suffice to explain what I mean.

1. Emma Lazarus, the first major Jewish poet in America, is most known today for her Statue of Liberty poem: "Give me your tired, your poor, / Your huddled masses yearning to breathe free." She cultivated Ralph Waldo Emerson as a mentor, and Emerson was initially charmed and honored by her enthusiasm. But her constant badgering, bothersome self-promotion, and sense of entitlement turned him off and made him not promote her name in the profession.

2. In a world where everyone, no matter how distant, is a Skype click or an e-mail away, the need to ration your time becomes more important than ever. Your Yoda is not there to coddle or comfort you, but to enter the deep, dark space with you. That's why small talk will sometimes kill a Yoda relationship. I have someone who wants me to be their Yoda, but I'm running the other way. Partly because this person will IM me with "Hi, Len, how ya' doing? Having a good day today? Is the weather nice? Are your kids staying healthy?" and any other number of small-talk greetings that I don't have the interest or inclination to invest in.

Askholes. At least that's what I call them: people who nag and gnaw, not at serious bones of contention, but at unimportant questions or meaningless gristle. My brain tires with both academicism's and popular culture's endless debates about the respective merits of the mediocre, whether it be books or TV shows or musical groups.

11

Lord, teach us to care, and not to care.
Teach us to sit still.[31]
—T. S. Eliot

11

3. Here is a final example: It is excerpted from an e-mail I received today from someone I have never heard of or talked to before: "Dr. Sweet, I'm a big fan of your writings and would like to learn more from you. Would you provide me a bibliography of the best books out there on apophatic theology and the importance of silence in the spiritual life? Since my project is due in the next couple of weeks I would appreciate a quick reply. Thank you."

Jesus never answered every question asked of him either.

Or to put my response in a more theologically correct way: There are many invitations that God presents to us that are not commands. We are free to accept or decline.

I humbly declined that one.

Yoda Interactives

1. Earl Creps testifies that "in countless hours of writing, talking, and counsulting about baton-passing, I had assumed the whole time that we had something that younger leaders wanted to inherit. But what if that's not true?"[32]

   Creps goes on to pose two questions for us:

   a) "Is the notion of 'baton-passing' just a Baby Boomer conceit? Would the Church be better served by more 'start-ups'?"

   b) "Is the Emerging Church mainly an example of being offered the baton and saying, 'No thanks'?"[33]

   What do you think? To explore this further, read the last chapter of Earl Creps' *Off-Road Disciplines* (Jossey-Bass, 2006), which is called "Legacy: The Discipline of Passing the Baton." It deals with the way Paul raised up Timothy to lead the next generation.[34]

2. Saint Francis Xavier referred to Ignatius as "under God, the father of my soul."[35] Do you have fathers/mothers of your soul? Can you name them? What do you do to honor them?

3. If there is one central theme in the Christian metanarrative, it is a sensitivity to suffering. How have your Yodas helped you integrate suffering into your spirituality?

4. To whom do you now look for guidance in your life? Are they all close by, or

withness 6: who's your peter/paul?   133

are some in other states or countries? If one of the key roles of a Yoda is to help you hear, listen to yourself, to others, and to God to discover who has been that Yoda in your life.

5. Schubert wanted to be buried next to Beethoven … his influence on him had been so great, and he admired him so much. Who do you admire so much you'd like to be buried next to him or her?

6. Some have said that the best way for mentors to learn something is to teach it. True or false? Why? If true, does that make the learning experience more reciprocal and mutual?

7. Is it true that every person's ability to understand the Scriptures is as good as every other person's? Or do some people have special gifts to teach others about lifting veils? Support your answer.

8. For an example of how a Yoda can exist in time but not in space, have someone read Winn Collier's *Let God: The Wisdom of Fénelon* (Paraclete Press, 2007) and report back to the group. Or better yet, work through the wisdom of Fénelon together.

9. Recall and tell some "passing the baton" stories—Moses to Joshua, Elijah to Elisha, Jesus to the twelve disciples. Can you think of others?

10. I contend that every true solution requires a "soulution." Have you ever

mistaken a solution for a "soulution"? Do you have a Yoda who helps you not settle for the solution?

11. Is it more important for your Yoda to teach you to love much or to think much? If your Yoda doesn't do it, who will help you understand and interpret your experiences of God?

12. How important is trust to a mentor-apprentice relationship? Who do you think takes the greater risk in trusting: the Peter/Paul or the Timothy? Why?

13. Do you think you can "know" something without first loving it? Does loving come before or after knowing?

14. Don't look for perfection in your abbas and ammas. Just as Peter and Paul didn't get everything right, so your Yoda will not be right about some things. All teachers make mistakes. The most brilliant minds in history have had some spectacular blind spots. One of my favorite painters, Gauguin, was a scoundrel: He dumped his family and moved to Tahiti, where he lived like a hedonist and betrayed one friend after another. Tolstoy was a husband from hell. A great genius like Einstein got some things wrong.[36] So did Mark Twain[37] … so did Aristotle,[38] Aquinas, Luther,[39] Calvin, and Wesley. It is possible to be very right about some subjects and very wrong about others at the same time. It's even possible to be spectacularly wrong about your own specialty: In 2005, H&R Block didn't get its tax return right.

Can you come up with your own examples?

Withness 7: Who's Your Deborah?
You Need a Back-Coverer

There's Jack, he's got your back!
—2005 film *Fun with Dick and Jane*

If you need a guide like Paul, you need a guardian like Deborah.

After all, revolutions are not tea parties.

Everyone who has made a dent or a difference for God in history has had "protectors"—people who have said to them, "I've got your back."

A young Augustinian friar named Martin Luther was only thirty-four when he "posted" his Ninety-five Theses to the chapel door at Wittenberg. When the religious establishment lashed back, Friedrich (1503–1554), the elector of Saxony, took Luther aside and said, "Marty, I've got your back."

Can you imagine what it must have been like for Luther to be able to say, "Somebody's actually got my back"?

Who is providing cover for you?

That's your Deborah.

In the history of Israel, only three people combined the offices of prophet, judge, and military leader: Moses, Samuel, and Deborah. When you add to the mix her ability as a poet, as revealed in the victory duet ("Song of Deborah")[1] she sang with Barak—the oldest extant Hebrew poem and one of the earliest writings in the Hebrew Scriptures—this "fiery spirit" is in a category all by herself.

In the mode of a prophet, Judge Deborah delivers an oracle (a message from God) to General Barak, commanding him to organize troops from two tribes to fight the Canaanites on Mount Tabor. At first the general does not live up to the meaning of his name: Lightning. But, reluctantly, the general agrees to face nine hundred iron chariots on the mountain ... but on one condition. He'll fight only if Deborah goes on the "journey" (her word) with him, only if Deborah covers his back.[2]

The Lightning won't strike without the Fire.

The Truth

It is not true that "behind every good man is an even better woman." But it is true that there is something behind every good man and good woman: a back-coverer. Let me share with you four truths that illustrate the need for and the need to be a Deborah.

Et tu, Judas?

1. You're going to get it in the back.

The longer you live, the more you can't escape the bleakest facts of human existence. Here they are: the deterioration of the body, the cruelty of illnesses, the humiliation of old age, the inevitability of death, and the absolute mess people make of themselves and each other. There are many kinds of monsters, many of them shaped like men and women.

The world is full of people who like nothing better than to kill—your reputation, your spirit, your mission. In England, when the Public Executioner died in 1883, the Home Office promptly received no fewer than fourteen hundred applications from people keen to take his job.

11

> 'Twere well it were done quickly.[3]
> —*Macbeth*

11

If your life is on mission for good and God, you'll be the first to be fired on by enemies and by friends. It doesn't matter how good you are; you're going to get criticism, and it usually comes via the back door. And it's going to be more than back-biting. It's going to be back-stabbing, or worse. If you recall, it was the religious establishment that told Jesus his healing was a work of the Devil.[4]

When people are on the attack, the object of their spleen will be sundry and surprising. Some have named Bob Dylan the world's greatest living artist. It's hard to imagine the music world without him or his influence. On his 1966 world tour, Dylan played electric rock for the first time. This scandalized many fans who saw it as "selling out," and when they turned on him, it became ugly. In Manchester, England, an enraged audience began drowning out his singing with shouts of "Judas!" As he traveled from Hawaii to London, he found his "fans" were greeting him each night with booing, hissing, slow hand-clapping, foot-stomping, and expletives.[5]

11

> Politics is an honest effort to misunderstand one another.[6]
> —Robert Frost

11

I was once invited to take part in a lion-feeding contest. The only problem was that I didn't know I was going to a coliseum. Plus I didn't know that I was the one being fed to the lions. The lion in this case was another author who has never cringed from criticizing me. Besides being a beautiful writer, this author is also a masterful communicator, and by the time I arrived on the scene I not only discovered the two-day "point-counterpoint" format ("You mean no one told you? Sorry …"), but the "counterpoint" had been turned into a knife-sharpening and knife-throwing contest. And guess which direction the knives were being hurled?

To say I was in a discombobulated state would be a kindness. The gathering was in another tribe, and I felt like I was in a drawing by Escher: looked at one way, the stairs appear to be going up; but look at the same picture long enough from another angle, and the stairs look like they're going down as well as up. In other words, I didn't know whether I was coming or going.

Last year I was asked to be part of a similar format, except in this case they wanted me to promise not to pray or read Scripture with them. "But we really need you to come and exegete the culture for us." I responded more like Jonah than Jeremiah: reluctant, eager to do anything else but what I was being called to do. Then someone from that tribe agreed to go with me and be my Deborah. He flew in from the other side of the country, at his own expense, and never left my side the entire time I was there. We spent every spare second debriefing what was happening and how I might respond more helpfully and less emotionally. The presence of a Deborah made all the difference in the world.

There are certain professions that are high in critical fiber: politics, ministry, the arts (acting, especially). But the church seems to be especially rampant with and flamboyant about its friendly fire. I'm not necessarily saying that the church is the only army that shoots its own wounded—that's just an old joke—but the church does seem to have more than its share of wounded warriors, and they're not laughing. It's one thing to beat a dead horse; it's another to beat a live one. The church can beat both with equal single-mindedness.

> 11
>
> To work in the church you need as high a doctrine
> of corruption as you have of glory.
> —saying of a friend
>
> 11

In fact, woundedness seems to attract attack like sharks smell blood. I think of this every time I turn on television poker. Poker is now eclipsing tennis and golf in fan interest and even prize money. Every mathematician will swear that poker is a game of total luck. But tell that to Chris "Jesus" Ferguson, or Phil "Unabomber" Laak, or Dave "The Devilfish" Ulliott, who keep walking away from the tables with the top pot. Why?

Because they can smell weakness. And once they get a whiff of a wound, they pounce on it with ruthless ferocity. The modus operandi of some Christians I've met is: If you see a belt, hit below it.

For leaders in the church today, the rear guard is needed for protection more than ever, since so much of the church is opposed to advancing and is clumped together at your rear where all they see is your back. Behavioral geneticists call the predisposition to be crabby, critical, and irritable "negative affectivity." When you're not where you're supposed to be—when the church digs in its heels or brings up the rear rather than positions itself in the vanguard of change—"negative affectivity" rears its hooting head. In the Bible, Deborah covered Barak's back so he could fight against the armies of the Canaanites; unfortunately, Deborahs today often cover your back so you can fend off the armies of the churches. This should not be so.

The ultimate betrayal is when the back-guard becomes the back-stabber. Look around you at your circle of closest friends. You can be certain of one thing: One of them will betray you. You say, "No, certainly not! Not my friends." I say, "Are you better than Jesus?"

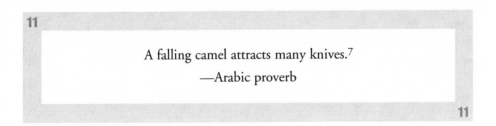

A falling camel attracts many knives.[7]
—Arabic proverb

I will never forget a Starbucks meeting with a pastor and his lead elder. They wanted some advice on how to take their staff to the next level. As we stood up to go, I felt moved to say to the pastor, "Remember one more thing: You can count on one of your confidants betraying you. Every time you see a picture of Leonardo da Vinci's *The Last Supper*, don't look for the hidden Mary. Look for the hidden Judas. Goethe in a famous essay suggested the whole picture was designed to convey Christ's words 'one of you shall betray me.'"

The lead elder laughed and said to the pastor, "You don't think it's me, do you?"

The pastor laughed back, "Just don't do it with a kiss."

A year later it came out that the pastor's wife and that lead elder were having an affair.

From a Distance

2. Sometimes Deborahs fight alongside you on the front lines, but mostly they cover you with prayer from a distance.

> For what are men better than sheep or goats
> That nourish a blind life within the brain,
> If, knowing God, they lift not hands of prayer
> Both for themselves and those who call them friend?[8]
> —Alfred, Lord Tennyson, "Morte D'Arthur"

In the opening battle scene of the movie *Gladiator* (2000), General Maximus (Russell Crowe) shouts to his men, "Unleash hell!" against the Visigoths. With great balls of fire crashing all around them, General Maximus feels the armor of someone brush against his back. He whips around, expecting to find an enemy to fight, but discovers his armor-bearer, protecting his rear.[9]

If you're a right-handed quarterback, one of your most trusted allies is the left tackle on the offensive line. This is your blind side, and the best defensive linemen are put here to intimidate you and make "reads and progressions." The success of every right-handed quarterback is a left tackle named Deborah who has his back.[10]

It is not always true, however, that those closest to you determine your level of success. Deborah didn't fight next to Barak, but she covered Barak's back with the fire of her words, her spirit, and her courage. She was always close enough to catch Barak's eye. Some people have a holy spirit, and the presence of that holy spirit in your life is enough to be your Deborah.

Sometimes we need a Deborah to protect us against ourselves. We are most vulnerable to "shooting ourselves in the foot" when we are riding the crest of the wave and when the puffery of the occasion makes us susceptible to puffs of evil. Very early in my ministry, a friend running for bishop started to believe all the nice things people were saying about him. I kept telling him, "Don't breathe in," but he kept breathing deeper and deeper until after a few months of "running" I didn't recognize him (and he didn't recognize me). He never became bishop, and he never recovered from what I now call "altitude sickness." Maybe that's the origin of the saying that a friend made bishop is a friend lost.

Timeless Little Debbies

The final two points go together under this heading because, well, they go together.

3. You can Deborah people you don't know.

I am the kind of person who doesn't like to be told what to do. So I'm prone to do just the opposite when I'm commanded to do something.

Take the sign: "PLEASE FLUSH!"

My first reaction to the person who put that sign there is, "Flush yourself!"

But when I think about the sign relationally, and begin to think about the person coming after me, suddenly I became very willing to "Please flush."

There are little Debbies we can do to cover the backs of people we don't know. Scripture refers to little Debbies as looking out for the least of these. You just might have someone come up to you in heaven one day and say, "Hey, you don't know me, but thanks for flushing! Really!"

4. We can Deborah generations that come after us and before us.

You can cover the back of people who aren't even there.

When a politician and a painter are friends, anything can happen. Former French Prime Minister Georges Clemenceau and Claude Monet, founder of French impressionism, were friends. They each lived to be old men, and each died within a few years of one another, Monet first.

A Deborah has keen radar for any sense of disrespect or danger. When Clemenceau saw a black shroud draping Monet's coffin, a sudden burst of fury overtook him. Rushing to a nearby window, he ripped a colorful curtain from its rod, cast the black shroud to the ground, and covered the coffin with the drape. For his friend to be buried in a color he had banned from his palette was the ultimate insult.[11] Even in death, Monet's back was being covered from the affront of black.

11

> Even a dog distinguishes between being
> stumbled over and being kicked.[12]
> —Oliver Wendell Holmes
>
> Even a dog knows the difference between being stepped on and kicked.
> —old Texas version

11

A Chivalrous Conclusion

Centuries ago it was the function of knights to be back-coverers for the weak and wounded. The role of medieval knights, especially in an age of chivalry, was to be protectors of the weak and unarmed, the priest, the peasant, the poor, and the child in a violent world. Like law-enforcement officers and military personnel today, knights often put their lives in jeopardy for the sake of others, even strangers, and an ethic of knighthood found classic expression in the "Knights of the Round Table." In the ethic of the "Round Table," personal glory came from royal service and selfless sacrifice.

Today we call knights "Deborahs," cardinal members of your round table of Withnesses.

Deborah Interactives

1. Who are your protectors now? Who have been your protectors? How important is it that you name your Deborah? What can you do to reinforce his or her identity as a back-coverer? When is the last time you thanked someone for covering your back?

2. Some people say Deborah was married to "Lappidoth," which means "fire" (Judg. 4:4). Other people say that "Lappidoth" describes her "fiery spirit" and her ability to "speak fire." Which do you think it was: married to a man named "fire" or married to a "fiery spirit"? Why?

3. What is the difference between a CYA (cover your rear) person and a CYB (cover your back) person? Why do you think backups mean so much to us?

4. Check out Paul's back as he bares it in 2 Corinthians 11:24–25—"Five times I received from the Jews the forty lashes minus one. Three times I was beaten with rods, once I was stoned."[13] Now describe Paul's back in as concrete terms as you can.

5. Jesus needed solitude after the multitude. Are your multitude Deborahs different from your solitude ones? Can they be the same?

6. Is having "roast pastor" for Sunday dinner one of those guilty pleasures, like watching the *Jerry Springer* show? Do you have any stories about people who

proudly lower horns and gore another preacher for the glory of God? What can you do to Deborah your pastor?

7. How do you feel when someone dislikes a person who likes you? What if that same person embraces your enemies? Should it make a difference?

8. Friendly fire is the worst kind. Did you see *Born on the Fourth of July* (1989), where a soldier is paralyzed by friendly fire? Or remember Cardinals football player Pat Tillman who volunteered for the military, was sent to Afghanistan, and then killed by friendly fire? Does the church do similar things as the military to "cover up" its friendly fire episodes? Give examples from your own experience.

9. Do you believe you have Deborahs in your life you don't know about? Have you ever been surprised by a Deborah at work? If so, describe your Deborah discovery.

10. When people try to prove us wrong and fire away at us, can we be proven in the fire? Can we prove ourselves? How? Can we maintain courage under fire? After all his courage under fire in World War II, George Patton died in a deadly car accident.

Withness 8:
Who's Your Zacchaeus?
You Need a Reject

It will do you no harm to find yourself ridiculous.
Resign yourself to be the fool you are.
—T. S. Eliot

The Wee Little Man

If we know the story of the slim, slimy Zacchaeus at all, it is most likely because of a wonderfully dense-with-detail Sunday school ditty. I memorized the song in a Salvation Army Sunday school (hence the British "tea" version):

Zacchaeus was a wee little man,
and a wee little man was he.
He climbed up in a sycamore tree,
   for the Lord he wanted to see.
And as the Savior passed him by,
   He looked up in the tree,
And he said, "Zacchaeus, you come down;
   for I'm going to your house for tea,
   for I'm going to your house for tea."

Zacchaeus came down from that tree,
as happy as he could be,
He gave his money to the poor,
   and said: "What a better man I'll be."[1]

Unfortunately, that's a wee, little interpretation of this important character you need in your life.

A real Zacchaeus? Well, do you know any street urchins? Seriously. Are jerks, buffoons, waifs, strays, cast-offs, wanderers, fifth-wheels, social misfits, and other rejects in your repertoire of relationships? Do any gypsies, tramps, and thieves have your business card or e-mail address?

One of the oddest people Jesus ever befriended was a short, wealthy, self-made entrepreneur named Zacchaeus. He got rich by climbing to the top rung of the most despised profession under Roman occupation: "chief tax collector."[2] If tax collectors were bad, the chief tax collector was the baddest of the bad, the chief of sinners, the sinner supreme, the ultimate social outcast. The more power and wealth Zacchaeus achieved in his profession, the smaller he became in the eyes of his community, who refused him any place in their midst and forced him into the public shame of having to climb a tree as the only way he could be part of the crowd that wanted to experience Jesus.

Some people are drawn to thoroughbreds. Others are drawn to mongrels. But almost nobody is drawn to misbehaving weirdos gifted in oddness.

Except Jesus, who expects us to do as he did.

Jesus' lineage closet was full of skeletons. Remember the story of Lot having sex with his daughters? Through the virtuous Ruth the Moabitess, one of these incestuously born children became an ancestor of Jesus. Jesus so surrounded himself with the freaks, misfits, and marginalized of his day that he was known as a "friend" of tax collectors and sinners.[3] Jesus associated with people who scandalized the gossips of Palestine. Which gossips are you scandalizing? Or have you made your "network" as hypoallergenic as possible?

> If you cannot get rid of the family skeleton,
> you may as well make it dance.[4]
> —George Bernard Shaw

As you think about who your Zacchaeus is and who you are a Zacchaeus to, keep this in mind: Most all of the 11 have something to give you; Zacchaeus requires something from you. If there were picture concordances, the verse "it is more blessed to give than to receive" would have a sketch of Zacchaeus beside it. It all begins with giving them your attention, looking "up in the tree," and seeing them. Your Zacchaeus will bestow gifts on you, but your arms and heart must be open first. With that in mind, here are some aspects of the wee, little Withness that invite your response-ability.

1. Remember that a Zacchaeus is someone who is "up a tree."

In the mountain culture from which I come, a worst-case scenario is being "up a creek without a paddle." Robber-baron Zacchaeus is up a tree with every known paddle but not able to go where he wants to go or even see what he wants to see. Get rid of every pretty picture of being "up a tree." This image of "up a tree" is grotesque, not picturesque. Misplaced, disgraced, isolated, and ashamed.

A Zacchaeus is someone who is "up a tree" either socially, mentally, physically, or economically. The *best* thing you can say about people who are "up a tree" is that they are round pegs in square holes (or vice versa). They don't do well in group conversation; a college education was not something they dreamed of; when the thought of exercise hits them, they lie down and elevate their feet until the thought passes; and they never pay their bills on time. They're messed up. But if we'll let them, their mess illuminates our own. This is one of their gifts to us.

The truth is we're all messed up. All of us are "cankered in the grain," as the world's greatest poet puts it.[5] We all have found ourselves "treed" by life because of some tragic flaw or fatal weakness. Each one of us is a steaming cauldron of moral failures and ambiguities. Not one of us is without spot or blemish. "No one is holy, not even one."

There is a rich vocabulary of human dysfunction in the Bible that is not adequately conveyed by the English word *sin*. Like the Inuit with their hundreds of words for *snow*, the English word *sin* is used to translate at least six Hebrew and seven Greek words. In fact, some have found over fifty words for our word *sin* in Hebrew alone, each one of which refers to relational dysfunctions of responsibility—to ourselves, to others, to creation, to God.

> Part of purgatory must be the realization of how little it
> would have to take to make a vice into a virtue.
> —novelist Flannery O'Connor

If Jesus' reputation bobbed in the wake of those who flowed toward him, he didn't seem to mind the ebb and flow. In fact, Jesus was less concerned about his reputation than about the rejects who were drawn to him, especially the two deemed most despicable and most routinely excluded from polite society: prostitutes and tax collectors—both of whom are Zacchaeus characters. One noted Jewish scholar has searched in vain throughout rabbinic literature to find a comparable measure of kindness toward prostitutes as Jesus meted out in both words and actions.[6] Jesus didn't relate to men as men and women as women, or to rejects as rejects, but to everyone he encountered as a person in need of love.

If Jesus is to be believed, and followed, there is no "other." There is only "oneanother." There are no "outsiders" because no one is outside the reach of God's love. Jesus taught us to see others not as "others" but as "one of us," as "oneanothers." We're all Zacchaeus. There is only *one*. Like an assault course, where a whole team with its quotient of mental laggards and physically unfit must finish within a given time, we are all in it together. We make it all together, or we don't make it at all.

The oneanother connection cannot be broken, only denied. We're all up the tree, in the creek, out to lunch, and looking for love.

> Whenever you find yourself in the majority,
> it's time to pause and reflect.
> —Mark Twain

2. Don't forget that a Zacchaeus is one-of-a-kind, an iconoclast.

In a world full of the "me-too" and "mini-me" mentalities, one-of-kind people—those who break mass habits of thinking—are rare.

If archaeologists of the future were to come from another planet and try to decipher human culture, how many of us would not fit the standard pattern? The real success of consumerism is its effectiveness in enforcing conformity. More than any pope or king, more than any totalitarian religion or regime, consumerism makes "coping" the same as "copying." In fact, the "coping strategy" *is* copying. In a world of franchised everything (even churches) and cloned dreams, we are programmed to be types following preordained circuits. Talk about predestination!

Remember those we used to call "copycats"? Copycats are now known as "fast followers." The fixation on "best practices" is another expression of this pursuit of uniformity and the laziness of our imagination.

A Zacchaeus prompts us to knock off the knockoffs and reminds us that copying is an expression of inauthentic living and inauthentic faith. In Christ all things are "new,"[7] and the Spirit frees us to be the one-of-a-kind, creative originals the Creator made us to be.[8] A Zacchaeus helps us to be iconoclasts, image-breakers, so we can be better incarnations and image-bearers.

A Zacchaeus breaks the mold. Like the Zacchaeus in the biblical story, they are both gifted rulers and abject sinners. There isn't a place for them in our world of boxes, which is one of the things that makes a Zacchaeus so strangely appealing.

11

Reporter: "What's the best thing about being 105?"
Centenarian: "Limited peer pressure."

11

The mark of an authentic community, or town, is the presence of a few good "characters." Orcas Island is such an interesting place to live because we have more than our share. There is the girl with the carefully groomed goatee. Then there is the wealthy resident who has made it her mission to be the county's early-warning system and environmental guard dog. Her letters to the editor warning of our island's impending doom as "another Nantucket" are the first things I read in the neighborhood rag. Then there is another landowner who enjoys mocking the sculpture and high-culture artwork that are increasingly seen on the island by collecting junk vehicles and scattering them around his lawn like tombstones. He then plants flowers in the radiators or grows trees in the engine blocks.

Every community needs a few good fools. They have their roles, even in temporary, makeshift communities like passengers on a plane. One seatmate of mine decided to get comfortable. He got out his pillow, covered himself in a blanket, then reached down, took off his socks, and proceeded to go to sleep. The smell that whooshed throughout that plane was nuclear. I thought the Patriot Act dealt with this kind of terror! We all started gagging and choking and trying not to breathe in the fumes. When people started looking at me to do something, I pretended to be sleeping too.

Suddenly a Zacchaeus appeared. He shook the sleeping passenger: "Buddy, you're killing us. Put those socks back on."

Everyone reading this can think of incidents where someone was doing something offensive or stupid, and we wished for the jerks and loudmouths to appear. "Where are you when we need you?"

What enabled that Zacchaeus to step out of his seat and solve the socks crisis was his refusal to conform to the conventions of Western culture; his uninhibited, out-of-context response was actually more true to our context than the polite awkwardness that straps us dutifully to our preassigned place. That's why your Zacchaeus often turns out to be one of the most important people you can have in your life … your zero-to-one person. The distance from zero to one is greater than the distance from one to any other number. And don't forget that there are moments when *you* are needed to be that zero-to-one person for someone else. "Where are *you* when they need *you*?"

11

> Being accepted isn't everything.
> —architect Frank O. Gehry's epigram he provided for the
> 1986 Walker Art Center (Minneapolis) exhibition of his works

11

Christians come from and are on a journey to a lyric land where they do things differently. Christians are a class unto themselves, but that class is not uniformed or monotone of voice. A copycat Christianity filled with quivering knee-jerk, butt-kissing, sound-the-same look-alikes is the exact opposite of authentic discipleship, which is as much at home with djembe drums, aboriginal didjeridoos, and Norwegian cow calls as with piano, organ, and guitar. A Jesus boom box surrounds you with a wash of sound: African kora and Asian Underground, Southern gospel and Saharan roots, and you can listen to it all beneath the shade of a sycamore tree.

11

> Woe to him who seeks to please rather than to appal! Woe
> to him whose good name is more to him than goodness!
> Woe to him who, in this world, courts not dishonor.[9]
> —sermon in the Nantucket chapel that launches Ishmael's voyage

11

3. Be mindful that a Zacchaeus is "out there."

Don't expect to find your Zacchaeus on the pew behind you at church; they no longer come to church. We have to go "looking for Zacchaeus" because they know they can't "fit in" church culture. When we do find a Zacchaeus, chances are many of them are "up a tree." Or sitting in the smoking section. Or at the bar. Or in the gutter …

The Sweet kids have a favorite directive for their Norwegian mother, who has found her fjord in Orcas Island and doesn't see the need to go "off island" for months at a time. Their words to her are, "Get out more."

Do walls make Christians?[10]

—late fourth-century philosopher Caius Marius Victorinus,

afraid to show up in church with his pagan friends

We have tried to "live in" rather than "live out" the gospel. It is time for Christians to "Get out more," to try alfresco forms of faith and community. The Christian church is too "in here" and not enough "out there."

"Out there" in love.

"Out there" in service.

"Out there" in relationships.

"Out there" in compassion.

There is no contact with Zacchaeus and other "outsiders" unless you're "out there" and start "living out" not "living in" the faith.

Why is it the purified (church people) most often resemble the petrified and the putrified? Because the energies of Christianity are outward, and too often the energies of the purified are all inward. Unlike many other religions (especially Islam), the movement of faith is not from the outward to the inward, or from the inward to the innermost inward, but from the inward to the outward. An outward thrust is one of the things that makes Christian faith unique. It is time our "acts of worship" become less what they really are—sits of worship—and more what they profess to be: real acts of the apostles.

Ah! There is nothing like staying at home

for real comfort.[11]

—Jane Austen, *Emma*

4. Be aware that a Zacchaeus is Trouble. And trouble starts with *T* that rhymes with *P*, which stands for …

A Zacchaeus is an "odd duck" where "odd" is not just agreeably odd, but disagreeably odd. When there's trouble, they're most likely right in the middle of it (of course through no fault of their own). A test of whether you have a Zacchaeus is whether you are now taking criticism for making room in your life for one of these unperfumed personalities. Take any flack for "the wrong crowd" lately? To everyone else, a Zacchaeus appears more an albatross to you than an asset. As is eating with a Zacchaeus today, any association with such a person usually grants you a response like "Why?"

A big picture making me look silly ended up in the center section of the *Wittenburg Door* because of my friendship with Willie Nelson and his acceptance of my invitation to serve a term on the board of a United Methodist seminary. Willie Nelson, as in the country-music-legend-tax-evader-friend-of-Waylon-and-the-boys. I received hundreds of letters accusing me of "condoning" his behavior. When we get this criticism, we can try arguing the point that "condone" technically does not mean approve or endorse. "Condone" means to pardon, forgive, overlook. You can condone an action without approving it.

Maybe that argument will work for you. It didn't work with the people I was dealing with. But the truth is a Zacchaeus doesn't just disturb others, they rub you the wrong way too sometimes. They may add force and farce to your life; they may prevent you from choking on the fricassee of faith. Their biggest gift may be that they give you perspective, a never-failing appreciation of what Louis MacNeice called "the drunkenness of things being various"; but these are people who are as unpredictable as a herd of wildebeest at the Limpopo. I shall never forget hanging out in the Honeysuckle Rose before a concert with actors and musicians I had only seen on TV, only to have one of them pass around a "joint for Willie" for everyone to share Communion-like.

> Just remember, the sweet is never as sweet
> without the sour, and I know the sour ...
> which allows me to appreciate the sweet.[12]
> —Jason Lee as Brian Shelby, *Vanilla Sky*, 2001

Protector of treed people beware: This Withness can get you in trouble. That's why you can't have too many Barnabases, but you can have too many Zacchaeuses. Life is already enough of a house of cards without stacking it with jokers. Life can collapse at a touch if you marry a Zacchaeus. Unless, like Hosea, God tells you to. More on that last sentence later.

5. Last, but not least, don't overlook the reality that a Zacchaeus is inefficient. But his or her inefficiency can reshape you in the image of Christ.

Note to self: Life runs so much more smoothly and efficiently without a Zacchaeus. But maybe it is time to make effigies of efficiency.

You need a person in your life to whom you are calling out and saying, "Come home with me." You need a person who is mocked by others, but to whom you stretch a healing, helping hand partly because only their hand can deliver you from worshipping at the foot of the god of efficiency. Zacchaeus is not interested in a well-oiled machine; however, they are quite fond of being broken and spilled out.

Conclusion

One of the most fascinating but least explored aspects of Jesus' life for me is his never-failing tender spot for "finding room"—whether in our homes or at our tables or in our hearts. Who knows the ways his mother's constant telling of the no-room-at-the-inn story shaped his soul and psyche. But the no-room refrain of Jesus' life is evident everywhere: from his promise "I go to prepare a place for you" to the sensitivity about Jesus having "no place to call his own" to the poignant detail ending the story of the Good Samaritan: finding room in his home for the wounded man. In fact, Jesus had a ready eye for chances to eat and spend the night with village fools and outcasts wherever they may be found: lepers,[13] tax collectors, mentally and physically disturbed, prostitutes, sex offenders, etc. For Jesus, it wasn't a sacrifice to do this—it was a passion. Even a pleasure!

To be sure, it is not easy living with a difficult person. That's why the call to *live* with Zacchaeuses is rare. One of my favorite Bible stories is of a young prophet from the northern kingdom named Hosea who was told by God to marry a Zacchaeus. Her name was Gomer, and she was known for two attributes: She was the most beautiful girl in Israel; and she shared her beauty with everyone, giving her the reputation of a prostitute and sex addict.[14]

Hosea was told to have three children with Gomer and to name each child symbolically for an action of Yahweh. No matter how many times Gomer left Hosea for other men, some of whom abused her terribly, Hosea kept buying and bringing her back. Gomer does not beg or woo Hosea to save her. Hosea simply shows her that there is nothing she can do to stop making him love her.

Gomer must have thought Hosea was a fool. But eventually Hosea's unfailing love rekindled in Gomer a spark of soul, and she ended up loving and being faithful to him. Come down from your tree, Gomer. Come home with me. I love you. Always have. Almost sounds like a country song—something Willie Nelson might sing, huh?

The *Today* show was never better than when Matt Lauer and Katie Couric sat side-by-side flirting with each another. One morning in 2004 my ears picked up when I heard them mention Hugh Hefner's "little black book." Actually there were a bunch of Hefner's "little black books," all from the 1950s. They were put on display as part of the fiftieth anniversary of the founding of *Playboy* magazine. As his sign off and segue to the next topic, Matt turned to Katie and asked incredulously, "Who would be interested in one of those books now?" Then they both snickered and shook their heads.

I yelled from my couch, "I would. You should." Talk about the triumph of the

Playboy ethic, where beautiful women become objects that are used for one's own gratification and then are tossed into the garbage heap when they are no longer useful. Something in me desperately wanted to get those black books so I could track down each name. Where were they now? What had happened to them? What had become of their dreams? Had anyone ever told them that before they were shaped in the womb, God knew all about them (Jer. 1:5)? Had they gotten the word that before the universe was created, God had them in mind and chose them as a focus of the Father's love (Eph. 1:4–5)?

Had they ever heard the news that each one of them is a child of God? Not a commodity. Not a play toy. Do they know that Jesus loves each and every one of them? That he wants to walk with them and have relationships with them? Not to take more of their selves away, as other men have done, but to give them more of who they were created to be.

Who would be interested in those books now?

Jesus would. We should.

Wee little men in trees and wee little girls in black books. Zacchaeus. Us.

Zacchaeus Interactives

1. Evagrius of Pontus (345–399), who invented the "Seven Deadly Sins" scenario (even though his original list had eight, not seven, and he called the eighth "thoughts" not "sins"), described the root of each sin as "forgetfulness of God's goodness."[15]

   Can you name the "Seven Deadlys"? Which ones are you most prone to? Your family? Our nation?

2. Søren Kierkegaard's definition of sin was a little different: Sin is the steadfast refusal to be your one true self.[16] Compare and contrast Kierkegaard's definition with Evagrius of Pontus's understanding of sin as based on a "forgetfulness of God's goodness."

3. Discuss this quote from novelist/theologian Chaim Potok in his book *The Chosen*. To what extent does it agree with and/or differ from the classical Christian understanding of "original sin"?

   > A man is born into this world with only a tiny spark of
   > goodness in him. The spark is God; it is the soul; the rest
   > is ugliness and evil, a shell. The spark must be guarded
   > like a treasure; it must be nurtured; it must be fanned into
   > flame. It must learn to seek out other sparks, it must
   > dominate the shell.[17]

4. Is it possible for your/an entire family to be a Zacchaeus? Why or why not?

If so, how does that relate to Scripture's notion of sins being passed from generation to generation? Are social curses passed down too?

5. Do you think we can expect to do all the harvesting in this life? To what extent do we leave the harvesting all up to God, and/or do we participate in it?

6. I have written elsewhere of authentic Christianity as a GOOD religion where GOOD is an acronym for Get-Out-Of-Doors.[18] How BAD (Behind A Door) is your church? How might you make it GOOD again?

7. The distinction between the "inner" and the "outer" used to be called the "withinforth" and "withoutforth." How withoutforth is your church? To what extent is your identity as a community of the faithful dependent on space bounded by stones or steel? How would you answer the philosopher Victorinus's query about whether walls make Christians? Do walls make Christians? By the way, Victorinus finally agreed to get walled: "Let us go to church. I wish to be made a Christian."

8. Here is a metaphor for "In Here" Christianity: Roman Catholic theologian Karl Rahner liked to talk about Thermos-bottle Christianity: It keeps everybody inside warm and sealed, and keeps everything outside cold and separate.[19] Explore the implications of this metaphor for the church. Do you like it? Will you use it?

9. Try greeting other Christians with a new phrase. Instead of "How you doing?" try instead "How you going?" What reaction do you get?

10. Describe a Zacchaeus Withness experience; for example, call to mind the story of someone you knew who was misunderstood by the community—a misfit, an outsider, an outcast who hurt from feelings of "outsideness." How did you and your friends handle such a person? Did you put her in the outcast box? Did you leave him alone? Did you make any extra efforts to get to know this person? How enriching were these initiatives?

11. Should we celebrate those kids who carry little baggage in the form of unwanted associations? How early should we encourage our kids to include Zacchaeuses in their network of friends? How would you encourage your kids to discover their "inner" Zacchaeus?

12. How many relationships have you shunned or social settings have you avoided to maintain the outward appearance of "a good Christian"? Did it work? Who are you trying to impress by doing so?

13. Where is the balance between having Zacchaeuses in our lives and allowing Zacchaeuses to reshape our lives? For an excellent book on the latter, check out Greg Paul, *God in the Alley: Being and Seeing Jesus in a Broken World* (Colorado Springs: WaterBrook, 2004).

14. Eric Harris was the son of a career military man. He was always moving from base to base, attending new schools every couple of years, never having the secure resources or stable relationships of other kids. You may know the name because he killed twelve of his classmates in Littleton, Colorado. Just before his violent rampage, he confided to a video his pain: "Everywhere I went I had to start again at the bottom."

Do you think that whole story might have been different if someone had seen in Eric Harris a Zacchaeus and treated him like Jesus did? Or are there some people who are just "bad seeds" and beyond reclamation?

15. In the movie *Forrest Gump* (2004), who is the Zacchaeus? Most would say that Forrest was. But in the relationship of Forrest and Jenny, wasn't she his Gomer?

Withness 9: Who's Your Rhoda? You Need a "Little One"

Children are just people in process of getting older,
vulnerable people learning to be human, and wise children know
that being men and women is much more interesting and
complicated that the state in which they are temporarily stuck.[1]
—A. S. Byatt

When it came time for Jesus to "get real" and showcase his "ideal" model of faith, he didn't tap on the shoulder of a scholar or parade an athlete before the onlookers.

He chose a baby face as faith's gold standard.

That's why you need a Rhoda.

Rhoda? Rhoda who?

The first voice heard from a Christian woman in the church of the book of Acts, that's who.

And that woman was a child.

God's Little Rosebud

Rhoda was a doorkeeper in the house of Mary in Jerusalem.[2] Even though a servant girl,[3] Rhoda (short for "Rosebud") participated in family prayer, no doubt because she not only believed in prayer, but also expected and watched for God to answer her prayers.

During one late-night prayer meeting, the adults were praying hard for an imprisoned Peter. James, one of Jesus' disciples, had already been executed, and everyone feared that Peter was next on Herod's list.[4] In the midst of all this praying, there was a knock at the gate. Rhoda went to answer it, and "in her excitement" from hearing Peter's voice, hastened back to the meeting without opening the door for Peter. Delirious with joy, she could barely voice the good news. Their prayers had been answered. Peter was standing outside, wanting to be let in.

They laughed and mocked "Crazy Rhoda," but she persisted. Then they dismissed her insistence with, "It must be his angel." A determined Rhoda finally convinced the adults to break away from their prayer exercises and see their prayers take flight. The adults were almost as much in jail as Peter, so busy being "prayer warriors" and enjoying the holy haze of "prayer meetings" that their gaze never lifted and their prayer life never got off the ground. It took a child to point out to them the reality of answered prayer.

For just as Rhoda said, there stood Peter at the gate, waiting to be let in.

Sometimes it takes a child to point out the obvious. And a child shall lead them.

Wifeless, Childless, Children-First Jesus

Jesus' startling affirmations of "children first" make strange with our expectations. Jesus lived without children of his own, but when he wants to show what discipleship is like, he plops a child in front of his disciples.[5]

Why a child? Because a child is innocent? Because a child is pure? Because a child is more truthful and trusting?

Are you kidding?

History, theology, and personal experience prevent any sweet, innocent, cheek-pinching sentimentalization of childhood. "Childhood" is largely a Victorian invention: Before 1800 the protected stage of "childhood" is missing from history. A crack in time can be seen in the Iranian version of Islamic law in which girls today can be "given" in marriage at age nine. Up until the Enlightenment, large numbers of children toiled in the worst possible places (mines, fields, sweatshops, etc.), and public hangings of children were common. As far as theology is concerned, Reinhold Niebuhr ventured that the greatest proof of original sin was a newborn. I admit it: No one can wrench out the Grinch in me faster than a sweet, innocent, untouchable, miniature Attila the Hun, who seems to fill up planes these days.

11

> It was no wonder that people were so horrible
> when they started life as children.[6]
> —Kingsley Amis

11

Then why a child? Because it was a child. And children were of no account in Jesus' day, enjoying a little lower status than women (some rabbis said better to burn a Torah than to give it to a woman), a little higher status than beasts. "Little ones" (especially women "little ones") were worthless, insignificant, despised, degraded, and neglected. But in the gospel according to Jesus, "little ones to him belong, they are weak but he is strong." The Jesus gospel showed how little is large, and Jesus' whole ministry was a sign system in how to be retrievers of the neglected, the maligned, the misfits, and the little, and how to trust the God of history to act in history in the Spirit of the Magnificat—who fills the hungry with "good things," and empties the pockets of the rich.

"Children first" was the Jesus motto because in the kingdom of God the last are first.

Don't leave the child behind. Yes, put away "childish ways"[7]—you enter adulthood when you stop eating multicolored breakfast cereal—but not children, for children keep you in childhood all your adult life.

"Childish" and "childlike" are vastly different. A childish faith needs to have an answer and needs it now—if not I will take my ball and go somewhere else. A childlike faith trusts the one in charge, not understanding it all but loving or honoring the one in charge.

11

> Do not be children in your thinking;
> be babes in evil, but in thinking be mature.[8]
> —apostle Paul

11

Difficult Stories

After the Harry Potter series took off, I knew some parents who banned all the books from their homes. I didn't think twice about it until I was speaking to a convention of Christian school principals. In the course of my first speech about the gospel as the telling of "difficult stories," I referenced J. K. Rowling. When I was finished speaking, a delegation of not-so-happy administrators met me at the edge of the platform.

"Dr. Sweet, don't you know that such stories lead children astray and glorify evil?"

"But these are just stories," I protested. "They are modern-day versions of the Brothers Grimm, Aesop's Fables, Mother Goose, Hans Christian Andersen, Lewis Carroll."

"There is no such thing as 'just stories' [they won that round!]. Harry Potter stories are not innocent, but insidious stories. They're full of magic and witchcraft and spells and all sorts of evil."

"And the Brothers Grimm aren't?" I countered, realizing that this approach was not going to get me anywhere. So I tried another.

"Besides, our children know that these stories are made up, not true, real-life stories."

"But they can't tell the difference."

I didn't say it out loud, but my next line would have curdled in the air of its utterance: "Wait a minute. Who is it who can't tell the difference?"

I failed to convince anyone of anything except me, and what I came away convinced of was this: Children can often be more grown-up than adults … and I'll never say "just stories" again.

You can't get real, grow up, and act infantile at the same time. But you can't do authentic adulthood without childhood either. When Anglican Bishop Michael Ramsey died, church historian Owen Chadwick said this about him: "Children thought he was the nearest thing to God: Michael Ramsey thought they were. There are those in this Abbey who think both were right."9

Once, Twice, Three Times a Rhoda

Jesus weaves three mantles of spiritual maturity around our Rhoda relationships.

One affirmation—"Let the little children come to me, for of such is the kingdom of heaven"—occurs right after Jesus discusses and justifies his own childlessness and singleness.[10] It is almost impossible for us to comprehend how truly odd a wifeless Jesus appeared in the Judaic tradition, although our fascination with and invention of stories of a married Jesus give evidence to how hard it is for even us to cope with his singleness. In a text Jesus would have read, Sirach (Ecclesiasticus) says that a man without a wife is a "fugitive and a wanderer."[11] Every Jewish father was expected to arrange marriage for his son after the age of twelve and before twenty-two. So for an older, never-been-married male to pick a child as the ideal of faith, and to rebuke those who were trying to prevent children's inclusion in adult conversations—"I tell you the truth, anyone who will not receive the kingdom of God like a little child will never enter it"[12]—was a double oddness.

The second time Jesus singled out a relationship with a child as the defining ideal for faith took place after the disciples were bickering with one another over who was "the greatest." A disgusted Jesus picked up a child in his arms and said that our ability to receive a child, and to become a child again, was the true measure of greatness: "Unless you turn and become like children, you will never enter the kingdom of heaven."[13] If you're too old to hold a child in yours arms or in your heart, you're too old to be alive. Be careful how you treat this child in your arms, Jesus warned. Children have specially assigned angels who have walkie-talkies with the Father in heaven.[14]

The special status of children was reinforced a third time in one of the harshest warnings Jesus ever uttered. If you harm a child or make a child stumble, "it would be better for you if a great millstone were fastened around your neck and you were drowned in the depth of the sea."[15] 'Nuff said.

11

Remembering When You Were a Rhoda

What is it about childhood that is so vital to our entrance into the kingdom of God?

Jerry Griswold has discovered what he believes is the secret to a successful children's book. After spending years studying the most influential children's books in history, he argues that the greatest are all alike in one simple way: The author could remember how it "feels like to be a kid."[16]

From a key to classic children's literature to Jesus' keys to the kingdom: Can you "become again like a child"?

> **11**
>
> A man is always a teller of tales, he lives surrounded by his stories and the stories of others, he sees everything that happens to him through them; and he tries to live his own life as if he were telling a story.[17]
> —Jean-Paul Sartre, *Nausea*
>
> **11**

Søren Kierkegaard came the closest to Griswold's perspective when he argued that there were only two good ways of reading stories to children: either so live the stories that you "own" the stories and in telling them you become a child yourself, or fake it by staging the story as if your life depended on it. Children need stories to stabilize and structure their existence. "Only when the child himself detects that the teller does not believe stories are the stories damaging—yet not because of the content itself but because of the untruth in regard to the teller—because of the mistrust and suspiciousness which the child gradually develops."[18]

The more storyless the culture, the more children will always be on the side of a good story. Philip Pullman, children's book author and winner of England's highest honor for children's literature,[19] argued in his acceptance speech that the wisdom of "once upon a time" determines more how we live and lasts longer than philosophy. "What characterizes the best of children's authors is that they're not embarrassed to tell stories. They know how important stories are."[20]

Pullman ended his speech with these words: "We don't need lists of rights and wrongs, tables of do's and don'ts: We need books, time, silence. 'Thou shalt not' is soon forgotten, but 'Once upon a time' lasts forever."[21]

What place do stories have in your life today? Are there any *once upon a times*? Or have they all been shelved away so you could get on with more important things? Your Rhoda can help you see the larger story, acts, scenes, dramatic monologues, and curtain calls.

Rhodas Don't Live by Bread Alone

One of the most brilliant and beautiful (though humorless) writers of the twentieth century, essayist George Steiner, believes that the storylessness of the modern world is the cause of many of our problems. He argues that the worst thing you can do to a child is to deprive him or her of stories (whether found in print or music or art), and especially of "the spell of the story":

> To starve a child of the spell of the story, or the cantor of
> the poem, oral or written, is a kind of living burial.... If
> the child is left empty of texts, in the fullest sense of that
> term, he will suffer an early death of the heart and of the
> imagination.[22]

This is why I would rather literalists read the Bible to my children than liberals, and why the reproduction rate for liberal Christianity is so low: The spell has been broken by critical detachment and demythologized discourse. When your lips tell a story without your limbs, or if you remember a story but your body doesn't, then you communicate a dead story. This kind of "romance" with the text has all the excitement of kissing through a kerchief. Martin Buber tells this story:

My grandfather was paralyzed. One day he was asked to tell about something that happened with his teacher— the great Baalschem. He told how the saintly Baalschem used to leap about and dance while he was at his prayers. As he went on with the story my grandfather stood up; he was so carried away that he had to show how the master had done it, and started to caper about and dance. From that moment on he was cured. That is how stories should be told.[23]

To be a Jesus follower means that "The Good News Story," the grand metanarrative, is the story that has shaped, is shaping, and will shape our multistoried lives.[24] A Rhoda keeps *once upon a time* alive and well and *happily ever after* something to be hoped for.

Rhoda Disciplines

The five recurring themes that Griswold's little gem of a book finds in classic children's literature are the five reasons why you need a Rhoda as one of your Withnesses.[25] Think of them as spiritual disciplines needed in life that won't happen unless you have a Rhoda. And when you learn them, you can pass them along to others, letting yourself be a Rhoda to them. Your ongoing relationship with a Rhoda will keep you snug, scared, small, light, and alive. True, those are not on the list of classic spiritual disciplines, but maybe they should be.

Rhodas Keep You Snug

As a child, my favorite places were in the land of "Make-Believe": a tepee I put up on our front porch that became the mobile headquarters for Hannibal as he was crossing the Alps; a do-it-yourself pup tent in the living room made up of a rugs-blankets-pillows building kit; an under-the-table fort where I could hide from my two bandit brothers. It goes without saying that "make-believe" was also a costume carnival, with each of us dressed up to fit the part we were playing in these original fantasy games.

My kids are no different today. Many times they would just as soon have the box as the prize it brings. UPS is another word for "Let's play make-believe," and the UPS truck is a Santa's sack of cardboard boxes greeted as complex puzzles.

Adults have their own hiding places and cardboard boxes: cabins in the woods, winter homes, summer rentals, spring-break beach houses—each one a place where you can not only sleep in peace, but also daydream to your heart's content.

It is that snugness that makes dreaming possible.[26] Without the snugness of the blankets at night, the snugness of the shelter by day, dreaming is difficult, not safe. "In this sense, every snug place is Plato's cave of ideas," wrote French philosopher Gaston Bachelard in his classic text *The Poetics of Space* (1964).[27] Just as we have a biological need to dream while sleeping, we have a spiritual need to dream while waking. Like our nocturnal dreams, these daydreams are shaped around narratives and metaphors that make sense of our lives. By night you're a poet working on a palette of images. By day you're a novelist, creating on the canvas of life your imagination at play, a dream sequence of "make-believes" made real in narratives of attachment and abandonment.

In keeping us dreaming, Rhodas unite our daydreams and our night dreams. God is both at work and at play in our lives. As adults, we separate "playtime" from "work time," making "play" a "recess" or a "vacation" from what is really important, i.e., "the real world." For children, however, "work and play are words used for the same thing under differing conditions," as Mark Twain would put it.[28] When separated from our night dreams, our daydreams become more reveries than revolutions.

In his novel *The Alchemist*, Paulo Coelho tells a compelling story about a young boy who is learning to follow his heart. The boy travels through the desert alongside a man who is simply identified as "the alchemist." As they journey the boy engages in a conversation with his heart. He learns that he, like everyone else, has a treasure waiting for him, and the heart's purpose is to encourage him to seek that treasure. But because people become preoccupied with so many other things, they no longer pay attention to their hearts. Only children, who have yet to be so distracted by life, have the ability to hear their hearts in a clear way. The boy learns from the alchemist that because of the pain of going unheard, the heart will eventually stop telling people to follow their dreams. The boy pleads with his heart to never stop speaking to him. Should he begin to wander away from his dreams, he wants his heart to sound the alarm and promises that he will hear it and follow.[29]

Can you still hear your heart? If you're not snug enough, you can't feel its vibrations or hear its voice. Being able to listen to your heart and dream the dreams God has planted in that heart sound like good reasons to have and be a Rhoda.

11

I have always studied to be simple.[30]
—John Calvin saying farewell to the pastors in Geneva

11

Rhodas Keep You Scared

A Rhoda in your life keeps you playing "Boo!" and "Grr!" games.

Witches, warlocks, and wolves, Voldemorts, vampires, and vultures, ogres and stepmothers—this is the stuff of which children's literature is made. Why? Because this is how children learn to master their fears.

We all do, all through life. Monsters are real, not just those under-the-bed but over-the-rainbow monsters, and we need to face our monsters and turn them into instruments of creativity and growth. Besides, you can't become a hero without a villain.

I wish I knew the name of the clever person who said, "Fear is the dark-room that develops negatives into positives." Maybe it's because only in the dark can we process the negative emotions of dread, anger, worry, etc. Maybe it's because the thrill of soaring begins with the fear of falling, and we need to be pushed out of the dark, cozy nests to discover how far we can go. Maybe it's because the dark breeds ghost stories, and those goose bumps of enjoyment give us a heightened sense of being alive. Or maybe it's because the older we get, the easier it is to pretend to be something other than we are, and Rhodas scare the real you out of you.

Whatever the reason, Rhodas rid us of the happy-minded mania that denies the fragile hold we have on life and the hard-won victories that come only to those scared enough to run the race. Folks without Rhodas in their lives see everything as a Thomas Kinkade painting. At first glance, it appears to be all light. But on further inspection, it's actually all trite. Rhodas shoo the trite out of the room.

Rhodas Keep You Small

> Its smallness is not petty:
> on the contrary, it is profound.[31]
> —novelist Jan Morris on Wales

A rediscovery of the little, and a contrite sense of our smallness in the grandness of the universe, is high on the list of "agenda items" if our twenty-second-century children are to make it through the twenty-first century. In fact, the mantra of the future might well be "Do Little Large." Here are three small hints. They all dove-tail somewhat, but they all have "small" differences.

1. Meaning and significance are in the small things. Jesus picked up a mustard seed and compared it to the power of faith in the kingdom of God. A mustard seed is supposed to be the smallest seed we can see with our eyes. To see life with mus-tard-seed eyes is to see right through the thicket of growth into the essence of things, to understand the primal as the primary, to never lose track of the simplic-ity in the midst of the complexity. Life is all about the small things and small spaces—of time, of relationships, of self—and filling the small with a large love for God, neighbor, and creation.

For this same reason Jesus took bread and wine, and in a moving show-and-tell moment of preaching without words, infused the elementary things of life with the elemental.[32] The essence of the incarnation is that God makes himself small for us.[33] God works little large. The whole of faith is encapsulated in a very small package: one act of love.[34]

> Most people simply don't know how beautiful the world is and how much splendor is revealed in the smallest things, in a common flower, in a stone, in THE BARK OF A TREE OR THE LEAF OF A BIRCH. Grown-up people, who have occupations and cares and who worry themselves about mere trifles, gradually lose the eye for these riches, while children, if they are observant and good, quickly notice and love with their whole heart.[35]
> —Rainer Maria Rilke

2. Living large by loving little.

I have visited the squatter camps of Johannesburg and am forever haunted by them. A squatter camp is a land where life resembles an overcrowded prison cell. In the squatter camp of Zandspruitt (a "suburb" of Johannesburg), approximately

35,000 people live in 1 square kilometer. Each person or family is crowded into a living space not much larger than 10 feet by 10 feet, with "homes" made of scrap metal and broken boards and cardboard boxes. The government has no interest in fixing up these hovels, or investing any money in these squatter camps, since upward of 90 percent of the adult residents either have AIDS or other terminal illnesses. Since they are going to be dead shortly anyway, why bother?

Amid all the squalor and decrepitude, one tiny "house" stood out. It had been painted white and black and had little planter boxes of flowers strategically placed under windows and around the "house." A little vegetable stand with a painted roof to protect the squash and tomatoes had been placed where you expected a mailbox to be. I stood there, frozen in awe at the beauty that was leaking out of this one person's life. I asked to meet her, but she hid in the shadows, peeking out at me nervously, a small woman who could have been fifteen or fifty. I did find out her name was Cecilia, and I have not stopped thanking God for Saint Cecilia ever since. I felt more of her soul in that 10-square-foot lot than I have in 10,000-square-foot homes that cost millions of dollars.

In the midst of the worst of human conditions, Cecilia had learned to live large by loving little. She may be the closest I have ever come to being in the presence of a saint.

David McDonald, a friend, colleague, and pastor at WestWinds (Jackson, Michigan), tells of meeting Maria in a dump in Juárez. Maria was known as the spiritual pillar of her community. Covered in open sores and infections, she asked for a prayer that she might continue bringing hope and love to the people who lived in the dump with her. When David was done, she rewarded him with a kiss on the eyes. "All night I tossed and turned, afraid I'd caught something from Maria," David confessed to me. "But then I had a moment of revelation: What if I hadn't caught her disease, but her grace? What if I'd been infected by her love? What if I'd been contaminated by her holiness?"

It's the little things that run the world.[36]
—Harvard insect biologist E. O. Wilson

3. Ask. Seek. Knock. A child's simple, small questions are often the most profound. If the greatest teachers (Socrates, Jesus) are those who ask the greatest questions, then Rhodas are master teachers. No wonder Jesus taught his disciples sometimes to sit at the feet of children. They ask questions so simple they are impossible to answer.

Rhodas have soul frequencies that are always tuned to the WYMI radio station: "Why am I?" or "Who am I?" or "What am I?" … Their jackhammering succession of "Who's-Who-and-What's-What" and "Whys" encourages us to tune in to the same frequencies ourselves of that WYMI station and ask nonadult (i.e., silly, stupid) questions. It was Thomas's willingness to ask a Rhoda question, "Lord, we don't know where you are going, so how can we know the way?" that elicited the words that have resounded through the ages: "I am the Way, the Truth, and the Life."

Jesus himself modeled the art of questioning:

✓ "Who do people say I am?" (Mark 8:27)
✓ "Who do you say I am?" (Mark 8:29)
✓ "What good will it be for a man if he gains the whole world, yet forfeits his soul?" (Matt. 16:26)
✓ "Why are you thinking these things?" (Mark 2:8)
✓ "What do you think?" (Matt. 17:25)
✓ "What is written in the Law?" (Luke 10:26)
✓ "What do you more than others?" (Matt. 5:47 NKJV)
✓ "What do you want?" (John 1:38)
✓ "Do you see anything?" (Mark 8:23)[37]

11

> A bird among the rain-wet lilac sings—
> But we, how shall we turn to little things
> And listen to the birds and winds and streams
> Made holy by their dreams,
> Nor feel the heart-break in the heart of things?[38]
> —Wilfred Wilson Gibson, "Lament"

11

Rhodas Keep You Light

One should be light like a bird, not like a feather.[39]
—Paul Valery

A Rhoda world is filled with lighthearted, even light-headed airborne characters (Peter Pan, Mary Poppins, Harry Potter, cupids, etc.) who are enchanting contrasts to the prosaic, predictable, grounded, weighed-down world of adults.

Gravity is an adult disease that leads to the grave. The more your body succumbs to gravity, the more your body starts to let you down. The more your soul succumbs to gravity, the more it sags, sheds desire, and the more dissolute it becomes. General Douglas MacArthur is known for the quote "Age wrinkles the body. Quitting wrinkles the soul." But what he actually said was much more profound: "You don't get old from living a particular number of years; you get old because you have deserted your ideals. Years wrinkle your skin; renouncing your ideals wrinkles your soul. Worry, doubt, fear, and despair are the enemies which slowly bring us down to the ground and turn us to dust before we die."[40]

Children of all types and cultures keep us young because they keep us flying. "The Lord wants only that there be flying," Rainer Maria Rilke wrote.

"Whoever happens to see to it, in that he has only a quite passing interest."[41] Once you discover lightness—the lightness of grace, the lightness of laughter, the lightness of music—you can fly again. Once you remember how to Jack-be-nimble, or reconnect with your Mary-Mary-contrariness, Humpty-Dumpty devilry, and Jack-and-Jill adventurousness, you are liberated into an aerial world of expanded possibilities where transfigurations are commonplace and transcendings routine.

For a child, it's natural to be an idealist; but it takes miracles to be a realist.

Children need novelty and surprise—new information must keep coming to them for them to survive. Rhodas keep us listening to new music, clothing ourselves in new styles, and generally keeping us from the ruts of inertia and the routines of life's logics and logistics.

> Lightness for me goes with precision and determination,
> not with vagueness and the haphazard.[42]
> —Italo Calvino, *Six Memos for the Next Millennium*

We are all running out of days, but Rhodas keep us from runaway crankiness and keep us taking off on runways of hope. When hope for this world and hope for the world to come kiss and make up,[43] the "Unhappy Hour" of old age can become life's most inebriating "Happy Hour." Old age is no day at the beach, but it can be your best day in the sun if you can join your Rhoda in common playgrounds and other sandboxes of the imagination.

Toward the end of his life, the genius Isaac Newton humbly confessed, "I know not what I appear to the world, but to myself, I seem to have been only like a boy playing on the sea-shore, and diverting myself, in now and then finding a smoother pebble or a prettier shell than ordinary, whilst the great ocean of truth lay all undiscovered before me."[44] No wonder Plato called the play of children *"spoudaios paizein"* or "serious play," which he believed was the calling of the true philosopher. Children play not for entertainment or distraction but to concentrate better and be creative.[45]

Without Rhoda, it's "I'm having a senior moment. Please excuse me."

With Rhoda's ripening, it can be "I'm having a God moment. Please join me."

Rhodas Keep You Alive

The sole origin of philosophy is wonder.[46]
—Socrates in Plato's *Theaetetus*

If you have children, you know about "animations." The word leads right into the universe of the child—"animation" is "anima," which means "alive."

In the world of a child, everything is alive, from talking animals to talking toys to talking nature. A child is never alone, and a child's friends come in surprising shapes and sizes. Griswold observes how in children's stories "all God's creatures seem chatty—whether they be bears, birds, cats, elephants, bugs, lions, pigs, dogs, monkeys, or fish in the sea."[47] The world of magic is the world of a child, because magic pulls the heartstrings of the universe. Children don't let daylight into the magic; adults don't let magic into the daylight.

Rhodas help us breathe different air because they live in a different time zone than the rest of us. We spend most of our days in the past and future. For children, there is only the "naked now." Rhodas refresh the everyday with surprises and disguises. Even though they move through parallel universes at breakneck speed, switching from spaceships to backyards in the blink of an eye, they do so only in the energy of the "now."

What does it mean to say that a person has "presence"? It's not what they say or do. It's their spirit. It's their ability to be present, to be "in the moment."

Rhodas "animate" the stale, pale platitude of the psalmist and make it into a living manifesto: *This* is the day the Lord has made; let us rejoice and be glad in it." If *spirituality* means "waking up,"[48] then your Rhoda is one of your prime spiritual directors. For your Rhoda helps you to wake up to life, to come alive to existence. "Most people, even though they don't know it, are asleep. They're born asleep, they live asleep, they marry in their sleep, they breed children in their sleep, they die in their sleep without ever waking up. They never understand the loveliness and beauty of this thing we call human existence."[49] Rhodas are our best mentors in exploring the "nowness" of the now, in inhaling the summit air of "the sacrament of the present moment."[50] That's why to let children loose in the backyard is like setting children loose in a candy shop. When we live in the simultaneity of past-present-future, every moment of our lives can become a form of communion with the divine love.

Sometimes I take my divinity students out for a meal and a movie, using both experiences as sign-reading ("semiotic") exercises. I shall never forget trying to convince one class to go with me to see *Toy Soldiers*. One of my front-row students blurted out that she despised movies that featured "inanimate" objects that talked. She gave up "animated" movies when she grew up. Her lost sense of being alive represented too much of grown-up society. To her it seemed foolish for things that are not alive to become alive. Heaven weeps at stories like that.

To children, "animation" is their reality.

Children remember nothing and see everything. That's why they are our best semioticians, for as they see everything for the first time, they help us see everything again as if for the first time[51] and become transparent to the world. Three times a day a practicing Jew prays a Rhoda prayer, thanking God "for thy miracles which are daily with us, and for thy continual marvels."

I shall never forget reading a newspaper account of billionaire Michael Bloomberg's visit to the Vatican. As befitting the mayor of New York City, Bloomberg got the VIP tour. Any run-of-the-mill tour of the Vatican bathes you in so much beauty that it leaves you in a lather. A cook's tour of the Vatican puts you into a stunned state of silence for days. Bloomberg got the pope's tour.

When reporters asked Bloomberg what he was most impressed with as he left the Vatican courtyard, he is quoted as responding: "You know what I'll never forget? They had Bloomberg Terminals in the Vatican!"[52]

Not Michelangelo's Sistine Chapel? Not Botticelli's *The Life of Moses*? Not Raphael's *The Transfiguration* or the Loggia? Not Leonardo's *Saint Jerome*? Not Bramante's octagonal courtyard? Not Saint Peter's Basilica? Not one of the innumerable Roman mosaics or Greek vases or French tapestries? But stock-trade terminals?

Without Rhodas and their animations, our souls can shrink, our minds can turn to mush or machines, our awareness atrophied by a consumer culture that defines reality in terms of trades and terminals. Rhodas keep the glint of adventure in our eyes, and when the Rhodas are released, doors previously closed for our whole lives start to open up.

My friend from South Africa, Peter Veysie, likes to talk about the "eggs" he's hatching. He's never more excited than when he calls up and says, "I've got a new egg I'm sitting on." When I finally asked him exactly what he meant, he said he got the language from his father, Donald, a retired Methodist pastor. All his life Donald would refer to his sermon or his theological insight as an "egg" in a nest. His job was to sit on these "eggs," keep them warm and turned, talked to and prayed over, until they were ready to hatch.

But timing is everything. The "egg" needs to come out as a baby chick. If the "egg" hatches as a crowing rooster or hard-to-grasp, full-grown hen, then the egg hasn't been sat on long enough. It needs a longer incubation period, more brooding and nurturing. Until the "egg" has been simplified to the point of childlike chirping, it's not a true hatch. When the "egg" breaks open and a baby chick emerges, then the thought has matured to the point of simplicity.

The Rhodas in our life keep us sitting on the eggs until they hatch as baby chicks, not dragons or dinosaurs that take flight and slay us.

Rhoda Interactives

1. Explore some other "Rhodas" in the Bible:

   a) The story of Miriam

   b) The story of Naaman's wife's servant, who told her mistress about God's prophet Elisha, and the ensuing changes in Naaman's life because of this child's little act of faith

2. Is anyone ever too old to hold a stranger in his or her arms or heart?

3. What are you doing to live Jesus' philosophy of "When you receive a child, you receive me"? Where are you receiving a child in your life? Here are some obvious ways of "Receiving Rhoda": a) You could serve in some capacity in children's ministry; b) You could teach a Sunday school class …

   What are some not-so-obvious "Receive Rhoda" ministries?

4. James Hillman invites us to "understand the decline and shrinkage that accompanies aging as 'value-added' rather than a literal loss."

   > The forgetful mind and lapses of attention, the vague fumbling of motor skills, the closing down of feeling responses and impoverishment of language may not be only as they seem to young eyes. Perhaps space is being made, the rest for a different music, a voiding of the usual for the sake of the unusual.[53]

Might not aging be the soul-making "space" for a deeper relationship with God?

5. Play "footsie" in a postmodern way. Integrate into your life some Billy Bray rituals.

Billy Bray (as described by William James) was an "illiterate itinerant English evangelist in the early nineteenth century who walked the countryside, lifting up one foot and saying 'Glory' and lifting up the other foot saying 'Amen.'"

Annie Dillard shows us how she plays footsie the Billy Bray way in her classic *Pilgrim at Tinker Creek*:

> Like Billy Bray I go my way, and my left foot says "glory," and my right foot says "amen"; in and out of Tinker Creek, upstream and down, exultant, in a daze, dancing, to the twin silver trumpets of praise.[54]

6. What were some of the "make-believe" games you played as a child? Can you identify some of the life skills you were learning while you were "making believe"?

7. Does play always need to be "productive play"? In other words, do you think that the experience of "sheer pleasure" might be one of those life skills we need to learn? Why or why not?

8. More than one biblical scholar has a negative view of Rhoda; for example, "Her emotion was out of proportion to her intelligence. Some people have too

little emotional luster; others have too much." For this commentator, Rhoda was the latter: not lacking in love, but with a "love out of harness."[55]

Is this such a bad thing? When might "love out of harness" be a compliment? When might it be a negative?

9. Do you think we as modern-day Christians still might not be ready to hear the voice of a Rhoda Withness? At least not without some effort?

10. Rhoda never saw Peter but just heard his voice and believed. The others (those inside the house and the disciples) had to see in order to believe.

    Discuss John 20:29: "Jesus told him [Thomas], 'Because you have seen me, you have believed; blessed are those who have not seen and yet have believed.'"

11. Do you see any similarities between Rhoda's recognition (verbally) of Peter and the risen Jesus' encounter with the disciples? (Compare Luke 24:31 and Matthew 28:8.)

12. Are you willing to do little? Is the little beneath you? Are you too big to do small? Children help us see the mustard-seed meaning to life.

Withness 10: Who Are Your VIPs? You Need a Lydia and Lazarus, Rich and Poor

Serve the poor and the rich will come.
—John King, lead pastor
Riverside Church, Peoria, Illinois

You've heard it said: It is more blessed to give than to receive. But forget what you've heard for a moment, and don't worry right now about getting that "blessing." It is more difficult to receive than to give. In fact, as important as it is to be generous givers, it's even more important to be gracious receivers.[1]

Greg Paul is a rock instrumentalist and composer whose music turned into a ministry on the streets of Toronto, Canada. *God in the Alley* (2004) is his story of the "Sanctuary" community that formed not as an outreach to the poor but that was (and is) being built around the poor. It is my favorite "here's the story of my church" book.[2]

Greg says one of the greatest problems he has when middle- or upper-income people come to Sanctuary is they immediately want to "serve." They go into a default "giving" mode. But this Sanctuary community of the poor and dispossessed also wants to give, and one of the hardest things Greg has to do is teach these middle- and upper-class "visitors" how to receive from the poor. Before they can give, they first must learn how to receive.

God is giver. We are receiver. God's fundamental category is "giving." Our fundamental category is "receiving." Not to like to "receive" is to prefer God's category. I am by nature a better giver than a receiver, which means I have one of the worst spiritual problems anyone can have: I have a God complex. To refuse to receive is tantamount to declaring war against the Gift (Holy Spirit), who proceeds from the Giver of Life (Father and Son).

Jesus was a good receiver. He was never the host at any designated meal (though he did feed five thousand surprise guests). Jesus never made up a list of invites. He was always a guest, always on the invitation list. He participated fully in the goodness of being.

We need to learn how to receive, how to be on the receiving end and participate in the gift of being. The two people we need to learn how to receive from the most are the rich and the poor, or what I'm calling your VIPs, your Lydia and Lazarus. To both Lydia and Lazarus we must learn never to say, "You shouldn't have!"

The rich need to discover their poverty, and the poor need to discover their riches.

Who's Your Lydia?

Who's your sponsor, your patron, your partner, and your provider?

Jesus was financed by well-to-do women. And so were almost all the early Christian communities.

Rich women like Lydia put their money where their faith was and provided the means for the spread of the gospel.

Lydia was a merchant of purple-dyed garments in Philippi,[3] a business-woman/organizer/go-getter who volunteered her home as a base for evangelization and for organization of Christian communities. After she and her entire household received baptism—suggesting both that she was the head of the household and that the whole household was loyal to her—she hosted house churches and presided at meetings. Her house must have been big enough to accommodate Paul, Silas, Timothy, and Luke, and her role was so important that Paul and Silas did not leave, even though expedience said to get out of town quick, until they first met with Lydia and "the brothers and sisters" in her home.[4]

Patrons practice hospitality and philanthropy, and Lydia's house of worship became a center for evangelization and education as well as worship. Some scholars who have studied the traditional Roman patronage system suggest that Lydia may also have received something in return: "It was customary for clients to maintain a relationship of *obsequium,* compliance, and submission. Did Paul give suitable tribute to his patrons Phoebe and Lydia and perhaps give them private instruction or repair leatherwork around the house in exchange for the hospitality and financial assistance he received from them?"[5]

We do wrong by vilifying the rich.

> **11**
>
> Is not a Patron, My Lord, one who looks with unconcern
> on a Man struggling for Life in the water and when he
> has reached ground encumbers him with help?[6]
> —Samuel Johnson's cynical definition of a *patron*
>
> **11**

True, the very rich have access to levers and resources we never knew existed. They can destroy anyone who is an annoyance or nuisance, or simply for their perverse pleasure.[7] But everyone who has grown up in a small town can testify to the power of the grapevine to destroy reputations in one de-story.

True, the rich have sins that garner the tabloid headlines: those old favorites of sex, greed, power addictions, six-figure bathtubs, cheating. But the poor have their sins too: jealousy, resentment, cheating.

True, the rich are spiritually more vulnerable than the poor. The Sermon on the Mount is Christianity's Mount Sinai. When Jesus said, "Happy are you who are poor," he used the word *ptochoi. Ptochoi* doesn't mean "poverty" as we know poverty; it means people who are utterly and completely dependent on God, people who have no alternative security other than God. This is why riches are so problematic for Jesus. The danger of wealth is that its default position moves us further away from God, while the default position of poverty moves us closer to God. The weakness of wealth is the default position: Money is our refuge and strength, a very present help in time of trouble. The strength of poverty is the default position: God is our refuge and strength, a very present help in time of trouble. Wealth means money in our pockets but a monkey on our backs.

True, income inequality is at a forty-year high. You know the drill: The rich are getting richer, and the poor are getting poorer.[8] The difference in per capita income between the world's wealthiest 20 percent and the poorest 20 percent was 30 to 1 in 1960; this ratio jumped to 74 to 1 in 2000.[9] But before we welcome each other to the global Plantation Economy of the twenty-first century, let us be aware of two interrelated things. First, the world as a whole is getting richer, and the poor are doing it faster than the wealthy.[10] In a global economy and its mitosis of the middle, the real losers are those in the middle.[11] Second, the wealth of the wealthy is not the problem. Just because the United States is consuming $10 trillion worth of goods and services each year doesn't mean that there is $10 trillion worth of goods and services out of circulation in the rest of the world.[12] Look at China and India. Almost overnight they moved out of poverty while the stock market set records moving northward.

Abraham Lincoln said long ago, "You don't make the poor rich by making the rich poor." Or in the words of George Kennan, "I know of no assumption that has been more widely and totally disproved by actual experience than the assumption that if a few people could be prevented from living well, everyone else would live better."[13] Our problems are not globalization, or global inequality, or unfair trade, or market injustices. Our problem is our failure to address the poverty of the rich and the richness of the poor.

In fact, my favorite toast is "Here's to having it all."

My mother heralded my father for being a "good provider"[14] for our family, yet my two brothers and I were born on a street called "Hungry Hill." My "good provider" father was a bank teller, and only late in his life made officer status ("Assistant Cashier"). When he died at age fifty-six, this "good provider" had worked his way up to an annual salary of $14,000. My parents were too proud for welfare assistance, but they weren't too proud to send me and my brothers across the street to beg from the poor.

"Marge, Mother sent me to see if you had anything for us." Thank God for Marge, who would often respond to my knocks on her back door with bricks of government-issued yellow cheese and brown flour sacks. This was the only time in my childhood when I had any inkling that we were so poor we "hardly had a roof to our mouths."[15] But it seemed less like the Sweet family was poor and out of food than that the Jackson family was rich in what Wordsworth called "the little nameless, unremembered acts / Of kindness and of love"[16]—although I do remember standing at that dilapidated back door and being amused by the irony of getting handouts from people getting handouts.

> **11**
>
> God does not need anything,
> but God rejoices over those who give to the needy.[17]
> —Sentences of Sextus
>
> **11**

We had nothing, but we had "it all." And "it all" came from a "provider" who gave me everything a child could possibly want: a family that loved me, brothers to play with, a safe household, music to learn, books to read, Bible verses to memorize, twice-daily family prayer, adventures to simulate the imagination, trips to complain about but be glad for later, historical monuments to photograph, open doors for strangers to enter, dreams to build. The Sweet family was rich beyond words and beyond money. We were "big spenders" thanks to my "provider" father and mother who labored to provide me with a working visa to a country called "Life."

You need VIP "providers"—persons who will lift up your arms financially for the ministry and mission to which God has called you. Ask any president of a 501-C-3. Ask any president of anything. Your success hinges on one thing: Is there someone out there who believes in you enough, and believes in the mission of your organization, to pony up to the table and put money where your mouth is? All it takes is one, but the presence of one Lydia galvanizes others and generates a momentum that enables you to function on the front lines.

Every one of us has been the recipient of wonderfully generous and charitable acts. When it came time for me to choose a seminary, one of my college professors, a then unpublished junior scholar named Emory C. Bogle, stepped up to the plate to bat on my behalf. He helped me choose a seminary, made a "cold call" to the president of that seminary, which coaxed out of them an academic scholarship. The domino effect of that one act is still with me today. Professor Bogle's patronage of someone only slightly more junior than himself launched a waterfall of wonders that continue to shape the course of my life. Typically, Lydias patron peers. Not enough Lydias are setting waterfalls in motion, especially for less-fortunate people than themselves.

But every one of us has stupidly rejected, whether knowingly or unknowingly, the largesse of patrons, and failed to recognize Lydias when they appeared. When I was finishing up my doctoral studies, I was appointed associate pastor of a church in Rochester, New York. My office was the first door on the right as you entered the side entrance of the church, and I quickly struck up a friendship with "Estelle." Every morning a disheveled, slightly pungent Estelle would stop by for her hug before she made her way to the kitchen, where the church made available to her leftover food to eat and clothes for her to wear. Some said Estelle was homeless. Others said Estelle rented a room somewhere. There were even rumors that Estelle, who couldn't throw anything away, lived with old newspapers stacked to the ceiling—although there was one church member who said, "They're not old newspapers; they're Xerox stock certificates."

One day when I gave Estelle her hug she whispered in my ear, "You're going to get a call." Estelle was always saying strange things to me, so I didn't think anything of it. But later that morning I received a call that went like this: "Dr. Sweet, this is Estelle's attorney. She wanted me to let you know that she has left you her entire estate in her will. She says she can't tell you this personally, but she wants to jump-start your ministry and wants you to purchase with her money a headquarters somewhere for you to set up the Leonard Sweet Evangelistic Association."

"This is a joke, right?"

"No, Estelle is very serious. As you know, Estelle lives very frugally. She can't spend money on herself. But she feels that God is calling her to give you what amounts to over a million dollars to set up your ministry."

"Did you say over a million?"

"Yes, well over a million. Maybe multiple millions, depending on the value of the stock when she dies."

"Sir, I am very flattered by this. But I am Estelle's friend in my capacity of serving as her pastor. She really needs to give this money to the church. It's not just me who is helping out Estelle. It's an entire body of disciples who love and care for her. I give her hugs and love her up in the morning. But there are others who set aside food and clothes for her and love her up the rest of the day."

"I'm sure that's the case, but she wants you to have the money."

"I can't take it."

"You don't have a choice. She's already given it to you."

"Sir, if Estelle gives me this money, she will not help my ministry; she will hurt it. In fact, she will kill my ministry. This money needs to go to the church, not to me personally."

"Then you will need to tell her that yourself, young man. She told me you would fight her on this, which is why she wanted me to call you to begin with. But you take this up with her. She's pretty stubborn, so good luck."

The next morning, when Estelle came in for her morning hug, she greeted me with an impish grin—like she knew she had done something naughty, but enjoyed doing it anyway. I explained to Estelle that I was honored by her gift, but that if she really cared for me and my ministry, she would give the money to the church. She shook her head no. I looked Estelle in the eyes and said, "Estelle, if you love me and care for me, you will not do this. You will give the money to the church. If you give the money to me, you will kill my ministry, not kick-start it."

When I said "kill my ministry," Estelle burst into tears. She couldn't stop crying, and collapsed in my arms, mumbling, "I only want to help," through her tears.

Three months later, Estelle died. She gave $25,000 to her paperboy. She gave $40,000 to one of the women who hid food for her in the church refrigerator. She gave $70,000 to someone who spoke to her on the street and another $50,000 to someone who had no idea who Estelle was. And on and on. She gave what was left to her attorney. Estelle could not give to an institution. She could only give to people, and a fortune was frittered away because I could not recognize a Lydia when she came knocking on my door.

Who's Your Lazarus?

There are two people, one real, one fictional, named Lazarus in the Bible. The real one was Jesus' true friend—Jesus' Jonathan. The story of Jesus raising Lazarus from the dead was so popular in the early church that it was second only to pictures of "The Good Shepherd" in catacomb frescoes.[18]

The fictional Lazarus (Hebrew for "God helps"), the only character to which Jesus ever attached a name in a parable, was the disabled, skin-diseased beggar who eked out an existence by soliciting alms from those who entered and exited the palatial home of Dives (Latin for "rich man").[19]

Dives is a biblical counterpart to Lydia—a person of wealth who is barred from paradise. His wealth is not what kept him out of heaven. In the story, after all, the fabulously wealthy Abraham is in heaven, acting as heaven's advocate.[20] Nor was it any crime or corruption that kept Dives out of those "eternal dwellings."[21]

11

> The richest people in the world?
> The Norwegians.

11

The fact that wealth per se is not the problem is a significant reason why liberal and socialist attack-the-rich approaches to poverty have failed. In the global-economic arena, where the rich are getting richer and the poor are getting poorer, why are the attacks against the rich from liberation theologians and Marxists not resonating with the poor, who are embracing Pentecostalism and a "prosperity" gospel? In USAmerica, where the "rich" are so super-wealthy they can buy entire countries, where the pay ratio of a CEO to a skilled worker is 412:1 (the ratio was 20 to 1 in the '60s), and where the middle class is being squeezed into oblivion, why is the backlash not against the rich, but against immigrants, the poor, and native-born minorities? Why isn't class warfare front-page news?

When the poor dream, what do they dream about? Becoming middle class? Simple living? A subsistence existence?

The poor dream rich dreams. The poor dream of becoming rich. To attack the rich and to vilify abundance is to attack the poor by taking away their dreams.

The problem with Dives was not his wealth. Rather, Dives lived his life without a relationship with Lazarus or any other poor person. In fact, Dives lavished more love and care on his pets than on this impoverished human being who begged on his doorstep. His VIPs in life were Very Important Pets and other "important" people like himself.

Have you noticed how Hollywood has no qualms about portraying people being blown to smithereens, but never pets? Almost a third of all pet owners admit to deeper affection and companionship with their pets than with other people. Almost four in ten pet owners talk to their pets either on the telephone or leave messages for them on the answering machine.[22] Eight in ten dog owners, and seven in ten cat owners, allow their pets to lick and kiss their faces. One in ten pet owners gives his or her dogs or cats massages.[23] When a culture "bow-wows" its pets, while making life increasingly "ruff" for people, something is awry.

Tell me what you get angry at, and I'll tell you who you are.

What makes your heart rip open your shirt? Is it dogfights in Virginia, or do doe-eyed children nodding off into terminal sleep register some beats? Does it hammer anyone's heart that billions of people have to subsist on less than a dollar a day or that tens of thousands of children die daily because water, the staff of life, is for them the drink of death? Just because we are dust, as David Pleins puts it, doesn't mean anyone should be treated as dust or have to live on dust.[24] Do we truly "hunger and thirst" for righteousness and holiness, or is success for ourselves our lives' main passion and drive? Are our lives lived for ourselves, which Jesus called a living death? Or are our lives lived for others, a "dying life" that burns itself out for others just as the sun does, a way of being in the world that theologian Don Cupitt calls in a marvelous metaphor "solar living"?[25]

> I would like to leave this world having asked less of it than I have given to it, without having much said about the matter either way.[26]
> —Paul Escamilla

What the rich need, even more than digging deep into their pinstriped pockets, is a relationship with the poor.

Ask anyone who heads up a homeless shelter or an inner-city rescue mission. They will tell you the same number one frustration. It isn't that the rich don't "visit" or "support" their ministry. The rich write checks and "visit" the poor all the time. It's that the rich don't "know" the poor or become friends with the poor. It is one thing to have a heart for the poor. It is another to use their bathroom. Rather, we treat the poor as anonymous recipients of charity rather than engage them as equals. Top-down "solutions" to poverty will never work. (For every $1 that goes for "foreign aid," only 14 cents gets to its intended recipient.) Only bottom-up relationships built on respect and reciprocity have any chance of making a different world. Anonymous relationships between donors and recipients are doomed to failure.

In the early church, the agape feast followed by the Eucharist was a "family reunion" where the rich and the poor shared food and fellowship together without regard to class distinctions or social status. But even our first-century ancestors struggled with social, economic, and theological divisions, causing Paul to warn the church that all families have differences and that these differences ought not to destroy our time together or derail the meaning of the meal we share.[27] For if that happens, we participate unworthily in the body and blood of Jesus.

The first followers of Jesus, when they gathered for worship, had to step past and sometimes over the poor who gathered outside entrances, begging for alms. The rich and the poor today are increasingly living geographically separate lives. Most people have not had twenty-five conversations with poor people in their whole lives. It is time to chip away the wall that separates the inseparable, the rich and the poor.

The major meaning of human existence comes from blind acts of human kindness and bold acts of leaping beyond the limits of human nature. This does not mean that we are ever free from self-interest. But these blind and bold acts help us to experience, if only for a fleeting moment, what it means to be human, to be fully conscious human beings in a world of unconsciousness and a world without conscience.

VIP Interactives

1. The philosopher Peter Singer has tried to estimate what the seriously rich should give. He finds that a modest but ethically defensible level of giving, which would not remove anyone from the list of the seriously rich and cause no hardship, would raise many times what the United Nations has estimated is needed to end world poverty—and that is only the seriously rich in America.

Here is what it looks like:

a) If the top .01 percent give a third ...

(0.01 percent of taxpayers earn an average of $12,775,000; that's 14,400 people who collectively earn a total of $184 billion a year. Minimum annual income in this group is $5 million ... If they gave away a third, leaving them an average income of $3.3 million) ...

b) If the rest of the top 0.1 percent gave 25 percent
(there are 129,600 in this group, with an average income of just over $2 million and a minimum income of $1.1 million) ...

c) If the rest of the top 0.5 percent gave 20 percent
(this consists of 575,900 taxpayers, with an average income of $623,000 and a minimum of $407,000) ...

d) If the rest of the top 1 percent gave 15 percent
(there are 719,900 taxpayers with an average income of $327,000 and a minimum of $276,000) ...

e) If the remainder of the nation's top 10 percent gave the traditional tithe
(there are nearly 13 million with an average of $132,000) ...

Then, Singer argues, we could eradicate poverty.[28]

Will we ever make poverty history? If you don't think so, is this any reason to stop trying?

2. In 2006, the Nobel Peace Prize was awarded to Muhammad Yunus for inventing a social network called the Grameen Bank. The Grameen Bank is not a bricks-and-mortar institution. It's a set of relationships that puts small amounts of capital in the hands of the poorest people in the world. Sometimes called "micro-finance," the Grameen Bank is unsustainable from the point of view of hard, cold, classical economics. It is however wildly successful in practice.

    Find ways to promote www.kiva.org in your church.

3. Do a book review of Daniel Pink's *A Whole New Mind: Moving from the Informational Age to the Conceptual Age* (New York: Riverhead Trade, 2005), which predicts the accelerating commoditization of technological creativity and even design. What's left? The right-brain skills that encourage imagination, innovation, and storytelling.

    How right brained is your church?

4. Why is it the least well off pay the most for basic goods and services, including higher interest rates? Discuss the "poverty premium" and what your church might be able to do to lower the "premium" placed on the poor.

5. Tell some Lydia stories.

6. Tell some Lazarus stories.

7. To what extent is "One Market Under God" replacing "One Nation Under God"? Do you think there is a growing problem with what might be called "marketolatry"?

8. When you read the Gospels, do you find a Jesus with a biting social edge? If so, give examples. If not, how would you describe Jesus' attitude toward the rich and the poor?

9. What do you think of this thesis: "It's not that the poor are getting poorer, or that more Americans are falling below the poverty line, so much as it is that poor Americans are falling further and further behind those who succeed"?[29]

10. Roman society was permeated by a firmly established, extensive system of patronage: Degrees of rank and influence in society were of the greatest importance. How do you think Paul's preaching of social and gender equality ("in Christ … there is neither Jew nor Greek, slave nor free, male nor female") fits into such a system of patronage?

11. If you're like me, the following reminder is often needed in one of three times: when what I think I've done in the past hasn't mattered, when what I'm doing presently isn't significant, or when I think I'm too busy or "big" to get involved. Print this out and put in a place where your eyes can always catch its message:

> Your care for others
> is the measure of your greatness.
> —Luke 9:48 TLB

Withness 11:
Where's Your Jerusalem?
You Need a Place

But now that I am in love with a place
which doesn't care how I look and if I am happy,
happy is how I look and that's all.

—Fleur Adcock

I have a new ambition in life. I want to be "a local."

If you had told me when I was starting out that someday "living a landscape" would be one of my greatest dreams, I would have responded, "It's one thing to be honest together, but let's not be stupid together."

But here I am: wanting to be "a local," with locavore hungers, longing to be "placed" and no longer to be "out of place."

Quote me: I'm going native!

And that's the focus of this chapter: place. Every person needs a place. Every person needs to live a landscape. You might find it odd that after all the emphasis on people, I'm including a place, but I'm hoping you'll consider this special Withness. I believe we all know this; we all just need a reminder.

In the mysterious alchemy of creation, spirit loves matter. In fact, spirit cares deeply about its life in matter, for spirit and body are one. The nature of your embodiment is central to who you are.

Some say Martin Heidegger was the most important and original philosopher of the twentieth century. If you're looking for reasons not to like Heidegger, you don't have to look far. His celebrated *Being and Time* (1927) is virtually unreadable (I've tried three times). All too readable are his anti-Semitic and Nazi sympathies in the winning days of Hitler. His affairs with Jewish graduate students (like Hannah Arendt) are too numerous to mention.

But Heidegger's theory of "grounding," which became so pivotal for twentieth-century theologians like Paul Tillich and Karl Rahner,[1] was itself "grounded" in a place. Heidegger's life revolved around his three-room, six-by-seven-meter hut in the southern Black Forest mountains in Germany. Heidegger's university teaching, lecturing, global travel, research, and writing did not revolve around where he had a home (Freiburg), but where he had a ski shack (Todtnauberg). His elegant suburban home at Rotebuckweg (on the western edge of the Black Forest) was merely a pit stop from which to get to his mountain hut (*chalet* is too misleading a word).[2]

> What is a compassionate heart? It is a heart on fire for
> the whole of creation. On fire for all of humanity, for the
> birds, for the animals, for all that exists.[3]
> —Saint Isaac of Syria

In fact, the reason Heidegger turned down the chair of philosophy in Berlin, the most prestigious appointment in Germany at the time (1934), was because he couldn't imagine life without his hut.

> This is my work-world.... Strictly speaking I myself never
> observe the landscape. I experience its hourly changes, day
> and night, in the great comings and goings of the seasons.[4]

His relationship with the hills of the Black Forest was one found "not in forced moments of 'aesthetic' immersion or artificial empathy," he confessed; rather, "one's existence stands in its work."[5]

> Sometimes the easiest answer to our difficulties is not so much
> to get outside ourselves as simply to get ourselves outside.[6]
> —William deBuys

In other words, Heidegger's academic "work" and his mountain "world" were so connected that to lose one would be to lose the other. Once again in his own words: "It is the work alone that opens up space for the reality that is these mountains. The course of the work remains embedded in what happens in this region."[7]

> On a deep winter's night when a wild, pounding snow-storm rages around the cabin and veils and covers everything, that is the perfect time for philosophy. Then its questions become simple and essential. Working through each thought can only be tough and rigorous. The struggle to mould something into language is like the resistance of the towering firs against the storm."[8]

What places represent holiness in your life? What are the coordinates of your "holy ground"? The intonations of your home space? Show me on the map your Beulah Land. What place exists that would cause you to say no to a dream job? It's not just kids who have a "nature-deficit disorder."

Roots and Wings

Every plant grows in two opposite directions at the same time: downward, more rooted and bound, clinging to the ground; but also upward, freer and more open, swaying in the breeze. Jewish mystic and literary scholar Walter Benjamin once observed that all storytelling emerges from two fundamental experiences: the state of being rooted to a particular place, and the act of traveling.[9]

In other words, there are two kinds of stories to tell: moving-in stories and moving-on stories. Moving-in stories are stories with roots: home-sweet-home books about sanctuary, security, and solitude. Moving-on stories are stories with wings: blue-highways books about pilgrimages, on-the-road-again restlessness, and homesickness.

Jesus told roots and wings stories back-to-back:

1. Roots: "The kingdom of heaven is like treasure hidden in a field" (Matt. 13:44).

2. Wings: "The kingdom of heaven is like a merchant in search of fine pearls" (Matt. 13:45 NRSV).

What Benjamin failed to point out, however, is that the storytelling of travel is not homeless—journeys do not occur in a vacuum. Instead, there is a major homecoming component that sometimes makes it more about a "home" place than even the storytelling of moving in.

In postmodern culture our moving-on, blue-highways books have no homecoming or homesickness. Homelessness has a variety of facets. Much of contemporary spirituality is placeless and homeless. In fact, you might call homelessness the hallmark of New Age spirituality: homeless words, homeless thoughts, homeless liturgies—all desperate attempts at "transient transcendence." When you hear on the evening news that homelessness is at an all-time high, they're not lying.

At the risk of throwing vinegar over caviar (to cite an old folktale about Russian foodways), or throwing ashes in one's ice cream (an old Appalachian saying), I must say that too many of our "homes" have become places where our kids can't wait to go from, not can't wait to come to. Even when the lights are on, nobody's home.

11

> If you want to see where you are you will have to get
> out of your spaceship, out of your car, off your horse,
> and walk over the ground.[10]
> —Wendell Berry from his home in Port Royal, Kentucky

11

This is an out-of-place culture with people living out-of-place lives. With no sense of place (location, grounding), our specious species has turned this planet into a consumer hell lined and linked with shopping malls, drive-throughs, and big-box megastores. One of the most Damascus Road moments in my life came when I read and interacted with Wes Jackson, the Kansas prairie geneticist and founder of the Land Institute. Upon reading his classic text *Becoming Native to This Place* (1994),[11] the lights came on and I wanted to get "home." I began to see myself as an aboriginal who could be boastfully local, boastfully indigenous, boastfully rooted.

Wes Jackson and his good friend Kentucky poet/farmer Wendell Berry (whom I believe is our country's greatest living poet) have taught me that becoming "native to our place" involves living out three questions:

1. Can you find your place?
2. Can you live in place?
3. Can you speak our place?

Finding Your Place

Jesus took the "local" seriously. We read of Jesus weeping twice, both times over "locals": once over a "local" person, the other time over a "local" place. Jesus cried over his best friend and his holy place, a dead Lazarus and a dying Jerusalem (see John 11:35 and Luke 19:41).

What's your holy place? Where do you cry to depart from? What land do you live in? Notice I didn't ask, "What land do you live *on?*" My favorite Walter Brueggemann book is *The Land* (1977), one of his earliest but most forgotten in the success of his later books. In *The Land*, Brueggemann argues that every person needs to be in a relationship with a piece of land, to "own" (as much as anyone can) some part of the planet, to bond with some bioregion, while at the same time make a place for others who are needing a place.[12] When Denise Levertov turned Wordsworth's lament upside down by writing "the world is / not with us enough," she was calling for the soul to sing a song of both time and place.

Nature speaks as though it were a lover.[13]
—Octavio Paz

Only the language of love seems to work when we've found "our place." Just as you give yourself heart and soul to a lover, so you give yourself heart and soul to a landscape: to smell its presence and to hear its voice at every season of its life.

With what place have you fallen in love? What place do you have on your screen saver along with what people? What terrain and what food own your heart and with which you are happily enslaved? Where do you pray best?

Or are you, like so many, a kingdom with no king? Hopelessly searching for spiritual roots without earth to plant in?

My Personal Dirt

I am a product of mountain culture. My father was from the foothills of the Adirondack Mountains, my mother from the part of the Appalachian Mountain Range known as the Alleghenies. Appalachia beats in my blood. Like poet W. H. Auden, who was never *not* thinking of Iceland, I am never *not* thinking of West Virginia: If Iceland is the land of pumice and geysers, winter light and brief summers, Appalachia is the land of hills and rills, the land of black nights, white winters, and rainbow autumns. The calendar of colors and rhythm of scents that come with four hardy seasons are imprinted in my soul.

Russell Hoban wrote the literary classic *The Mouse and His Child* (1967) that is as much a spiritual masterpiece as a children's book. The mouse father and child are caught in the middle of an animal territorial war. When the child mouse asks, "What is territory?" he is told:

"A territory is your place," said the drummer boy. "It's where everything smells right. It's where you know the runaways and hideouts, night or day. It's what you fought for, or what your father fought for, and you feel all safe and strong there. It's the place where, when you fight, you win."

"That's *your* territory," said the fifer. "Somebody else's territory is something else again. That's where you feel all sick and scared and want to run away, and that's where the other side mostly wins."

The father walked in silence as a wave of shame swept over him. "What chance has anybody got without a territory?"[14]

So it is.

Since 1992 the San Juan Islands have become my "territory." So far north in the Pacific Northwest that parts of Canada (e.g., Victoria on Vancouver Island, British Columbia) are south of it, the best description of what the Native Americans called the Salish Sea (we say Puget Sound) is in Jim Lynch's *The Highest Tide* (2005). The book tells the story of a thirteen-year-old spending the summer in the tidal flats of where I live, a place where land and sea meet in gentleness, where "the Pacific Ocean comes to relax."[15] There are also other creatures that come to relax in our gentle waters: whales, eagles, osprey, otters, salmon, the world's biggest octopus, the world's largest number of sand dollars, and all sorts of marine and land life. When you're tired of Orcas Island, you're tired of life.

Even though I now have an adopted territory, my Appalachian heritage will always be my home place. As much as I love Orcas Island, the affected bonhomie of left-coast aristocracy sticks in my Appalachian gullet, making me all the more passionate about preserving my tribal tongue and customs through thick and thin:

"creek" is always and everywhere pronounced "crik"; funeral parlors are "slumber rooms" (my gramma was laid out in "the slumber room"); when I whisper in your ear "you've left the barn door open" you better look down; every kitchen table needs a lazy susan (fancy ones have napkin holders) which enables you to put all the dishes on the table at once.

West Virginia may be an easy place to get away from, but a place impossible to leave behind. And that's how it should be: no more smug attempts at leaving and forgetting the places that have shaped us—that continue to shape us.

Where are you most at home? Where must you go to be buried? Where are you most alive, and thus, where do you most want to die? At what location does death have the least dominion over you?

West Virginia is also a place with an underside: a region of willful ignorance and intrigue, of blood feuds, weepings-wailings-and-gnashings of gums, and limited horizons—"Can anything good come out of West Virginia, except an empty bus?" The Jerusalem of Jesus' day is now buried underneath twenty feet of "fill": garbage, debris, dust, soil, etc. But when Jesus cried over the mountain city and its forty thousand inhabitants, the Jerusalem of Solomon's Temple also lay buried underneath feet of "fill." No "place" is without "fill." And no one can escape the "fill."

But Appalachia will always be my womb with a view, and I speak of it as Christians should speak of Christ: never in the past tense, only in the present and future tense ... and as the Bible ends speaking of the "new Jerusalem," a shalom city rising up from the earth, where every man rests secure "under his vine and under his fig tree, and none shall make them afraid."[16]

None of our Beulah Lands are "holy." Not yet. But they combine the future and the present in the process of becoming the "holy" lands we dream them to be.

Living in Place

Where are you "situated"? Where do you "situate" yourself? Is part of our struggle to find our "place" on earth that we try to get "situated" without truly situating ourselves? What patch of the earth's surface do you claim as your own? What land-scape are you living? Might not our uncommittedness be a reflection of our unplacedness?

I now cherish more than home-cooked meals; I want a home-cooked life.

I used to think that to be a monk or nun meant to take a vow of chastity, poverty, and obedience. But that's the vow Franciscans take.

Seven hundred years earlier Benedictines began taking a different vow: Obedience, Stability, and Community.[17] When probation ends for Benedictine monks, this vow of stability binds them to a particular monastery for life. In this community, and in this place, they will practice their faith until they die. It's their home for life. Benedictines thus practice the Pauline priority of place: The natural comes first, then the supernatural.[18] Benedictine spirituality is by design a community in place. The elixir of place is partly the elixir of community.

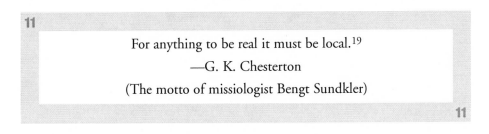

11

For anything to be real it must be local.[19]
—G. K. Chesterton
(The motto of missiologist Bengt Sundkler)

11

Who we are is shaped by where we are. An embodied faith involves emplacement—learning the local narratives, developing rituals that celebrate the local, conducting local conversations not just with other humans but with the native landscape, its terrain, its climate, its colors, its creatures. Relocalization also involves a move toward more cooperative living situations.

There is a complex relationship between geography and theology, between coordinates and creativity, your commitment to place and your commitment to spiritual practices, your philosophy and your placement. When you're living in place, you are engaging in "homecoming rituals" and feng shui (literally "wind and water") practices that celebrate the local and ritualize local narratives. Architecture at its best is a theology of place that takes material form.

Unfortunately, "local" is the last thing the "local church" often is. For the church to be "local" it needs to incarnate the life of faith within the local culture. Or as my pastor friend puts it, "Sometimes going is staying." Maybe it is time to place less value in convenience and cost than loyalty to community and place.

An aboriginal community will have a unique personality that reflects the quirkiness of the place where it lives and affects and has its being. The church isn't near quirky enough. A truly "local church" would enjoy an intimate familiarity with the world that lies outside its walls.[20] It would experience God through local elements and expressions while re-creating the local with transcending universals. The "local communion" that emerges within that indigenous culture both animates and enriches the universal church and "builds up" the body of Christ to "full stature."[21]

Instead, too many churches "do business" like too many strip malls: cookie-cutter planning from detached, centralized corporate offices. The spiritual result: Christian "nomads," traveling congregation to congregation, Sunday after Sunday, looking for a "home" that can't be manufactured.

Living in place is an emblem for new types of spiritual practices and postmodern spiritual disciplines.

Example 1: Eat locally, buy locally. The more we globalize, the more we need to deglobalize and localize.

One of my favorite restaurants is the Farmers Diner in Quechee, Vermont, an inexpensive 60-seat eatery that gets about 70 percent of its food—including meat—from organic produce within a 60-mile radius. Why are there not thousands of such eateries across USAmerica? Why are we not buying our best food from local farmers and farmers' markets?

> We have ecology; there's the possibility of a sacred ecology;
> eventually we'll have a sacred economics.[22]
> —poet, environmental activist Gary Snyder

The reason why Italians have such a rich food culture is because of regional variations. Unlike French cooking, which Paris dominates, Italian food is local, not governed by a single, central, or national place, and the endless variations of sauces and pastas are each presented with local pride.

Example 2: Eat seasonally. Community Supported Agriculture (CSA) is a cooperate effort between farmers (usually organic) and people who desire to have fresh vegetables and fruits on their dinner tables during the local growing season. Why not celebrate the glory of life by feasting on seasonal glories: daffodil cakes in the spring, peach cobbler in the summer, grape pie in the fall, plum pudding in the winter—and Sharon's carrot cake all year round?

Example 3: Eat genius: Love and live genuinely.

Both the words *genuine* and *genius* come from the same German word *genie*. A genie is, in its oldest and broadest sense, the unique character of a person or place. Everyone has a "genie," a spirit that inspires and animates a person with the gift of genius, which is both a blessing and a curse. It puts you in a special posture and place, but separates you from the everyday. Anyone can learn a skill or craft, but genius is unique to its possessor. It is something that cannot be cultivated or acquired.

In other words, everyone is a genius. But a genuine person lets the genie of their soul out when someone strokes it and uncorks them. If you keep your genie corked, eventually there may be no genie left to come out. Don't suffocate the spirit.

To live in pace with place doesn't mean a stationary, sedentary life. We need to rethink our concept of space and place for a missional people on the move, whether moving in or moving on. Christians are people who can be at home when on the road or in a foreign country.

For example, "place" for young eagles is not the nest, but the air. When learning to fly, too much time in the nest is not wise. But neither is abandonment. A good parent keeps a watchful eye on all that is happening, leaves the learner alone when possible, and intervenes only when necessary. Maybe it's time for the church to learn from the birds.

One of humankind's oldest professions gives us another clue as to the importance of our origins. No, not *that* profession—the other one: gardening.

One of the most ideal places for relationships? A garden. The meeting between God and Adam and Eve took place in a garden. What more fitting place could we grow, thrive, and be nourished than in the company of other created things doing the same? One of the pressing issues facing people of faith in the twenty-first century is our relationships with nonhuman neighbors.

Unfortunately, for many decades, the only green space reserved or protected by most of our cities was for the dead. Maybe we need to be less anthropocentric and more anthropomorphic.

In biblical Hebrew there is no word for "nature," because "nature" is not something separate from us. We are a part of it, and it is a part of us.[23] The two traditions that seem to produce people with the greatest poetic sensibilities—Roman Catholicism and Quakerism—are also those with the highest "sacramental" sense. With Catholics, a heightened sense of Christ's presence in the Eucharist. With Quakers, a heightened sense of Christ's presence in the world, which is why Quakers don't do the "sacrament of communion," since you can find God anywhere and everywhere. The Catholic sense of sacrament, which also extends to all of life, and the goodness of all of life, is expressed in these words of Hilaire Belloc:

> Wherever the Catholic sun doth shine
> There's always laughter and good red wine.
> At least I've always found it so.
> *Benedicamus Domino!*[24]

People suffer today from both a nature deficit and a spiritual deficit, and religious groups that bring the two together are booming. For example, trends in growth for the Wiccan religion have been staggering over the last twenty years. From 8,000 adherents in 1990 to 134,000 in 2001, the trend continues today. Why? One of the foundational components of Wicca is its worship of nature—

recognizing the sacred and the spiritual in creation. As a mirror, the church can see in Wicca's growth an area too long neglected in its own liturgy and spiritual formation.

In our one-planet society, where six billion inhabitants consume more than forty thousand liters of oil every second, we've got to learn to like mud and green over asphalt and gray. Can we turn from our wicked ways?

Speaking Our Place

Every place has a personality. When you speak, can people hear the personality of your place? Do you speak with an accent? Does your "speech betray you," as it did Peter with the servant girls?[25] The incarnation means that disciples of Jesus speak not only with a gospel accent, but with a geographic accent as well. The intonations of place get deep inside and change us. If you're a part of a "place," it changes you.

One of the worst things you can do in life is to betray your heritage and lose your accent.

11

> For a man who no longer has a homeland,
> writing becomes a place to live.[26]
> —Theodor Adorno

11

Martin Luther King Jr.'s speech "I Have A Dream" has now become part of the sacred canon of USAmerican civil religion right up there with Abraham Lincoln's Second Inaugural Address and the Declaration of Independence. This speech is perhaps best known for its ending words: "Free at last, free at last; thank God Almighty I'm free at last."

But these aren't King's words. They were the words felt from a Charles A. Tindley song called "I Shall Get Home Some Day."[27] What made King's words resonate so powerfully is that they were spoken out of the accent of the black church. The pain and particularity of the struggle for freedom gave King's words universal resonance.

It is only when we're bound and bonded to a place that we can be free to inhabit all places.

Jerusalem Interactives

1. Do you routinely honor the experiences of life God gives you by enjoying them? Can you sing praises for that pot of beans or pint of beer that goes with them?

2. What are some "homecoming rituals" that your family practices? Any "reunions"? What about holidays as "homecoming rituals"?

3. One of the critiques of "globalization" is that it leads to a monoculture of sameness and a wiping out of differences. Yet in Sydney, Australia, one McDonald's opened as a café; in one Asian country, teenagers used McDonald's facilities as study halls after school, becoming a new locus for community.[28] And what McDonald's have you been in that wasn't soliciting donations for some local cause or family?

    Do you think it is possible that sometimes McDonald's global operations may exhibit more diversity and expression of local social values than Christian churches? Why or why not?

4. Have you heard of "Freegans"? These are people who eat only thrown-away food.

    Timothy Jones, an anthropology professor at the University of Arizona, conducted a 10-year study that concluded the country wastes 40 percent to 50 percent of its food. A 1997 U.S. Department of Agriculture study put the loss at 27 percent of total U.S. food production, or 96 billion pounds of food.

"The number one problem is that Americans have lost touch with what food is for," Jones said. "We have lost touch with the processes that bring it to the table and we don't notice the inefficiency."[29]

What do you think? Do you agree with him? Why or why not? Do you know any "Freegans"? Any "Freegans" in your church?

5. Have someone look up *bioregionalism* and discuss what it might mean for you and your church.

6. In light of what I said above, do the birds take better care of their young than the church does?

7. Gary Snyder tells the story of an old pine tree in a Korean nunnery. Once a year the nuns pour a gallon of rice liquor around the root perimeter "to cheer it up."[30]

Are you doing anything to "cheer up" your Jerusalem? Do you think that the more toxins we release into the environment, the more "cheering up" nature needs? Did you know that toxic chemicals drift northward and accumulate in Arctic food chains, making the breast milk of some mothers in Greenland now technically qualifying as hazardous waste?

8. In ancient cultures you were largely defined by your "place": Jesus of Nazareth, Simon of Cyrene, etc. But it appears that Jesus never allowed either the place he was born (the princely city of David known as Bethlehem) or the place he was brought up (the nowhere place of nobodies known as Nazareth) to define

him. If anything, he loved to hang out in Bethany but had a special spot in his heart for a place whose very name meant peace and unity but whose history was just the opposite: Jerusalem. After his last journey to Jerusalem, Jesus wept over the city because it never knows "the things that make for peace."[31] Some things never change.

9. What is the difference between a moving-in story and a moving-on story? Are you better at living one story than the other? Which one? Why?

10. The patriarch of the Eastern Orthodox Church recently argued that we need to develop a sense of "sin" when we offend against the earth and the natural world. What do you think? Where might we be "sinning" right now if that is the case?

11. Have you ever done any spiritual ecotourism (these are environmentally benign travel experiences that focus on the "spiritual")? Other religions have their form of "spiritual" pilgrimages—think Australian walkabouts, Tibetan monks, Native American vision quests, etc. Can you think of any Christian pilgrimages?

12. Have someone research the difference between "Dark Greens" and "Bright Greens." Which are you? If you're neither, how would you describe yourself vis-à-vis the environment? How stupendous do you think will be the costs of our stupidity and environmental mismanagement?

The Invisible 12th
You Need the Paraclete

Thy mercies how tender, how firm to the end!
Our Maker, Defender, Redeemer and Friend.[1]
—hymn "O Worship the King"

Sometimes ... Jethros fail.

Sometimes ... Yodas are no-shows.

Sometimes ... Jonathans turn into Judases.

Sometimes ... Deborahs fall asleep.

Sometimes ... your VIPs turn out to be DUDs.

Sometimes ... Jerusalem gets paved and they put in a parking lot.

In Saint Paul's words, who is sufficient for these things?

That's when we have another promise: "He who watches over Israel will neither slumber nor sleep."[2] God works the late shift. God *always* has your back. And every other part of your being as well.

Sports have the tradition of "the 12th man." Texas A&M first introduced the metaphor almost a century ago, but when the Seattle Seahawks made it their moniker, it suddenly became every team's pride. The invisible but tangible energy of the home crowd is "the 12th man on the field."

Disciples of Jesus have a mysterious "12th Withness" on the field of their lives. The 12th Withness may not fully manifest himself until the eleventh hour,[3] or when you've touched the third rail, but he never fails to appear.

The Invisible 12th is known as the "Paraclete." The word *Paraclete* is most often used for the Holy Spirit. But it is also the same word Jesus sometimes uses to describe himself. We translate *Paraclete* as "comforter." But the Holy Spirit as

"The Comforter" doesn't mean a cuddly blanket or a hot water bottle but a bracing friend who helps us bear every burden, lift every load, climb every mountain, ford every stream. In the Bayeux Tapestry, commissioned in the eleventh century to portray the events of the 1066 Norman invasion of England, Bishop Odo pokes the troops in the back with his spear. The Latin transcription reads, *Hic Odo episcopus baculum tenens confortat pueros:* "Here Bishop Odo, holding his staff, comforts the troops."[4]

But we can think of "comforter" as a garment, something given to us and we "put on":

Professors receive a black bathrobe garment to battle ignorance and stupidity.

Medical doctors receive a white coat garment to battle disease, suffering, and death.

Soldiers receive a Kevlar garment to battle forces of oppression.

Grasped in this manner, the Paraclete can be felt much like the prized robe of the father that the prodigal received upon coming to his senses and returning home. As in the case of the prodigal, the robe doesn't so much signify a position of power as it does a position of privilege; *this is my beloved son or daughter with whom I'm well pleased!* This garment is given to us as we step into the life God has prepared for us, suiting up to battle the evil forces of poverty, racism, pharisaism. It is said that you should never give a sword to a soldier who can't dance. It could also be said that you should never send a soldier into battle without his robe. Our battles are not scripted movie reenactments; they are wrestlings with principalities and powers.

The Holy Spirit is our 12th Withness—our garment of protection, our "armor of light," our spiritual bodyguard and battle companion. Some people estimate that 65 to 75 percent of the total value of Fortune 500 companies resides in their intangible assets.[5] Have you stocked your warehouses full of product with no demand? Is your inventory sitting unused for this current marketplace? Is your heart building a shoddy foundation with physical materials, or do you endeavor and invest in the unseen glory of an unseen God?

Our greatest asset is invisible and intangible. The Paraclete goes out into life's conflicts with us and protects not only our backs, but also our sides, our fronts, our insides, the whole being!

This is not the place for a much-needed discussion about the parsed and polarized, one-dimensional treatments of the Holy Spirit by current denominations and church orientations. The Charismatic/Pentecostals have simplified (and cheapened) the Holy Spirit to little more than emotional experience. The old-line denominations have chosen to keep the Spirit at a "safe" distance, preventing genuine, unpredictable movement and manifestation. Whatever extreme you choose, the effect is the same: constraining the nature of relationship with the Paraclete. This chapter encourages you to allow the Spirit to be both/and/neither/other.

The Paraclete is over our heads, under our feet, behind our backs, in front of our faces. In many Bible dictionaries, the word *Paraclete* means "one called to the side of."[6] This is the job description of the Holy Spirit: to stand at the side of all those who follow Jesus. When Jesus gave us the Paraclete, he gave on a permanent basis what the psalmist sang about: "The angel of the LORD encamps around those who fear him, and he delivers them."[7] One thing a Jesus disciple is not is an insufferable sufferer. For this Paraclete is the ultimate fulfillment of every promise. Like this one from Isaiah: "When you pass through the waters, I will be with you; and when you pass through the rivers, they will not sweep over you. When you walk through the fire, you will not be burned; the flames will not set you ablaze."[8]

It's part of our own job description as followers of Jesus to be on the front lines of mission and ministry. The Withnesses are our comrades in arms, and the ties of mutual trust that develop in this new world of intersection and interdependence are major sources of life's satisfaction and meaning. As part of their oath to fight, not to flee, ancient Greek soldiers vowed never to expose the person standing to their left in battle. Each held a shield in his left hand and a sword in his right hand. The integrity of the "fighting unit" was based on this mutual defense and dependability.

But sometimes the fighting unit collapses. One or more of life's Withnesses go AWOL or get wounded in battle. Often we are not the best judge of character and mistake an "assistant" for an "assassin." When French Prime Minister Jacques

Chirac met with Saddam Hussein in 1975, he embraced him as one of his life's Withnesses and said, "You are my personal friend…. You are assured of my respect, my consideration and my affection."[9] Every disciple will experience a Judas betrayal, just as every disciple will face the temptation to *be* a Judas *at some juncture.* People on the front lines need Paraclete presence and protection, which is what Jesus promises us when we feel left behind and left alone to fend for ourselves.

As with all these Withnesses, God is the epitome. The Lord is our chief "Advocate," who braces us for impact, who goes with us. Under no circumstances and in no condition do we not have the Withnessing presence of the Holy Spirit. We are never without what we need for life's missions, the guards and guides, the goads or gifts. The 12th enables us to have the attitude of Saint Paul: "If God is for us, who can be against us?"[10]

11

First frend He was, best frend He is,
all tymes will try Him trewe.[11]
—Robert Southwell's poem in praise of Christ

11

One of the most astonishing claims of the Bible is that God created humans to be the "friends" of God, and that Jesus calls us no longer "servants" but "friends."[12] In the First Testament, God calls Abraham and his offspring God's "friend,"[13] and God speaks to Moses "as one speaks to a friend."[14]

If Gentiles found the wisdom of the cross scandalous,[15] Greek philosophers like Aristotle found this idea of friendship with God "blasphemous." But this is precisely what the gospel promises: a friendship life. We are summoned by the Paraclete to be friends with God. In fact, Thomas Aquinas believed that the life of faith was nothing more or less than this: a life of friendship with God.

But this is no "Buddy Jesus" of trendy T-shirts or kitschy action figures. What we learn in relationship with the 11 Withnesses becomes the framework and cornerstone for our relationship within the 12th. With the Paraclete Spirit, God gives us closeness and intimacy with Christ, but do not mistake the near for the casual. Our relationship in the Holy Spirit is not one of equals, though it is one of lovers. The Paraclete covers, surrounds, and fills us, protecting our hearts and our minds in righteousness and love. Surely this is the most sacred of relationships a human can experience, and in humility we reverence this comforter and friend.

When I sing "What a Friend We Have in Jesus,"[16] I don't see myself as a "sinner in the hands of an angry God" so much (if I may be so bold as to emend the great Jonathan Edwards) as a sinner in the hands of a forgiving God, a giving God, a loving God, a hugging God. When I sing "What a Friend We Have in Jesus," I have the image of a loving parent, holding on in a big bear hug as a rebellious child flails away, struggling with all the child's might to break free … yet all the while hoping that those strong, protective arms never let go.

God exists as a friendship community. And we are empowered by the Spirit to participate in the divine friendship, which is happiness. The Bible makes the "secret" no longer a "secret." The secret is out: The secret of a happy life is friendship with God. Happiness has little to do with "having a good time" but everything to do with "entering the Joy of the Lord" that comes from a relationship with God. In fact, the apostle Paul made what he called the "secret"[17] of a happy life very explicit: "I can do everything through [Christ] who gives me strength."[18]

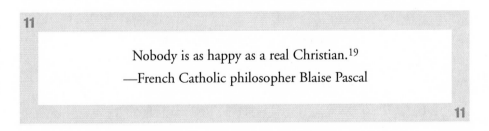

11

Nobody is as happy as a real Christian.[19]
—French Catholic philosopher Blaise Pascal

11

A friend of God means more than to love God. It means to be in a right relationship with God where three marks of the Paraclete, three signs of the Spirit, reign supreme: confidence, humility, and courage: "I can do everything through [Christ] who gives me strength."[20] God's "friends" have a "right spirit"[21]—the courage of humble confidence.

Crises and trials in life can either break you down or break you open: Whether it causes a breakdown or break open depends on your ability to triangulate the three signs of the Spirit. The three-pronged strategy that gets you through every challenge in life is the confidence of "I can do everything"; the humility of knowing that the only way you can do "everything" is "through [Christ]"; and the living out of the "strength" or courage that comes from a nondual experience of life and of God that connects the humility of "And yet!" to the confidence of "But, God!"

11

Art always says "And yet!" to life.[22]
—Georg Lukács

11

When you look at this planet and all its problems with the Paraclete Withness at your side, you bring together two extremes: pessimism of the mind with optimism of the will, a full awareness of your worth and worthlessness, a sense of your importance and impotence at the same time. We're all made up of opposites: good and evil, love and hate, altruism and selfishness, courage and cowardice, pride and humility.

With every person Jesus met, he combined maximalism and miniaturism: the highest of ideals with the lowest of expectations. No one had loftier dreams for humanity than Jesus did. No one had deeper compassion for humanity than Jesus.

The Trifecta of Truth: Confidence, Humility, Courage

Charity is the soul of the Christian paradox, for charity is the love which demands our self, but charity is also the love which promises a self.[23]
—Passionist priest Paul J. Wadell

Confidence

Because of the Paraclete, disciples of Jesus can be "confidence men" and "confidence women."

The term *confidence man* has an interesting origin. A century ago a well-dressed individual would approach a stranger on the street. "Do you have enough confidence in humankind to let me hold your watch?" he asked. When handed the watch, the man walked away with it.

Our confidence is not an earned confidence, it is an alien confidence.[24] The biblical notion of confidence is a gift from outside ourselves, not a condition we achieved or earned. It is a hope that arises from a deep faith in the providence and protection of the Paraclete. Our confidence is not in ourselves, in our own greatness and goodness. Our confidence is in God's grace and goodness and greatness.

Timothy Radcliffe tells the African story of a tortoise about to meet a leopard in battle. Beforehand he went to the battleground and made marks all over the place, suggestive of a hard struggle. When he was asked what he was doing, he replied: "Because even after I am dead, I would want anyone passing by this way to say, 'A fellow and his match struggled here.'"[25]

I love that turtle.

Humility

We descend by exaltation and we ascend by humility.[26]
—Rule #7 of Saint Benedict of Nursia

But along with our unwarranted confidence we bring a monstrous modesty. Without humility, confidence is always pride, always overconfidence. The disciple of Jesus stoops to conquer.

The world is divided, not so much between conservative and liberal, Red and Blue, as between those who think they have it all worked out, and those who remained baffled and awestruck by the wonder of it all and the mystery of the universe.

Humility comes from *humus*, which means "good earth." A humble person is rooted in the earth and grounded in reality. In fact, Saint Benedict's "Rules" has a whole chapter (7) on how to climb the "ladder of humility." Note: *not* the ladder of success. But the twelve-rung ladder of humility.

Ancient societies regarded humility as a vice. In terms of classical thought, the "theological virtues" of faith, hope, and love made little sense. In Aristotle's ethical system, pride or self-confidence held pride of place, and all Greek terms related to humility had modifiers of "insignificant," "base," "obscure," or "mean." In the words of Alasdair MacIntyre, "The only place in Aristotle's account of the virtues where anything resembling humility is mentioned, it is as a vice, and patience is not mentioned at all by Aristotle."[27]

11

> The foundation of our philosophy is humility.[28]
> —Saint John of Chrysostom

11

In marked contrast is the biblical virtue of humility, where you can't be exalted without being humbled. In fact, humility was the condition for Jesus' own exaltation.[29] We are called throughout the Scriptures to humble ourselves and to serve God in all humility of mind[30] or lowliness of mind.[31] In fact, in an inversion of the world's hierarchy of values, the meek inherit the earth, the last are first, and in the famous refrain from the Magnificat, *"Deposuit superbos et exaltavit humiles"* ("He hath put down the proud and exalted the humble").

To whom better to give a last word than Augustine? "That first way, however, is humility; the second way is humility, and the third way is humility, and as often as you ask, I would say this.... When the most distinguished orator was asked what he thought one ought first of all to observe in the rules of eloquence, he is said to have answered, 'Delivery.' And when he was asked what came second, he said again, 'Delivery.' And asked what came third, he said only, 'Delivery.' So too, if you ask and as often as you ask about the rules of the Christian religion, I would answer only, 'Humility.'"[32]

Courage

> Courage is that virtue that makes all other virtues possible.[33]
> —Aristotle at the dawn of Western civilization

The Withnessing power of the Paraclete brings along with it Jesus' ultimate gift: the courage of his "peace," the "peace" that Paul said "transcends all understanding" in this world, and in its storms. Not the kind of peace "the world gives," peace that is achieved only for moments and only enforced by the power of the state. Jesus promised his "peace" to all who live with the Paraclete courage of humble confidence.

11

Cowardly Lion: Courage! What makes a king out of a slave?
Courage! What makes the flag on the mast to wave? Courage!
What makes the elephant charge his tusk in the misty mist, or
the dusky dusk? What makes the muskrat guard his musk?
Courage! What makes the sphinx the seventh wonder?
Courage! What makes the dawn come up like thunder?
Courage! What makes the Hottentot so hot? What puts the
"ape" in apricot? What have they got that I ain't got?
Dorothy, Scarecrow, Tin Woodsman: Courage!
Cowardly Lion: You can say that again![34]
—"If I Were King of the Forest," *The Wizard of Oz*

11

The Invisible 12th means we are never alone, never abandoned, never at the mercy of the world's whims and wickedness. The Paraclete Withness enables us to live our lives to the fullest, to face our greatest fears, to be more than conquerors in life's conflicts and confusions.

11

May the Spirit
Bless you with discomfort
At easy answers, half-truths, and
Superficial relationships so that
You will live deep in your heart.

May the Spirit
Bless you with anger
At injustice and oppression,
And exploitation of people and the earth
So that you will work for Justice, equity and peace.

May the Spirit
Bless you with tears to shed
For those who suffer
So that you will
Reach out your hand
To comfort them.

And may the Spirit
Bless you with the foolishness
To think you can make a difference
In the world,
So you will do the things
Which others say cannot be done.[35]

11

12th Interactives

1. Read Ephesians 6. Notice that the list of the armor has only the front described, with nothing to protect your back. Why? One explanation has been that if you're advancing, you only need armor in the front; that's the front line of battle. You don't need it in the rear. But that's ridiculous. You never leave your rear exposed.

   So, what do *you* think?

2. There are many explicit connections between the Paraclete and each one of the 11 Witnesses. For example, the Paraclete directly connects with Jethro in that *Paraclete* also means "one who ends the curse." Wherever you are being cursed, wherever the forces of evil are up to no good, the Spirit works his curse-breaking powers.

   Can you think of other explicit biblical connections with other Witnesses?

3. Here's an explicit connection with the Paraclete and your Yoda: "But the Counselor, the Holy Spirit, whom the Father will send in my name, will teach you all things" (John 14:26).

   If the Paraclete is our teacher, we are always in school. We are never too old to learn.

   How are you always learning?

4. Which of the 11 Witnesses help you enjoy life, and which help you endure life?

5. If one of the Withnesses was a plant, which one would you choose?

   If one of the Withnesses was an animal, which one would you choose?

6. Watch the end of *Saving Private Ryan*,[36] where the lines have been breached and a wounded and fatigued Captain John Miller (Tom Hanks) is firing his last bullets at an approaching tank. Just before all is lost, the close air support comes and saves the day. He rightly calls them "angels on our shoulders."

   Have you ever felt "angels" on your shoulders?

7. I heard a story once of a mother who was ill and could not go to church. When her young son came home, she asked him the subject of the pastor's sermon. He said, "The preacher said God is going to send us another bed quilt."

   The surprised mother then asked him if he remembered the verse of Scripture he used. The lad said the preacher said, "He shall give you another comforter."

   Why do you think this "comforter" image rather than the "companion" image has stuck so stubbornly to the word *Paraclete*?

8. Where's your backup?

   People are looking for backups—even artificial, fake, false-hope backups. Give some examples of our attempt to "back up" our lives.

To prime the pump, here is a quote from Bart Kosko, who is in his thirties but is a tenured professor in electrical engineering at USC. He has written three textbooks, as well as the best-selling *Fuzzy Thinking*:

> It's a hell of a thing to live in a machine that has no backup. I am one of 500 or so who has a cryonic bracelet and hopes to see if future nanotech can rebuild those cells and synapses. That, too, is a form of backup. The better thing is just to upload in a chip. The brain stores about a billion billion bits of information and runs at about 10 million bits per second. Today you would need a chip the size of a house. But if Moore's Law keeps doubling the circuit density of chips every two years or so, by around 2020, your brain should fit to the last bit on a chip the size of a sugar cube. You could last until your last chip fell into a black hole or star. On chip time, that may be as close to eternity as we can come in a universe made of matter and energy. Heaven or hell in a chip. Until then, it's burn, bury, or freeze. I wouldn't bet my life on cryonics, but I am happy to bet my death on it.[37]

9. When visiting his close friend Teddy Roosevelt at Sagamore Hill, the famous naturalist William Beebe tells of a bedtime ritual he shared with Roosevelt:

> After an evening of talk, we would go out on the lawn, where we took turns at an amusing little astronomical rite. We searched until we found, with or without glasses, the faint, heavenly light-mist beyond the lower left-hand corner of the Great square of Pegasus, when one or the other of us would then recite:

That is the Spiral Galaxy in andromeda.

It is as large as the Milky Way.

It is one of a hundred million galaxies.

It is 750,000 light years away.

It consists of one hundred billion suns,

each larger than our sun.

After an interval Colonel Roosevelt would grin at me and say "Now I think we are small enough! Let's go to bed."[38]

What "Your God is too small" rituals do you have in your life?

10. Have someone report on Jim Collins' classic management text *Good to Great* (2001),[39] where he classified the characteristic feature of "good to great" companies as these dialectical virtues of humble confidence: Invest $1 in a range of Dow Jones Index companies, and you get back $56 after 15 years. Invest $1 in good to great companies, and you get back $470 after 15 years. What's the difference? The critical turning point in the life of a company turned out to be the arrival of a CEO: not a savior CEO, but a CEO who combined two qualities: "extreme personal humility with intense professional will" or confidence.

11. How would you respond to this thesis by Alexander Solzhenitsyn:

A decline of courage may be the most striking feature that an outside observer notices in the West today. The Western world has lost its civic courage, both as a whole and separately, in each country, in each government, in each political party, and of course, in the United Nations. Such a decline in courage is particularly noticeable among the ruling and intellectual elites, causing an impression of a loss of courage in the entire society.[40]

Notes

Acknowledgments

1. Quoted in Jennifer Cognard-Black, *Narrative in the Professional Age: Transatlantic Readings of Harriet Beecher Stowe, George, Eliot, and Elizabeth Stuart Phelps* (New York: Routledge, 2004), 32.
2. Gilbert Meilaender, *The Limits of Love: Some Theological Explorations* (University Park: The Pennsylvania State University Press, 1987), 1.
3. John Aubrey, "Brief Lives," *Chiefly of Contemporaries, set down by John Aubrey, Between the Years 1669 and 1696,* ed., Andrew Clark (Oxford: Clarendon Press, 1898), 1:220.
4. Quoted in Frederick M. Tisdel, "Rossetti's 'House of Life,'" *Modern Philology* 15 (1917): 264.

Introduction

1. Martin Buber, *I and Thou*, trans., Ronald Gregor Smith (Edinburgh, U.K.: T. & T. Clark, 1937), 18.
2. Both Percy Bysshe Shelley (see for example his "Epipsychidion" [1820], where section X ends: "The dreariest and the longest journey go"); and E. M. Forster (see his *The Longest Journey* [Edinburgh, U.K.: W. Blackwood, 1907]) nastily dubbed marriage "the longest journey."
3. See John 21:18.
4. Ursula K. Le Guin, *The Left Hand of Darkness* (New York: Walker, 1969), 158.
5. Mark Nepo, *The Exquisite Risk* (New York: Harmony Books, 2005), 12.
6. I wish to thank Michael Blewett for finding this one. See his "The Tides Are Turning," in *The Church of The Perfect Storm*, ed., Leonard I. Sweet (Nashville: Abingdon, 2008), quote toward the end of the chapter.
7. Larry Crabb, *The Safest Place on Earth: Where People Connect and Are Forever Changed* (Nashville: Word Publishers, 1999), 21.
8. Quoted in *Boswell's Life of Samuel Johnson,* ed., George Birkbeck Hill, rev. and enl. ed., ed., L. F. Powell (Oxford: Clarendon Press, 1934), 3:230. For more on journeying lifestyles, see my *11 Genetic Gateways to a Spiritual Awakening* (Nashville: Abingdon, 1998).

9. For the role of summoning, see my *Summoned to Lead* (Grand Rapids, MI: Zondervan, 2004).

10. Matthew 10:22b.

11. 2 Timothy 4:7.

12. Jesus' desire for disciples as a desire for community is best made clear in Lauren F. Winner's *The Voice of Matthew* (Nashville: Thomas Nelson, 2007).

13. Blewett, "The Tides Are Turning," *The Church of The Perfect Storm,* quote toward end of the chapter.

14. John writes of Jesus' agape love that "having loved his own who were in the world, he loved them to the last" (John 13:1).

15. John 14:3 NRSV.

16. Or in terms of a metaphor I have developed elsewhere, what crew do you take with you as you travel through "The Perfect Storm"? See Leonard Sweet, ed., *The Church of The Perfect Storm* (Nashville: Abingdon, 2008).

17. The quote appears in Saint Thomas Aquinas, *Lectura Super Matthaeum* (p. 100), as referenced in Paul Murray, *The New Wine of Dominican Spirituality* (New York: Burns & Coates, 2006), 150–51. The Aristotle quote "Anyone who lacks the capacity to share in community, or has no need to because of his self-sufficiency, is no part of the city and as a result is either a beast or a god" is from *The Politics of Aristotle,* trans., Peter L. Phillips Simpson (Chapel Hill: University of North Carolina Press, 1997), 12.

18. The West Front of Westminster Abbey now contains ten figures of twentieth-century martyrs.

19. Ignazio Silone wrote not long before his death: "If my literary work has any meaning, in the last analysis it is this: At a certain moment writing meant for me an absolute necessity of bearing witness." Ignazio Silone, *Emergency Exit* (New York: Harper & Row, 1965), 46.

20. Luke 6:12–16.

21. Mark 3:14.

22. Hebrews 11.

23. Genesis 2:18.

24. I introduced the concept and language of "relationship repertoires" in *Out of the Question ... Into the Mystery: Getting Lost in the GodLife Relationship* (Colorado Springs: WaterBrook Press, 2004). The wonderful phrase "friendship repertoires" is that of Liz Spencer and Ray Pahl in their cliché-busting book, *Rethinking Friendship: Hidden Solidarities Today* (Princeton: Princeton University Press, 2006), 54. The idea came from their study "of the bases of actual friendships where we found that, not

only did people have different types of friends, but they also varied in the range or constellation of friends they included in their personal community."

25. See the story of the sheep and goats in Matthew 25:32–46. Or consider the Trinitarian nature of God, which means that my very "self" cannot be found outside of relationships, outside the "three hypostases" of communion with (or "hypostatic union" of) God, self, and neighbor.

26. Letter to "My Dear Theo," July 1880, in *The Complete Letters of Vincent van Gogh* (Boston: New York Graphic Society, 1978), 1:199.

27. Marilyn McCord Adams, *Wrestling for Blessing* (London: Darton, Longman & Todd, 2005), 101.

28. For a metaphoric use of the phrase, see Deryn Rees-Jones, *Consorting with Angels: Essays on Modern Women Poets* (Highgreen, Tarset, Northumberland: Bloodaxe Books, 2005). The title is borrowed from Anne Sexton's 1963 poem, "Consorting with Angels" (11).

29. Frederick Buechner, *Beyond Words: Daily Readings in the ABCs of Faith* [electronic resource] (New York: PerfectBound, 2004), 352.

30. Dawna Markova, *I Will Not Die an Unlived Life: Reclaiming Purpose and Passion,* (Berkeley, CA: Conari Press, 2000), 189.

31. Michael Bywater, *Big Babies, Or: Why Can't We Just Grow Up?* (London: Granta Books, 2006), 137.

32. John Ed Mathison, *Tried and True: Eleven Principles of Church Growth from Frazer Memorial United Methodist Church* (Nashville: Discipleship Resources, 1992), 1.

33. Tracy Goss, *The Last Word on Power: Reinvention for Leaders and Anyone Who Must Make the Impossible Happen* (New York: CurrencyDoubleday, 1996), 96.

Chapter 1

1. Quoted in Huston Smith, *The World's Religions: Our Great Wisdom Traditions* (New York: Harper Collins, 1991), 55.

2. Thanks for Terry O'Casey and Earl Pierce for helping me see this.

3. 2 Samuel 7; 1 Chronicles 17:1–15.

4. 2 Chronicles 29:25.

5. See Nathan's role in getting Solomon, the son of David and Bathsheba, to be next in line (1 Kings 1:11–40).

6. 2 Samuel 12:7.

7. Quoted in "The Leadership Survey: Pastors Viewing Internet Pornography," *Leadership,* (Winter 2001) 22:89.

8. 1 Chronicles 17:16 NASB.

9. Cecil Day-Lewis, "On Not Saying Everything," in *Complete Poems of C. Day Lewis*, ed., Jill Balcon (Stanford, CA: Stanford University Press, 1992), 601.

10. Welty's exact quote is "My wish, indeed my continuing passion would be not to point the finger in judgment but to part a curtain, that invisible shadow that falls between people, the veil of indifference to each other's presence, each other's wonder, each other's human plight." Eudora Welty, *One Time, One Place: Mississippi in the Depression: A Snapshot Album* (New York: Random House, 1971), 8. Thanks for this reference found in Paul L. Escamilla, *Longing for Enough in a Culture of More* (Nashville: Abingdon, 2007), 4.

11. Joseph R. Myers, *Organic Community: Creating a Place Where People Naturally Connect* (Grand Rapids, MI: Baker Books, 2007), 132–43.

12. Ibid, 137.

13. Isaiah 8:19.

14. This phrase has been made popular in prayer and song by the Taize movement. The Latin reads: *Ubi caritas et amor, Deus ibi est.* www.taize.fr/en_article504/html. (Accessed September 1, 2007.)

15. As quoted in the review of Millicent Bell, *Meaning in Henry James*, in the Harvard University Press Catalog. www.hup.harvard.edu/catalog/BELMEA. (Accessed September 1, 2007.)

16. Henry James, "The Younger Generation," *The Times Literary Supplement*, April 2, 1914, 158.

17. William Blake, "Jerusalem," in *The Complete Poetry and Prose of William Blake*, newly rev. ed., ed., David V. Erdman; commentary by Harold Bloom (Berkeley: University of California Press, 1982), 152: "I took the sighs & tears, & bitter groans: / I lifted them into my Furnaces; to form the spiritual sword. / That lays open the hidden heart."

18. Ephesians 4:15 NEB.

19. Galatians 6:1 NRSV.

20. James 1:22 RSV.

21. Exodus 3:5 NRSV.

22. John 2:5 NRSV.

23. William Butler Yeats, "Anima Hominis," in his *Per Amica Silentia Lunae* (New York: Macmillan, 1918), 29. The phrase "or if we have a moral sense, sanctity," which was a part of the original manuscript was later cut by Yeats. See R. F. Foster, *W. B. Yeats: A Life II: The Arch-Poet, 1519–1939* (New York: Oxford University Press, 2003), 2:79.

24. Matthew 4:1–11.

25. Galatians 5:19–21, 26 NRSV.

26. The actual quote is as follows: "Tully [i.e. Cicero], the greatest author of the Roman language, says of a certain person, 'He never uttered a word that he would want to take back' [Cicero, *Fragmenta incerta* 1,11]. Though this praise seems very high, it is easier, nonetheless, to believe this of someone very stupid rather than of the perfect sage. For to the extent that those whom the ordinary people call 'morons' are out of touch with common sense and are more absurd and silly, they are more likely not to utter any word that they would want to take back. For to regret saying something bad or foolish or inappropriate is the mark of an intelligent person." See Augustine, "Letter 143" [3], in his *Letters 100–155*, vol. 2, pt. 2 of *The Works of Saint Augustine: A Translation for the 21st Century* (Hyde Park, NY: New City Press, 2003), 302.

27. Ralph Keyes, *The Post-Truth Era: Dishonesty and Deception in Contemporary Life* (New York: St. Martin's Press, 2004), 247.

28. Judges 16:20 NRSV.

29. This is Bernard Williams's famous phrase. See Bernard Williams, "Persons, Character and Morality," in *The Identities of Persons*, ed., Amélie O. Rorty (Berkeley: University of California Press, 1976), 214.

30. See 1 Chronicles 17:2–4, where God straightens Nathan out.

31. Mark Nepo, *The Exquisite Risk: Daring to Live an Authentic Life* (New York: Harmony Books, 2005), 276.

32. Cicero, *De Amicitia*, in his *De Senectute, De Amicitia, De Divinatione*, trans., William Armistead Falconer (Cambridge, MA: Harvard University Press, 1964), 187.

33. Marilyn McCord Adams, *Wrestling for Blessing* (New York: Church Publishing, 2005), 97.

34. Thanks to Terry Hershey for this insight.

35. Quoted in Daniel Pinchbeck, *2012: The Return of Quetzalcoatl* (New York: Jeremy P. Tarcher/Penguin, 2006), 121–22.

Chapter 2

1. See Bono's introduction to *Selections from the Book of Psalms: Authorized King James Version*, Pocket Canon series (New York: Grove Press, 1999), vii–xii. Also quoted in Bono, "Psalms Like It Hot," *The Guardian* (U.K.), 31 October 1999, www.atu2.com/news/article.src?ID=668&Key=psalms&Year=&Cat. (Accessed May 11, 2006.)

2. Joseph Heller, *God Knows* (New York: Laurel, 1984), 13–14. With thanks to John

Buchanan for this reference.

3. 1 Samuel 20:16–17 details what Jonathan was to David.

4. 1 Samuel 18:1. At Jonathan's death, David testified that Jonathan's love was so "wonderful" that it "surpassed the love of women" (2 Sam. 1:26). The friendship of Ruth and her mother-in-law Naomi might be another example of a true friend: "Where you go I will go . . . your people shall be my people, and your God my God" (Ruth 1:16 RSV).

5. Cicero, "On True Friendship" (*De Amicitia*) [xxi.80], trans., Frank Copley, in *Other Selves: Philosophers on Friendship*, ed., Michael Pakaluk (Indianapolis, IN: Hackett, 1991), 108.

6. Martin Luther also called depression "the devil's pool." Even earlier Saint Jerome (ca. 347–420) called melancholia "the Devil's bath." See Johann Weyer, *Witches, Devils, and Doctors in the Renaissance*, ed., George Mora (Binghamton, NY: Medieval & Renaissance Texts and Studies, 1991), 346.

7. Aristotle, *Problems* [30.1], trans., W. S. Hett (Cambridge, MA: Harvard University Press, 1937), 2:155.

8. David's kingship depended on Jonathan's sacrifice, because Jonathan was in the royal lineage.

9. John 3:30.

10. John 15:13–14. Truly, as the nineteenth-century song by Joseph M. Scriven says, "What a friend we have in Jesus."

11. Aelred of Rievaulx has written "the most important treatise on friendship to emerge from medieval monastic life," according to Gilbert C. Meilander. "It is clear, then, … what the fixed and true limit of spiritual friendship is: namely, that nothing ought to be denied to a friend, nothing ought to be refused for a friend, which is less than the very precious life of the body, which divine authority has taught should be laid down for a friend. Hence, since the life of the soul is of far greater excellence than that of the body any action, we believe, should be altogether denied a friend which rings about the death of the soul, that is, sin, which separated God from the soul and the soul from life." As quoted in Gilbert C. Meilander, *Friendship: A Study in Theological Ethics* (Notre Dame: University of Notre Dame Press, 1981), 55–56. The original Aelred of Rievaulx quote is from his *Spiritual Friendship*, trans., Mary Eugenia Laker (Washington, DC: Consortium Press, 1974), II:69.

12. Quoted in Nicky Hayes, *Principles of Comparative Psychology* (New York: Psychology Press, 1994), 22.

13. Proverbs 18:24 TNIV and NRSV. Also see, "A man of many companions may come to ruin, but there is a friend who sticks closer than a brother" (ESV).

14. Mark Nepo, *The Exquisite Risk: Daring to Live an Authentic Life* (New York: Harmony Books, 2005), 267.

15. Simone Weil, *Waiting for God*, trans., Emma Craufurd (New York: G. P. Putnam's Sons, 1951), 74.

16. Carlos Fuentes, *This I Believe: An A to Z of a Life,* trans., Kristina Cordero (New York: Random House, 2005), 104.

17. Quoted in Jon Winokur, ed., *The Portable Curmudgeon* (New York: Plume, 1992), 104.

18. Quoted in Adele M. Fiske, "Saint Anselm," in her *Friends and Friendship in Monastic Tradition*, Cidoc Cuaderno, 51 (Cuernavaca, Mexico: Centro Intercultural de Documentacion, 1970), 15/21. For more on Anselm and his friendships, see Brian Patrick McGuire, "Love, Friendship and Sex in the Eleventh Century: The Experience of Anselm," *Studia Theologica*, 28 (1974), 111–52.

19. William Blake, "Jerusalem" (Plate 91), in *The Poetry and Prose of William Blake*, ed., David V. Erdman (Garden City, NY: Doubleday, 1965), 248.

20. As quoted in Jeff Astley, *Christ of the Everyday* (London: SPCK, 2007), 47.

21. Dan Montgomery, *Beauty in the Stone: How God Sculpts You Into the Image of Christ* (Nashville: Thomas Nelson, 1996), 190.

22. Ibid.

23. Sidney M. Jourard says that a psychologically healthy person is one "who displays the ability to make himself fully known to at least one other significant human being." See his *The Transparent Self* (New York: Van Nostrand Reinhold, 1964), 27.

24. "You've Got a Friend": Song Lyrics, http://oracleband.net/Lyrics/youve-got-a-friend.htm. (Accessed December 19, 2007.)

25. Quoted in Michael Holroyd, *Bernard Shaw* (New York: Random House, 1898), 2:317.

Chapter 3

1. Edward Abbey, *Desert Solitaire: A Season in the Wilderness* (New York: Ballantine Books, 1985), xii.

2. Exodus 3:1.

3. Exodus 4:18.

4. 2 Samuel 18:9.

5. 2 Samuel 18:33.

6. Ruth Scott, "Forgiveness—A Lifetime's Work," *The Tablet*, March 11, 2006, 5.

7. Rabbi Dr. Jonathan Magonet noted this first. See Ruth Scott, "Forgiveness—A

Lifetime's Work, *The Tablet*, March 11, 2006, 5. Rabbi Dr Jonathan Magonet is Principal of Leo Baeck College. He is coeditor of the three volumes of *Forms of Prayer for Jewish Worship* (London: Reform Synagogues of Great Britain, 1977–1995), the prayerbooks of the Reform Synagogues of Great Britain. He is a lecturer in the area of Bible studies and has published *A Rabbi's Bible* (SCM Press, 1991) and *Bible Lives* (SCM Press, 1992). He has gained much experience in inter-faith dialogue through coorganizing the annual "Jewish–Christian Bible Week" and "Jewish-Christian-Muslim Student Conference" at the Hedwig Dransfeld Haus in Bendorf, Germany.

8. Dante Alighieri, *The Divine Comedy*, vol. 3: *Paradiso*, Canto III.

9. Cynthia Ozick, *Trust* (Boston: Houghton Mifflin, 2004), 629. (First published 1966.)

10. Vladimir Nabokov said that "a wise reader reads the book of genius not with his heart, not so much with his brain, but with his spine. It is there that occurs the tell-tale tingle," which telegraphs good writing. The quote concludes, "Then with a pleasure which is both sensual and intellectual we shall watch the artist build his castle of cards and watch the castle of cards become a castle of beautiful steel and glass." Vladimir Nabokov, "Good Readers and Good Writers," in his *Lectures on Literature*, ed., Fredson Bowers (New York: Harcourt Brace Jovanovich, 1980), 6.

11. For the surprising power of ingratiation in bagging prestigious board seats, see James Westphal and Ithai Stern, "Flattery Will Get You Everywhere (Especially If You Are a Male Caucasian): How Ingratiation, Boardroom Behavior and Demographic Minority Status Affect Additional Board Appointments at U.S. Companies," *Academy of Management Journal* 50 (April 2007): 267–88.

12. This is part of the appeal to me of George Hunter's book *The Celtic Way of Evangelism: How Christianity Can Reach the West Again* (Nashville: Abingson Press, 2000).

13. The title of John Stands In Timber's favorite Warrior Song, as quoted by Margot Liberty in John Stands In Timber and Margot Liberty, *Cheyenne Memories* (New Haven: Yale University Press, 1998), vi.

14. From the William Cowper hymn, "God Moves in a Mysterious Way," *The Covenant Hymnal* (Chicago: Covenant Press, 1973), 99. John Henry Cardinal Newman quoted these words in "Christianity and Scientific Investigation: A Lecture for the School of Science, 1855," in his *The Idea of a University Defined and Illustrated* (London: Longmans, Green, 1907), 467.

15. Robert Desnos, "Dove in the Arch," www.poemhunter.com/poem/dove-in-the-arch. (Accessed July 23, 2007.) Also the E-book *Robert Desnos Poems* (Poem Hunter.Com,

2004), 3. http://poemhunter.com/i/ebooks/pdf/robert_desnos_2004_9.pdf. (Accessed
July 25, 2007.)

16. Romans 8:19.

17. Saint John of the Cross, *The Dark Night of the Soul* (Garden City, NY: Image Books,
    1959); and Thomas H. Green, *Drinking from a Dry Well* (Notre Dame, IN: Ave
    Maria Press, 1991) respectively.

18. Nehemiah 4:6 NRSV.

19. *Joys and Sorrows: Reflections by Pablo Casals as told to Albert Kahn* (New York: Simon
    & Schuster, 1970), 17.

20. John Stackhouse, *Humble Apologetics: Defending the Faith Today* (New York: Oxford
    University Press, 2002), 77.

21. Quoted in Richard P. McBrien, "Karl Rahner and Thea Bowman," Viewpoints,
    Tidings on Line, Friday, March 30, 2007, www.the-tid-
    ings.com/2007/033007/essays.htm. (Accessed November 7, 2007.) The quote is also
    attributed to Will Rogers.

22. Thomas H. Green, S. J., *The Friend of the Bridegroom: Spiritual Direction and the
    Encounter with Christ* (Notre Dame, IN: Ava Maria, 1999), 52.

Chapter 4

1. 2 Timothy 3:10–11 TNIV.

2. 1 Peter 5:13.

3. Alan Jamieson, *Journeying in Faith: In and Beyond the Tough Places* (London: SPCK,
   2004), 137.

4. Acts 5:38–39.

5. Reggie McNeal, *A Work of Heart: Understanding How God Shapes Spiritual Leaders*
   (San Francisco: Jossey-Bass, 2000), 48.

6. 1 Kings 1:3–4.

7. Well into the seventeenth and eighteenth centuries, scientific physicians such as the
   Englishman Thomas Sydenham (1624–1689) and the Dutchman Hermann
   Boerhaave (1668–1738) were advising their elderly patients (in Boerhaave's case, an
   elderly burgomaster in Amsterdam) to lie down between two young women, "assur-
   ing him that he would then regain his strength and energy." See Gérard Régnier,
   Pablo Picasso, Neil Kroetsch, Jeffrey S. Moore, *The Body on the Cross* (Montreal:
   Montreal Museum of Fine Arts, 2002), 64. Quotation from Frank Gonzales-Crussi,
   Trois Cas de Mort Soudaine: Et Outres Reflexions sur la Grandeur et la Misere du Corps
   (Paris: Le Promeneur-Quai Voltaire, 1989), 41. For an alternative exegesis of David

and the Shunammite woman, see Norman H. Snaith's work on 1 Kings 1:1–4 in *Interpreter's Bible* (New York: Abingdon, 1954), 3:19–20.

8. Here is the quote in context: "Love is the luminous will willing the person ... in his or her irreducible uniqueness.... Love is seen to be the light of knowledge. A knowledge of the finite that is not willing to understand itself in its ultimate essence as reaching its own fulfillment only in love, turns into darkness.... Thus love is the light of the knowledge of the finite and since we know the infinite only through the finite, it is also the light of the whole of our knowledge. In the final analysis, knowledge is but the luminous radiance of love." Karl Rahner, *For a Philosophy of Religion*, trans., Joseph Donceel, ed., Andrew Tallon (New York: Continuum, 1994), 81.

9. From 1984 to 1995, when I was president of United Theological Seminary in Dayton, Ohio.

10. See http://aullwood.center.audubon.org. (Accessed July 27, 2007.)

11. See my *Quantum Spirituality: A Postmodern Apologetic* (Dayton, OH: Whaleprints, 1991), vii, xi.

12. Judges 2:10 NRSV.

13. Quoted in Thomas Friedman, "Wanted, An Arab Sharon," op-ed column, *New York Times*, January 11, 2006, 29.

14. Quoted in Nick Gillespie, "Editors Note: The Next Two Years," *Reason*, February 2007, 2. *Reasonline*, www.reason.com/news/show/118172.html. (Accessed February 17, 2006.)

15. For an argument of this in print, see "S Is for Studio" in Leonard Sweet, Brian D. McLaren, and Jerry Haselmayer, *A Is for Abductive: The Language of the Emerging Church* (Grand Rapids, MI: Zondervan, 2003), 271.

16. As quoted by Michael Mayne, *Pray, Love, Remember* (London: Darton, Longman & Todd, 1998), 22.

17. Edmund Morris, *Beethoven: The Universal Composer* (New York: AtlasBooks/HarperCollins, 2005), 130.

18. Adaptation of "A friend is someone who knows the song in your heart and can sing it back to you when you have forgotten the words" —Anonymous (popular Web quote).

19. Walter Ong, *The Presence of the Word: Some Prolegomena for Cultural and Religious History* (New York: Simon and Schuster, 1970), 262–86.

20. Ibid., 113: "The word as sound establishes here-and-now personal presence."

21. For more on this, see my *Summoned to Lead* (Grand Rapids, MI: Zondervan, 2004).

22. Virginia Danielson, *The Voice of Egypt: Umm Kulthum: Arabic Song and Egyptian Society in the Twentieth Century* (Chicago: University of Chicago Press, 1997), 193,

249. It is estimated that Nassar attracted four million while Umm Kulthum drew more. See also Martha Slud, "Umm Kulthum: 1904–1975," *The International Magazine on Arab Affairs: Special Report*, http://dwc.hct.ac.ae/lrc/arab%20women/Um_%20Kulthum1.htm. (Accessed April 25, 2006.)

23. I read on the Internet where grape growers are playing classical music to help grapes grow faster and bigger. The owner of the vineyard has only tried classical music; refuses to try rock.

24. Matthew 5:47 NKJV.

25. Ethel Merman, *Who Could Ask for Anything More*, as told to Pete Martin (Garden City, NY: Doubleday, 1955). Of course, the phrase is originally from Ira Gershwin's "I Got Rhythm," written for the musical *Girl Crazy* (1930), starring Ethel Merman and Ginger Rogers.

26. As quoted by Lilian Calles Barger, *Chasing Sophia: Reclaiming the Lost Wisdom of Jesus* (San Francisco: Jossey-Bass, 2007), 108.

27. For the value of making "better and worse" distinctions as opposed to right and wrong, see John Stackhouse, *Humble Apologetics: Defending the Faith Today* (New York: Oxford University Press, 2002), 89. "When we are trying to discern 'right and wrong,' or 'true and false,' or 'beautiful and ugly,' therefore, it would be more accurate for us to speak of 'better and worse' *hypotheses* to explain our experiences."

28. As reported by the American Marketing Association Foundation, www.london.edu/assets/documents/PDF/Berry-AMA_Press_Release.pdf. (Accessed October 15, 2007.) The book: Patrick Barwise and Seán Meehan, *Simply Better: Winning and Keeping Customers by Delivering What Matters Most* (Boston: Harvard Business School Press, 2004).

29. David Edgerton, *The Shock of the Old: Technology and Global History Since 1900* (New York: Oxford University Press, Books, 2006), 72: "Such products make [IKEA's] founder and owner, it is alleged, the richest man in the world, richer than Bill Gates of Microsoft."

30. Robert Venturi, *Iconography and Electronics upon a Generic Architecture: A View from the Drafting Room* (Cambridge, MA: MIT Press, 1996), 248. The full quote is, "Was it not I who said in the mid-sixties: 'less is a bore'?—although now I wonder if more is a bore."

31. Thanks to Donald S. Deer for this research.

32. Nintendo makes 70 percent of its game software, whereas Sony produces only 15 percent of what it sells. See Mark White, "Nintendo Targets 35 Million Wii Console Sales in U.S.," May 23, 2007,

www.bloomberg.com/apps/news?pid=newsarchive&sid=ayyjKZmA1o6s. (Accessed
September 15, 2007.)

33. Henry Pleasants, "Elvis Presley," in *Popular Music: Critical Concepts in Media and
Cultural Studies*, ed., Simon Frith (New York: Routledge, 2004), 3:251.

34. *The Rule of St. Benedict in Latin and English with Notes* [63.10], ed., Timothy Fry
(Collegeville, MN: Liturgical Press, 1981), 279.

35. This quote is from Matthew Sturgis, "Bewildered, Betrayed," *Times Literary
Supplement*, June 1, 2007, 26. For the story, see Caspar Wintermans, *Alfred Douglas:
A Poet's Life and His Finest Work* (Chester Springs, PA: Peter Owen, 2007), 149–50.

36. See Donald Miller and John MacMurray, *To Own a Dragon: Reflections on Growing
Up Without a Father* (Colorado Springs: NavPress, 2006).

37. James Mawdsley, *The Iron Road: A Stand for Truth and Democracy in Burma* (New
York: North Paint Press, 2002), 145–46.

38. See Luis Muñoz, *Being Luis: A Chilean Life* (Exeter, UK: Impress Books, 2005),
150–53. See also Caroline Moorehead, "In Another Room," *TLS: Times Literary
Supplement*, January 27, 2005, 31.

39. "Sony's new PlayStation 3 video game has gone from top dog to underdog in record
time." See Mike Snider, "PlayStation 3 Is Down 2-to-1 to Nintendo's Wii," *USA
Today*, March 20, 2007,
www.usatoday.com/tech/gaming/2007-03-19-ps3-woes_N.htm. (Accessed September
15, 2007.)

Chapter 5

1. J. R. R. Tolkien, *The Fellowship of the Ring: Being the First Part of The Lord of the
Rings* (Boston: Houghton Mifflin, 1994), 83.

2. Michael Marmot, The Status Syndrome: How Social Standing Affects Our Health
and Longevity (New York: Times Books, 2004), 21–22. "Academy Award–winning
actors and actresses lived an astonishing four years longer than their costars and the
actors nominated who did not win…. Winning the Oscar is like reducing your
chance of dying from a heart attack from about average to zero…. The winners had a
lower risk of death from heart disease, but from other causes too."

3. Acts 4:36–37.

4. Acts 9:26–27.

5. Acts 11:22–24.

6. Acts 11:25–26.

7. 1 Thessalonians 5:11.

8. "John left them to return to Jerusalem." From Acts 13:13 on, Paul is the lead member of the team.

9. David L. Edwards, *Yes: A Positive Faith* (London: Darton, Longman & Todd, 2006), 73.

10. Acts 15:36–40.

11. I love that phrase "sacred and secular scriptures," and thank Nicholas Boyle for coming up with it. See his wonderfully rich and provocative *Sacred and Secular Scriptures: A Catholic Approach to Literature* (Notre Dame, IN: University of Notre Dame Press, 2005). Alas, Boyle does not mention Sayers in his work.

12. Proverbs 25:11 NRSV.

13. See the chapter on "Cheer Rivals from the Bench," in my *SoulSalsa: 17 Surprising Steps for Godly Living in the 21st Century* (Grand Rapids, MI: Zondervan, 2000), 104–12.

14. Gerard Manley Hopkins, "As Kingfishers Catch Fire," in *The Poems of Gerard Manley Hopkins*, ed., W. H. Gardner and N. H. Mackenzie, 4th ed. (New York: Oxford University Press, 1967), 90.

15. Philip Larkin, "For Sidney Bechet," in his *Collected Poems*, ed., Anthony Thwaite (London: Marvell Press, 1988), 83.

16. Ralph Waldo Emerson, "Music," in his *Poems* (Boston: Houghton Mifflin, 1911), 365.

17. Colossians 1:7; 4:12.

18. James 4:2 KJV.

19. One etymology of *obedience* is from "ob-audio," or "listen thoroughly."

20. Hebrews 2:1.

21. A. S. Byatt, "Justice for Willa Cather," *New York Review of Books* 47 (November 30, 2000): 52.

22. Wendell Berry, "Manifesto: The Mad Farmer Liberation Front," in his *The Country of Marriage* (New York: Harcourt Brace Jovanovich, 1973), 17.

23. In the Christian tradition the "gift of tears" is called the "*donna lacrimarium.*"

24. Ruth 1:16 KJV; and the song based on this verse and made famous by Les Paul and Mary Ford. It is now a popular wedding song: "Whither Thou Goest," words and music by Gary Singer.

25. For example, see Paul's use of *makrothumia* in Galatians 5:22.

26. Dan Wakefield, *Spiritually Incorrect: Finding God in ALL the Wrong Places* (Woodstock, VT: SkyLight Paths, 2004), 81.

27. The full quote is as follows: "To try to understand the meaning of the commandments through study and reading without actually living in accordance with them is

like mistaking the shadow of something for its reality. Only by participating …" As quoted by Christopher Bamford in "Thinking as Prayer: Lectio Divina," *Parabola*, 31 (Fall 2006), 10.

28. Quoted in David Homer Bates, "The Turning-Point of Mr. Carnegie's Career," *The Century: A Popular Quarterly* 76, (July 1908): 334.

29. Dostoevsky, *The Brothers Karamazov: A Novel in Four Parts with Epilogue*, trans., Richard Pevear and Larissa Volokhonsky (San Francisco: North Point Press, 1990), 322, [Bk 6, ch. 2, sect. (I)].

30. Exodus 2:4–8.

Chapter 6

1. "And from my pillow, looking forth by light / Of moon or favoring stars, I could behold / The antechapel where the statue stood / Of Newton, with his prism and silent face / The marble index of a mind forever / Voyaging through strange seas of thought, / alone." William Wordsworth, "Residence at Cambridge," in his *The Prelude, or Growth of a Poet's Mind*, ed., A. J. George (London: D. C. Heath, 1888), 43.

2. Or the original quote: "If I have seen further it is by standing on ye shoulders of Giants," Newton to Hooke, February 5, 1675/6, in *The Correspondence of Isaac Newton*, ed., H. W. Turnbull (Cambridge: For the Royal Society at the University Press, 1959), 1:416. Actually, Newton himself was quoting the medieval scholar Bernard of Chartres, whose original version was this: "In comparison with the ancients we stand like dwarfs on the shoulders of giants." As quoted in George Sarton, *Introduction to the History of Science* (Baltimore: For the Carnegie Institution of Washington by Williams & Wilkins, 1931), 2.1:196.

3. *Tractate Sotah*, trans., Jacob Neusner, volume 17 of *The Talmud of Babylon: An American Translation* (Chico, CA: Scholars Press, 1984), 139 [Sotah 22a].

4. Acts 4:13 TNIV: "When they saw the courage of Peter and John and realized that they were unschooled, ordinary men, they were astonished and they took note that these men had been *with* Jesus."

5. Plato's entire doctrine of the immortality of the soul was based on this one fact: Plato could not envision a world without his dead teacher and friend Socrates in it.

6. "I have had time to think and pray about my situation and that of my nation. I have come to the conclusion that I have made a mistake in coming to America. I must live through the difficult period of our national history with the Christian people of Germany.… Christians in Germany will face the terrible alternative of either willing

the defeat of their nation in order that Christian civilization may survive, or willing the victory of their nation and thereby destroying our civilization. I know which of these alternatives I must choose, but I cannot make the choice in security." As quoted in Reinhold Niebuhr, "The Death of a Martyr," *Christianity and Crisis*, June 25, 1945, 6. Bonhoeffer spent two years in prison and was executed a few days before the end of the war: April 9, 1945.

7. Hebrews 13:17.

8. Galatians 6:6.

9. "Every night after supper before opening my large dark green manuscript book I used to limber up by turning the pages of the 1933 plum-coloured Macmillan edition." Philip Larkin, "Introduction to the North Ship," in his *Required Writing: Miscellaneous Pieces 1955–1982* (New York: Farrar Straus Giroux, 1983), 29.

10. John E. King, *Captive Notions: Concise Commentaries on the Commonplace* (Seattle: Little Philosophies Press, 2005), 34.

11. I was tempted to speak here of Theophilism, after "Theophilus," as found in Luke 1:3 and Acts 1:1, a name that means literally "friend of God." Theophilism then would be the teaching of followership, not leadership: a mentoring in how to be a Christ follower, and to love God with all our hearts, minds, souls, and strength, and the study and embodiment of God's love for us.

12. There is also a difference of temperament between those who are most comfortable with Pauline, authoritative (or respect-based) mentoring and Petrine, authoritarian (or position-based) mentoring. For the difference between the two in leadership literature, see Manfred Kets de Vries, *The Leadership Mystique: An Owner's Manual* (New York: Prentice Hall, 2001), 61.

13. For more insights in the master-pupil relationship, see Alexander Berzin in his book on Tibetan practices, *Relating to a Spiritual Teacher: Building a Healthy Relationship*, which lists six attributes of the student-teacher relationship:

    a) Almost all spiritual seekers progress through stages.

    b) Most practitioners study with several teachers during their lifetimes and form a different relationship with each.

    c) Not every spiritual teacher is equally accomplished.

    d) The appropriate relationship between seeker and teacher depends upon the spiritual level of each.

    e) The relationship between students and teachers usually deepens as they proceed along the spiritual path.

    f) Each teacher may play a different role in each seeker's spiritual life.

    See Alexander Berzin, *Relating to a Spiritual Teacher: Building a Healthy*

Relationship (Ithaca, NY: Snow Lion Publications, 2000), 67.

14. Quoted in David Lipsky, *Absolutely American: Four Years at West Point* (Boston: Houghton Mifflin, 2003), 56.

15. Anna Karenina's words: "If there are as many minds as there are heads, then surely there must be as many kinds of love as there are hearts." Leo Tolstoy, *Anna Karenina*, Christian Classics Ethereal Library online text: www.ccel.org/ccel/tolstoy/karenina.html, 100. (Accessed December 14, 2007.)

16. As quoted in Paul Benjamin, *The Vision Splendid: Book One: Believing* (Washington, D.C.: American Press, 1981), 21.

17. John 13:7.

18. Quoted in Mark Albion, *Making a Life, Making a Living: Reclaiming Your Purpose and Passion in Business and in Life* (New York: Warner Books, 2000), 10.

19. See my chapter on "disciple" as "learner," titled "What Big Ears You Have!" in *Summoned to Lead* (Grand Rapids, MI: Zondervan, 2004), 117–41.

20. For my personal tribute to Dr. Hudson, see my "Winthrop S. Hudson: A Personal Perspective," *Foundations* 23 (April–June 1980), 155–60. For a tribute I wrote for Dr. Hudson's Festschrift, see "'A Nation Born Again': The Union Prayer Meeting Revival and Cultural Revitalization," in *In the Great Tradition: Essays on Pluralism, Voluntarism, and Revivalism: In Honor of Winthrop S. Hudson*, ed., Joseph D. Ban and Paul R. Dekar (Valley Forge, PA: Judson Press, 1982), 193–221.

21. See *The New Oxford Book of Literary Anecdotes*, ed., John Gross (Oxford: Oxford University Press, 2006), 233. See also Constance Babington Smith, *John Masefield: A Life* (New York: Macmillan, 1978), 199, n.1.

22. Quoted in Valerie Trueblood, "A Fellow Feeling," *The American Poetry Review* 28 (November–December 1999): 31.

23. James Worley, "Mark Van Doren," first published in Christian Century, Oct 17, 1979, 1006.

24. Sa'di's advice: "I have reserved it for such an occasion because wise men have said: 'Do not give so much strength to the friend that, if he becomes thy foe, he may injure thee.'" *The Gulistan or Rose Garden of Sa'di*, trans., Edward Rehatsek, ed., W. G. Archer (New York: G. P. Putnam's Sons, 1964), 105–6. For online version see Sa'di, "The Wrestler," www.humanistictexts.org/sa'di.htm#_Toc483886327. (Accessed May 1, 2007.)

25. For more on this, see "Is Your Clay Moist?" in my *A Cup of Coffee at the SoulCafe* (Nashville: Broadman & Holman, 1998), 6–16.

26. Louis Jacobs, "Vaethanan," in his *Jewish Preaching: Homilies and Sermons* (Portland: Vallentine Mitchell, 2004), 175.

27. 1 Timothy 5:17–19.
28. Quoted in Abel Stephens, *History of the Methodist Episcopal Church in the United States of America* (New York: Eaton & Mains, 1896), 2:217.
29. William Blake, "Marriage of Heaven and Hell," in *The Poetry and Prose of William Blake*, ed., David V. Erdman; commentary by Harold Bloom (Garden City, NY: Doubleday, 1965), 41.
30. John Wesley, "To Vincent Perronet, December 1748," *The Letters of the Rev. John Wesley, A.M.*, ed., John Telford (London: Epworth Press, 1931), 2:300–1.
31. T. S. Eliot, *Ash-Wednesday* (New York: G. P. Putnam's Sons, 1930), 15.
32. Earl Creps, "Will Anyone Want the Baton I Am Passing," *Monday Morning Insight*, http://mondaymorninginsight.com/index.php/site/comments/will_anyone_want_the_baton_I_am_passing/. (Accessed March 22, 2007.)
33. Ibid. For more, see also Earl G. Creps, *Off-Road Disciplines: Spiritual Adventures of Missional Leaders* (San Francisco: Jossey-Bass, 2006), ch. 12, 173–84.
34. See also Earl Creps, "Will Anyone Want the Baton I Am Passing," *Monday Morning Insight*, http://mondaymorninginsight.com/index.php/site/comments/will_anyone_want_the_baton_I_am_passing/. (Accessed March 22, 2007.)
35. As referenced in Thomas H. Green, S. J., *Drinking from a Dry Well* (Notre Dame, IN: Ave Maria Press, 1990), 9.
36. The speed of light it appears is not constant and has been broken.
37. Mark Twain idolized Ulysses S. Grant. Twain thought that Grant was the greatest president in history.
38. Aristotle had the idea of happiness as the free flourishing of one's powers and capacities. But Aristotle did not include in that "one" either women or slaves.
39. Look no further than Luther on the Jews, or Aquinas on masturbation. Aquinas, in the *Summa Contra Gentiles*, in a chapter on "The Reason Why Simple Fornication Is a Sin According to Divine Law, and That Matrimony Is Natural" treats both masturbation and contraception as a crime against humanity, second only to homicide. "The inordinate emission of semen … after the sin of homicide … appears to take next place" (146). See Thomas Aquinas, *Summa Contra Gentiles*, trans., Vernon J. Bourke (Notre Dame, IN: Notre Dame Press, 1956), 142–47.

Chapter 7

1. Judges 5.
2. Judges 4:6–9, 14.
3. William Shakespeare, *Macbeth*, Act 1, Scene 7.

4. Matthew 12:24.

5. See "Judas! [shout]" in Michael Gray, *The Bob Dylan Encyclopedia* (New York: Continuum International, 2006), 365–66; for the booing, etc., see Howard Sounes, *Down the Highway: The Life of Bob Dylan* (New York: Grove Press, 2001), 191–92.

6. *Notebooks of Robert Frost*, ed., Robert Faggen (Cambridge, MA: Belknap Press of Harvard University Press, 2006), 445.

7. Used as an opening to novelist Robert Ferrigno's *Prayers for the Assassin* (New York: Scribner, 2006), vii.

8. Alfred, Lord Tennyson, "Morte D'Arthur," in *The Poetic and Dramatic Works of Alfred Lord Tennyson* (Boston: Houghton Mifflin, 1898), 67.

9. *Gladiator* [video recording]; produced by Douglas Wick, David Franzoni, Branko Lustig; directed by Ridley Scott; screenplay by David Franzoni, John Logan, William Nicholson (Universal City, CA: DreamWorks Home Entertainment, 2000).

10. It was Lawrence Taylor coming from the left side who ended Joe Theismann's career, sandwiching him (between another famous Giants linebacker Harry Carson), fracturing both tibia and fibula.

11. Herman Pleij, *Colors Demonic and Divine: Shades of Meaning in the Middle Ages and After*, trans., Diane Webb (New York: Columbia University Press, 2004), 94.

12. Oliver Wendell Holmes, *The Common Law* [electronic resource] (Boston: IndyPublish.com, 2004), 3.

13. The best resource on Paul's back is Thomas Schmidt, *Scandalous Beauty: The Artistry of God and the Way of the Cross* (Grand Rapids, MI: Brazos Press, 2002), 75–85.

Chapter 8

1. For a more traditional version of this anonymous ditty set to music by Mrs. N. R. Schaper in 1943, see "Zacchaeus," Alfred B. Smith, *Action: A Collection of Gospel Songs and Choruses Compiled Especially for Boys and Girls* (Grand Rapids, MI: Zondervan, 1944), 27.

2. The Greek word *architelones*, which we translate as "chief tax collector" is not used elsewhere in all of the New Testament, nor has it been found in any extant Greek writing.

3. Matthew 11:19.

4. This aphorism by George Bernard Shaw is projected on the screen as a backdrop for the first scene change of the 2006 movie version of Shaw's *Mrs. Warren's Profession*.

5. Shakespeare.

6. Schalom Ben-Chorin, *Brother Jesus: The Nazarene through Jewish Eyes*, trans., Jared S.

Klein and Max Reinhart (Athens: University of Georgia Press, 2001), 98: "I can think of no other words that express greater depth and kindness than those spoken by Jesus to the sinful woman anointing him."

7. The key to Paul, according to N. T. Wright's book *Paul: In Fresh Perspective* (Minneapolis: Fortress, 2005), 10, 12, etc.

8. For more on this, see my *Jesus Drives Me Crazy* (Grand Rapids, MI: Zondervan, 2003), esp. 45.

9. Herman Melville, *Moby Dick, Or, The Whale* (New York: Russell & Russell, 1963), 1:58–59.

10. As told in *St. Augustine's Confessions*, with an English translation by William Watts (Cambridge, MA: Harvard University Press, 1968), 1:411.

11. Jane Austen, *Emma* (Boston: Houghton Mifflin, 1957), 212.

12. "Memorable Quotes from *Vanilla Sky* (2001)". www.imdb.com/title/tt0259711/quotes. (Accessed August 31, 2007.)

13. En route to Jerusalem, Jesus stayed at Simon the leper's house, where he was anointed with a year's salary worth of perfume.

14. Gomer may have been a cultic prostitute for Baal. These prostitutes were to engage in sexual relations to frenzy the gods into sexual acts. They were also called temple prostitutes because they would give their money earned through promiscuity to the temple fund.

15. Quoted in Gerard W. Hughes, *Seven Weeks for the Soul* (Chicago: Loyola Press, 2001), 53.

16. "Ultimately there is only one sin, and that is the steadfast refusal to be one's own true self." Søren Kierkegaard, *Sickness Unto Death*, 77.

17. The quote continues: "Anything can be a shell, Reuven. Anything. Indifference, laziness, brutality, and genius. Yes, even a great mind can be a shell and choke the spark." Chaim Potok, *The Chosen: A Novel* (New York: Simon and Schuster, 1967), 276.

18. See my *Eleven Genetic Gateways to Spiritual Awakening* (Nashville: Abingdon, 1998), 100–11.

19. See Tamara Cissna's interview, "'God Sent a Person Not a Proposition': A Conversation with Len Sweet," *George Fox Journal* 1 (Fall 2005), 1. www.georgefox.edu/journalonline/emerging.html. (Accessed December 26, 2005.)

Chapter 9

1. I have taken immense pleasure in this quote by A. S. Byatt's essay in *The Pleasure of*

Reading, ed., Antonia Fraser (London: Bloomsbury, 1992), 131.

2. Acts 12:12. Tradition claims that this house of Mary was the place where the Last Supper was held and perhaps was the headquarters of the Jerusalem church.

3. The Greek word used to describe her is *paidiske,* meaning "little girl, damsel, maid."

4. Acts 12:5.

5. Mark 9:33–37; Matthew 18:1–5.

6. Kingsley Amis, *One Fat Englishman* (New York: Harcourt, Brace & World, 1963), 162.

7. This is the apostle Paul's phrase in 1 Corinthians 13:11, as he is admonishing disciples of Jesus to "Grow up!" without losing their childhood.

8. 1 Corinthians 14:20 RSV.

9. Quoted in Michael Mayne, *Pray, Love, Remember* (London: Dartman, Todd, 1998), 35.

10. For Jesus' self-understanding as a eunuch for the kingdom, see Matthew 19:12.

11. Sirach (Ecclesiasticus) 36:30 NRSV.

12. Mark 10:15; Luke 18:17.

13. Matthew 18:3 (1–5). Also see Mark 9:33–37; Luke 9:46–48. Matthew and Luke omit the physical pickup.

14. "Watch that you don't treat a single one of these childlike believers arrogantly. You realize, don't you, that their personal angels are constantly in touch with my Father in heaven?" (Matt. 18:10 MSG).

15. Matthew 18:1–6.

16. Jerry Griswold, *Feeling Like a Kid: Childhood and Children's Literature* (Baltimore: Johns Hopkins University Press, 2006), 4.

17. Jean-Paul Sartre, *Nausea*, trans., Lloyd Alexander (New York: New Directions Publishing Co., 1964), 39.

18. "Childhood, Children," Journal entry for 1837, in *Søren Kierkegaard's Journal and Papers*, ed. and trans., Howard B. Hong and Edna H. Hong (Bloomington, IN: Indiana University Press, 1967), 1:113. Here is Kierkegaard's own description of the two ways: First, the way storytellers who "*are* basically children" can "open up a whole world of fantasy to the child," by being "sincerely convinced of the truth of their stories"; second, the way a storyteller "who knows *how to be* a child," "who knows what this life [of childhood] requires, [and] who knows what is good for it, … [can offer] children intellectual-emotional nourishment which is beneficial for them."

19. Pullman won the Carnegie Medal in 1996 for his *The Golden Compass*.

20. Philip Pullman, "Carnegie Medal Acceptance Speech," www.randomhouse.com/features/pullman/author/carnegie.html. (Accessed July 17, 2007.)

21. Ibid. Here is another flavor of Pullman's speech: "Now I don't mean children are supernatural wise little angels gifted with the power of seeing the truth that the dull eyes of adults miss. They're not. They're ignorant little savages, most of them. But they know what they need, and they go for it with the intensity of passion, and what they need is stories. Why do they spend so much time watching TV? They're not watching documentaries about Eastern Europe or programs about politics. They're watching drama, film, story. They can't get enough of it."

22. George Steiner, *Real Presences* (Chicago: University of Chicago Press, 1989), 190–91.

23. Quoted by Michael Mayne, *The Enduring Melody* (London: Darton, Longman & Todd, 2006), 204–5.

24. For more see my *The Three Hardest Words in the World to Get Right* (Colorado Springs: WaterBrook Press, 2006).

25. The five themes of classic children's literature according to Jerry Griswold are Smugness, Scariness, Smallness, Lightness, and Aliveness. See his *Feeling Like a Kid: Childhood and Children's Literature* (Baltimore: Johns Hopkins University Press, 2006), 1–6.

26. Jerry Griswold, *Feeling Like a Kid: Childhood and Children's Literature* (Baltimore: Johns Hopkins University Press, 2006), 25.

27. See Gaston Bachelard's *The Poetics of Space*, trans., Maria Jolas (Boston: Beacon Press, 1964), 6.

28. For more on this by "play experts" such as Stuart L. Brown, founder of the National Institute for Play, early childhood professor and author Vivian Gussin Paley, and Yale research scientist Dorothy G. Singer, see Stuart L. Brown, "Concepts of Childhood and Play," interview with Brian Sutton-Smith, *ReVision* 17 (1995), 35–43. T. Vivian Gussin Paley, *A Child's Work: The Importance of Play* (Chicago: University of Chicago Press, 2005); Dorothy G. Singer, Roberta M. Golinkoff, Kathy Hirsh-Pasek, *Play=Learning: How Play Motivates and Enhances Children's Cognitive and Social-Emotional Growth* (New York: Oxford University Press, 2006). Also see Edgar Klugman, *Play, Policy, and Practice* (St. Paul, MN: Redleaf Press, 1995).

29. As referenced by Gary Shockley, *The Meandering Way: Leading by Following the Spirit* (Herndon, VA: Alban Institute, 2007), 96–97. See also the words spoken to the boy by Fatima in Paulo Coelho, *The Alchemist*, trans., Alan R. Clarke (San Francisco: HarperSanFrancisco, 1998), 97. See also "Tell your heart that the fear of suffering is worse than the suffering itself. And that no heart has ever suffered when it goes in search of its dreams, because every second of the search is a second's encounter with God and with eternity." Words spoken by the Alchemist in Paulo Coelho's *The Alchemist*, 135.

30. As quoted by John Stott, *Between Two Worlds: The Art of Preaching in the Twentieth Century* (Grand Rapids, MI: Eerdmans, 1994), 128.

31. Quoted in Jerry Griswold, *Feeling Like a Kid: Childhood and Children's Literature* (Baltimore: Johns Hopkins University Press, 2006), 73.

32. When we do this, in Paul's words, we "proclaim the Lord's death until he comes" (1 Cor. 11:26 NRSV).

33. In the words of Pope Benedict XVI's Midnight Mass on December 24, 2006, delivered to Saint Peter's Basilica, Vatican: God "makes himself small for us. This is how he reigns. He does not come with power and outward splendor. He comes as a baby—defenseless and in need of our help. He does not want to overwhelm us with his strength.... There we read: 'God made his Word short, he abbreviated it' (Isa. 20:23; Rom. 9:28). The Fathers interpreted this in two ways. The Son himself is the Word, the Logos, the eternal Word became small—small enough to fit into a manger. He became a child, so that the Word could be grasped by us. In this way God teaches us to love the little ones. In this way he teaches us to love the weak. In this way he teaches us respect for children." See his "Solemnity of the Nativity of the Lord," *Vital Speeches of the Day* 73 (January 2007): 43.

34. Matthew 22:37–40.

35. Rainer Maria Rilke, "Die kleinen Dinge":

Die meisten Menschen
wissen gar nicht, wie schön die Welt ist
und wie viel Pracht in den kleinsten Dingen,
in irgendeiner Blume, einem Stein,
einer Baumrinde oder
einem Birkenblatt sich offenbart.
Die erwachsenen Menschen,
die Geschäfte und Sorgen haben
und sich mit lauter Keinigkeiten quälen,
verlieren allmählich ganz den Blick
für diese Reichtümer,
welche die Kinder,
wenn sie aufmerksam und gut sind,
bald bemerken
und mit dem ganzen Herzen lieben.
http://fhoelderslyrikseite.blogspot.com/2007_02_01_archive.html. (Accessed July 27, 2007.)

Rilke said something similar in a more accessible form: "We can recall that all beauty in animals and plants is silent and [sic] enduring form of love and longing.... The existing order transcends desire and grief and is mightier than will and resistance. The earth is full of this secret down to her smallest things. Oh, that we would only receive this secret more humbly, bear it more earnestly, endure it, and feel how awesomely difficult it is, rather than to take it lightly." Rainer Maria Rilke, *Letters to a Young Poet*, trans., Joan M. Burnham (Novato, CA: New World Library, 2000), 36–37.

36. Quoted in Jeanna Bryner, "Flower Buds: World Famous Scientist E. O. Wilson Speaks Out on the Importance of Saving the Planet's Pollinators," *Science World*, March 7, 2005. http://findarticles.com/p/articles/mi_m1590/is_11_61/ai_n13648067. (Accessed August 15, 2007.)

37. There are many books on the questions of Jesus. Two of the best are M. Basil Pennington's *Who Do You Say I Am? Meditations on Jesus' Questions in the Gospels* (Hyde Park, NY: New City Press, 2005; originally published 1999); and my personal favorite, John Dear's *The Questions of Jesus: Challenging Ourselves to Discover Life's Great Answers* (New York: Image Books, 2004). Both books have appendixes that provide a complete listing of Jesus' questions in the Gospels.

38. Wilfred Wilson Gibson, "Lament," in *Georgian Poetry 1916–1917* (London: Poetry Bookshop, 1917), 123. Also available online at www.fullbooks.com/Georgian-Poetry-1916-172.html. (Accessed July 26, 2007.)

39. As quoted in Jerry Griswold, *Feeling Like a Kid: Childhood and Children's Literature* (Baltimore: Johns Hopkins University Press, 2006), 89.

40. As quoted in Paul Tournier, *Learn to Grow Old* (New York: Harper and Row, 1972), 192.

41. Rainer Maria Rilke, Letter "To Princess Marie von Thurn und Taxis-Hobenlobe, Paris, December 17, 1913," in *Letters of Rainer Maria Rilke*, trans., Jane Bannard Green and M. D. Herter Norton (New York: W. W. Norton, 1948), 2:100. I discovered this quote in Stephen Frech, "A Conversation with Gary Miranda"—interview with poet/playwright Gary Miranda, *Image*, 46 (Summer 2005): 61. www.imagejournal.org/back/045/miranda_interview.asp. (Accessed August 16, 2007.)

42. As quoted in Jerry Griswold, *Feeling Like a Kid: Childhood and Children's Literature* (Baltimore: Johns Hopkins University Press, 2006), 89. But check Italo Calvino, *Six Memos for the Next Millennium* (London: Vintage, 1996).

43. For the two kinds of hope, see Austin Farrer, "The Ultimate Hope," in Leslie Houlden, ed., *Austin Farrer: The Essential Sermons* (Cambridge, MA: Cowley Publications, 1991), 199.

44. Quoted in Louis Trenchard Möre, *Isaac Newton, 1642–1727* (New York: Charles Scribner's Sons, 1934), 664.

45. Quoted in Hugo Estenssoro, "Serious Player," *TLS: Times Literary Supplement*, May 21, 2004, 10. Estenssoro is quoting from Fernando Savater, *Jorge Luis Borges* (Madrid: Omega, 2004), which is published in Spanish.

46. The translated full quote of Socrates is "This sense of wonder is the mark of the philosopher. Philosophy indeed has no other origin." Plato, "Theaetetus," (155d), in *The Collected Dialogues of Plato Including the Letters*, eds., Edith Hamilton and Huntington Cairns (Princeton, NJ: Princeton University Press, 1961), 860.

47. Jerry Griswold, *Feeling Like a Kid: Childhood and Children's Literature* (Baltimore: Johns Hopkins University Press, 2006), 104.

48. This is Anthony de Mello's definition of *spirituality*.

49. Anthony de Mello, *Awareness: A de Mello Spirituality Convergence in His Own Words*, ed., J. Francis Stroud (New York: Doubleday, 1990), 5.

50. This is the phrase of the eighteenth-century French priest Jean-Pierre de Caussade in his book *Self-Abandonment to Divine Providence*.

51. This is called by some philosophers "the second naiveté."

52. Jennifer Steinhauer, "The Arts Administration," *New York Times*, October 23, 2005, 2.1: "During a private tour of the Vatican in 2000, the thing that piqued his [Bloomberg's] interest was the church's collection of Bloomberg terminals, an aide who traveled with him recalled."

53. James Hillman, *Kinds of Power: A Guide to Its Intelligent Uses* (New York: Currency Doubleday, 1995), 62.

54. Annie Dillard, *Pilgrim at Tinker Creek* (New York: Harper's Magazine Press, 1974), 271.

55. Theodore P. Ferris, in his exposition on Acts 12:13–15, in *The Interpreter's Bible: The Holy Scriptures in the King James and Revised Standard Versions with General Articles and Introduction, Exegesis, Exposition for Each Book of the Bible* (New York: Abingdon, 1954) 9:160.

Chapter 10

1. For more on my theology of receiving, see chapter 4, "Bounce Your Last Check" in my *SoulSalsa: 17 Surprising Steps for Godly Living in the 21st Century* (Grand Rapids, MI: Zondervan, 2000), 52–61; and my Web site article, "'Freely You Have Received, Freely Give': Toward a Post-Tithing, Post-Stewardship, Postmodern Theology of Receiving,"

http://leonardsweet.com/includes/ShowSweetenedArticles.asp?articleID=91. (Accessed September 13, 2007.)

2. Greg Paul, *God in the Alley: Being and Seeing Jesus in a Broken World* (Colorado Springs: WaterBrook Press, 2004).

3. Acts 16.

4. Acts 16:14–15, 40 NRSV.

5. Carolyn Osiek, Margaret Y. MacDonald with Janet H. Tulloch, *A Woman's Place: House Churches in Earliest Christianity* (Minneapolis: Fortress Press, 2005), 11.

6. Samuel Johnson, "To Lord Chesterfield, Friday, February 7, 1755," in *The Letters of Samuel Johnson*, ed., Bruce Redford (Princeton, NJ: Princeton University Press, 1992), 1:96.

7. "One night over dinner in a restaurant in Ciudad Juárez, Mexico, a businessman was telling me about a Middle Eastern potentate who owned a 747, with a gyroscopically rotating prayer room perpetually oriented toward Mecca. The potentate had a serious heart condition, the businessman continued, so he converted the plane's upper deck into a cardiac intensive-care unit with all the latest technology. I made suitable murmurings of awe. The businessman smiled patiently until he got to the part that had impressed even him: 'The plane was also equipped,' he said, 'with a living donor.' A heart donor, that is. It was a poor man of compatible tissue type whose reward, it seemed, was living well for a little while and the promise that his family would live well afterward." Richard Conniff, *The Natural History of the Rich: A Field Guide* (New York: W. W. Norton, 2002), 135.

8. Matt Bai refines the mantra thus: "It's not that the poor are getting poorer, or that more Americans are falling below the poverty line, so much as it is that poor Americans are falling further and further behind those who succeed." Matt Bai, "The Poverty Platform," *New York Times Magazine*, June 10, 2007, 69.

9. Stein Ringen, "Fewer People: A Stark European Future," *TLS: Times Literary Supplement*, February 28, 2003, 9ff.

10. See the findings of the former World Bank economist Surjit S. Bhalla in his book *Imagine There's No Country: Poverty, Inequality, and Growth in the Era of Globalization* (Washington, D.C.: Institute for International Economics, 2002), esp. 130, 195–96.

11. Between 2000 and 2005, middle-class workers with a four-year college degrees saw their wages fall 3.1 percent when adjusted for inflation. Here is a Congressional Budget Office Report: Between 1979 and 2003, the top 1 percent of households enjoyed a 129 percent gain in after-tax income, adjusted for inflation. The middle class saw a 15 percent gain. The bottom fifth, an income increase of only 4 percent. Those making more than 1.7 million a year saw a 181 percent gain.

12. "A Question of Justice? Poverty and Inequality; (Understanding Global Inequality)," *The Economist*, March 13, 2004, 13.

13. George Kennan, *Around the Cragged Hill: A Personal and Political Philosophy* (New York: W. W. Norton, 1993), 121.

14. I can't be sure, but I'm assuming this term comes from 1 Timothy 5:8, which reads: "And whoever does not provide for relatives, and especially for family members, has denied the faith and is worse than an unbeliever."

15. As the father of one of my favorite poets, Les A. Murray, liked to put it. Murray, an Australian poet, dedicates all his books "to the glory of God." Murray's father liked to say "We were poor people—hardly had a roof to our mouths." See Peter Alexander, *Les Murray: A Life in Progress* (New York: Oxford University Press, 2000), 241 (on dedication); 20 (quote).

16. William Wordsworth, "Lines Composed a Few Miles Above Tintern Abbey, on Revisiting the Banks of the Wye During a Tour, July 13, 1798," *The Complete Poetical Works of William Wordsworth*, with an introduction by John Morley (New York: A. L. Burt, 1888), 92.

17. "The Sentences of Sextus, [382]," in *The Nag Hammadi Library: The Definitive Translation of the Gnostic Scriptures Complete in One Volume*, ed., James M. Robinson (San Francisco: HarperOne, 2004), 508.

18. Philip F. Esler and Ronald Piper, *Lazarus, Mary and Martha: Social-Scientific Approaches to the Gospel of John* (Minneapolis: Fortress Press, 2006), 146–47.

19. Luke 16:19–31.

20. Genesis 13:2.

21. Luke 16:9.

22. "VIPs (Very Important Pets)," *American Demographics*, 23 (March 2001): 16.

23. Ibid., 18.

24. J. David Pleins, *The Psalms: Songs of Tragedy, Hope, and Justice* (Maryknoll, NY: Orbis Books, 1993), 81.

25. Don Cupitt, "The Radical Christian Worldview" *Cross Currents* 50 (Spring–Summer 2000): 56–67, exp. 58, 63–65. See also his *Solar Ethics* (London: SCM Press, 1995).

26. Paul Escamilla, *Longing for Enough in a Culture of More* (Nashville: Abingdon, 2007), 5.

27. Paul complains, "When you come together, it is not really to eat the Lord's supper" (1 Cor. 11:20). For the metaphor of the "family reunion," see John A. Huffman, Jr., "Have You Been to a Real Family Reunion Lately?" Sermon preached June 25, 2006. © 2006 www.standrewspres.org/sermons/serm062506.htm. (Accessed September 6, 2007.)

28. Peter Singer, "What Should a Billionaire Give—and What Should You?" *New York Times Magazine*, December 17, 2006, 58–63, 80–85.
29. Matt Bai, "The Poverty Platform," *New York Times Magazine*, June 10, 2007, 69.

Chapter 11

1. See for example Tillich's discussion of "the ground of being as sources of the courage to be" and "the courage to be as key to the ground of being," in his *Courage to Be* (New Haven, CT: Yale University Press, 1952), 156–90. Other theologians influenced by Heidegger include Rudolf Otto and Rudolph Bultmann.
2. I am predicting that hermit huts will be all the rage in the future, as a culture of solitude seekers look for and find sanctuary in small places.
3. Quoted in François Bovon, "The Child and the Beast: Fighting Violence in Ancient Christianity," *Harvard Theological Review* 92 (October 1999): 373. Quoting from *The Heart of Compassion: Daily Readings with St. Isaac of Syria*, ed., A. M. Allchin (London: Darton, Longman & Todd, 1989), 20.
4. Heidegger's explanation was first recorded as a radio address and published as a newspaper article, translated as "Why Do I Stay in the Provinces?" Adam Sharr, *Heidegger's Hut* (Cambridge, MA: MIT Press, 2006), 64.
5. Sharr, *Heidegger's Hut*, 64.
6. William deBuys, *The Walk* (San Antonio, TX: Trinity University, 2007), 10.
7. Sharr, *Heidegger's Hut*, 64.
8. Ibid.
9. Walter Benjamin, "The Storyteller: Reflection on the Works of Nikolai Leskov," in his *Illuminations*, ed., Hannah Arendt (New York: Schocken Books, 1969), 84–85. He calls the former "the tiller of the soil" and the latter "the trading seaman."
10. Wendell Berry, "Out of Your Car, Off Your Horse," in his *Sex, Economy, Freedom and Community: Eight Essays* (New York: Pantheon Books, 1993), 20.
11. Wes Jackson, *Becoming Native to This Place* (Lexington: University of Kentucky Press, 1994).
12. Walter Brueggemann, *The Land: Place as Gift, Promise, and Challenge in Biblical Faith* (Minneapolis, MN: Fortress Press, 2002), 4–6, etc.
13. As quoted by Alison Hawthorne Deming, *Writing the Sacred into the Real* (Minneapolis, MN: Milkweed Editions, 2001), 5.
14. Russell Hoban, *The Mouse and His Child* (New York: Camelot Books, 1967), 45.
15. Jim Lynch, *The Highest Tide* (New York: Bloomsbury, 2005), 3.
16. Revelation 21:2; Micah 4:4 RSV.

17. "Community" is an admittedly inadequate translation of the Latin *Conversatio morum*, which features a now-obsolete Abbott Christopher Jamison, *Finding Sanctuary: Monastic Steps for Everyday Life* (Collegeville, MN: Liturgical Press, 2006), 116.

18. "The spiritual did not come first, but the natural, and after that the spiritual" (1 Cor. 15:46 TNIV).

19. See Marja-Liisa Swantz, *Beyond the Forestline: The Life and Letters of Bengt Sundkler* (Leominster, MA: Gracewing, 2002), 49.

20. An excellent resource toward this end is Daniel G. Deffenbaugh, *Learning the Language of the Fields: Tilling and Keeping as Christian Vocation* (Cambridge, MA: Cowley Publications, 2006), 130.

21. See my "Manifold Witness," appendix to *The Three Hardest Words in the World to Get Right* (Colorado Springs: WaterBrook Press, 2006), 151–69.

22. Quoted in Trevor Carolan, "Grounded in Humanity: An Interview with Gary Snyder" in *The Bloomsbury Review*, July/August 2007, 24.

23. Check out Psalm 148.

24. Quoted in Benedict J. Groeschel, *The Virtue Driven Life* (Huntington, IN: Our Sunday Visitor, 2006), 81.

25. "Surely you are one of them; for your speech betrays you" (Matt. 26:73 NKJV).

26. Theodor W. Adorno, *Minima Moralia: Reflections from Damaged Life*, trans., E. F. N. Jephcott (London: New Left Books, 1974), 87.

27. "Beams of heaven as I go, / Through this wilderness below, / Guide my feet in peaceful ways, / Turn my midnights into days. / When in darkness, I would grope, / Faith always sees a star of hope. / And soon from all life's grief and danger, / I shall be free some day.
[Refrain:] I do not know how long 'twill be, / Nor what the future holds for me, / But this I know, if Jesus leads, / I shall get home some day. /
Often times my sky is clear, / Joy abounds without a tear. / Though a day so bright begun, / clouds may hide tomorrow's sun. / There'll be a day that's always bright, / A day that never yields to night, / And in its light the streets of glory / I shall behold some day. /
[Refrain]
Harder yet may be the fight, / Right may often yield to might, / Wickedness awhile may reign, / Satan's cause may seem to gain. /
There is a God that rules above, / With hand of pow'r and heart of love. / If I am right, He'll fight my battle, / I shall have peace some day. /
[Refrain]

Burdens now may crush me down, / Disappointments all around, / Troubles speak in mournful sigh, / Sorrow through a tear-stained eye. / There is a world where pleasure reigns, / No mourning soul shall roam its plains, / And to that land of peace and glory, / I want to go some day. /

[Refrain]

Charles A. Tindley, "Some Day," *Songs of Zion, Supplemental Worship Resources 12* (Nashville: Abingdon, 1961), 10.

28. See Benjamin R. Barber, "Jihad vs. McWorld" The Atlantic.com, http://www.theatlantic.com/doc/199203/barber. (Accessed December 15, 2007.)

29. Desmond Butler, "That's Not Trash, It's Dinner, Freegans Say," *Seattle Times*, December 6, 2005, http://seattletimes.nwsource.com/html/nationworld/2002645365_dumpsters25.html. (Accessed September 21, 2007.)

30. Gary Snyder, "Thinking Toward the Thousand-year Forest Plan," in his *Back on the Fire: Essays* (Emeryville, CA: Shoemaker & Hoard, 2007), 42.

31. Luke 19:41–44 (NRSV).

Chapter 12

1. Closing lines of Robert Grant, "O Worship the King" (1833).
2. Psalm 121:4.
3. For the metaphor of "the eleventh hour," see Matthew 20:5–6.
4. In the tapestry, Bishop Odo of Bayeux, an appointee of William the Conquerer, shares the scene from the Battle of Hastings with William, who turns toward the troops and lifts his headpiece to assure the troops he is still alive. See Lucien Musset, *The Bayeux Tapestry*, new edition trans., Richard Rex (Woodbridge, Suffolk, UK: Boydell Press, 2005), 248–51, 270.
5. As cited in Jack Neff, "J&J Targets Red Cross, Blunders into PR Firestorm," *Advertising Age*, August 13, 2007, 22. The statistic comes from Lowell Wallace, managing partner of the consulting firm Marketing Valuation Partners.
6. G. W. H. Lampe, "Paraclete," *Interpreter's Dictionary of the Bible: An Illustrated Encyclopedia* (Nashville: Abingdon, 1962), 3:654.
7. Psalm 34:7.
8. Isaiah 43:2.
9. Manfred Kets de Vries, *The Leadership Mystique* (London: Financial Times Press, 2001), 279–80.
10. Romans 8:31.

11

11. Robert Southwell, "A Childe My Choyse," *The Complete Poems of Robert Southwell*, ed., Alexander B. Grosart, The Fuller Worthies' Library (New York: AMS Press, 1971; reprinted from London: Printed for Private Circulation, 1872), 71.

12. John 15:15.

13. Isaiah 41:8; 2 Chronicles 20:7.

14. Exodus 33:11.

15. See 1 Corinthians 1:23.

16. Joseph M. Scriven, "What a Friend We Have in Jesus," (written ca. 1855); music by Charles C. Converse (1868).

17. Philippians 4:12.

18. Philippians 4:13.

19. Quoted in Paul Murray, *The New Wine of Dominican Spirituality: A Drink Called Happiness* (New York: Burns & Oates, 2006), 45.

20. Philippians 4:13.

21. See Psalm 51:10.

22. Georg Lukács, *The Theory of the Novel: A Historico-philosophical Essay on the Forms of Great Epic Literature* (Cambridge, MA: The MIT Press, 1974), 72.

23. Paul J. Wadell, C. P., *Friendship and the Moral Life* (Notre Dame, IN: University of Notre Dame Press, 1989), 121.

24. This is an adaptation of Martin Luther's phrase about our "alien righteousness."

25. Timothy Radcliffe, *What Is the Point of Being a Christian?* (New York: Burns & Oates, 2005), 70.

26. *The Rule of St. Benedict in English*, ch. 7, ed., Timothy Fry (Collegeville, MN: Liturgical Press, 1981), 32.

27. Alasdair MacIntyre, *After Virtue: A Study in Moral Theory*, 3rd ed. (Notre Dame, IN: University of Notre Dame, 2007), 177.

28. Quoted in John Calvin, *Institutes of the Christian Religion*, trans., Fort Lewis Battles (Philadelphia: Westminster Press, 1960), 1:267.

29. Philippians 2:9–11.

30. See Acts 20:19.

31. See Colossians 2:18, 23; 3:12; and 1 Peter 5:5.

32. Augustine, "Letter 118" [22, 23], *Letters 100–155*, vol. 2, pt. 2 of *The Works of Saint Augustine: A Translation for the 21st Century* (Hyde Park, NY: New City Press, 2003), 117. For the reference to Cicero, see his *The Orator*, bk. 3, ch. 56.

33. As quoted by James Schlesinger, "Patriotism in Our Eyes," *Vital Speeches of the Day*, 73 (April 2007): 153.

34. Quoted in Harold Myerson and Ernie Harburg, *Who Put the Rainbow in the Wizard*

of Oz? Yip Harburg, Lyricist (Ann Arbor: University of Michigan Press, 1993), 151.

35. Interfaith Council for Peace and Justice, as quoted in Alan Jamieson, *Journeying in Faith: In and Beyond the Tough Places* (London: SPCK, 2004), 137–38. Quoted in *On the Road Again: Newsletter of the Anabaptist Association of Australia and New Zealand, Inc.*, November 2004, 16. Also quoted in Alan Jamieson, *Called Again: In and Beyond the Deserts of Faith* (Wellington, New Zealand: Phillip Garside, 2004), 141. Jamieson cites as his source the Interfaith Council for Peace and Justice, quoted in Peter Millar, *Finding Hope Again: Journeying through Sorrow and Beyond* (London, SCM-Canterbury Press, 2003), 192. But the Interfaith Council for Peace and Justice cannot verify the source, as per May 2, 2006 e-mail from chuck@icpi.net. A version of this prayer also appears as "A Franciscan Blessing," cited as from *Troubadour: A Missionary Magazine* published by the Franciscan Missionary Society, Liverpool, UK, Spring 2005, and quoted in *The Beatitudes Society Newsletter*, January 2006. www.beatitudessociety.org/newsletter/january_2006.html. (Accessed May 27, 2006.)

36. *Saving Private Ryan* [video recording], (Universal City, CA: DreamWorks Home Entertainment, 1999).

37. Sheldon Teitelbaum, "Fuzzy Thinker: Fuzzy Logic Guru Bart Kosko Explains Spock's Worst Nightmare," *Wired* 3 (February 1995), 135.

38. Paul Russell Cutright, *Theodore Roosevelt: The Making of a Conservationist* (Urbana: University of Illinois Press, 1985), 261–62.

39. James C. Collins, *Good to Great: Why Some Companies Make the Leap, and Others Don't* (New York: HarperBusiness, 2001).

40. Alexander Solzhenitsyn, A World Split Apart: Commencement Address Delivered at Harvard University, June 8, 1978 (New York: Harper & Row, 1978), 9, 11 (Russian text on 8, 10).

Bible Resources